IF GOD IS MY FATHER, WHO IS MY MOTHER?

P.J. FISK

BALBOA.PRESS
A DIVISION OF HAY HOUSE

Balboa Press books may be ordered through booksellers or by contacting:

Balboa Press
A Division of Hay House
1663 Liberty Drive
Bloomington, IN 47403
www.balboapress.com
844-682-1282

Print information available on the last page.

ISBN: 978-1-9822-6139-9 (sc)
ISBN: 978-1-9822-6140-5 (e)

Balboa Press rev. date: 01/07/2021

CONTENTS

Dedicated to
My daughters
Trudy, Kimberly, Lori, Brenda

The experience in this book is mine.
The stories are as I remember them.
Names have been changed.

1

THE TWO-STORY BUILDING needs paint and stands on a lot where more weeds than grass grow. One of four apartments in this used-to-be-house became a home for me just hours ago, and now feels like a prison.

I sit on the top of dingy, wooden stairs with a much-worn carpet beneath my buttocks. I shiver with bared arms and legs in my baby-doll pajamas. The single-bulb light fixture hanging down overhead casts shadows across the stair railing creating the image of bars. Stale cigarette smoke drifts to my nostrils from the hall bathroom we share with a young married couple and the groom's father who uses the bathroom as his cave and flicks ashes onto the floor.

It is January 17, 1961. Two days ago, I married in a borrowed dress and veil, then spent a one-night honeymoon in my husband's family cabin. I am eighteen years old, and three months pregnant. My husband of forty-eight hours has locked me out of our three-room apartment. He is asleep in the rented bed in our bedroom.

There is a sealed door from the hall into the bedroom. I rise and tip-toe gingerly across a dirty wooden floor to knock on it gently. Whispering so I will not awake neighbors, I plead, "Please let me in. I am sorry."

Three times I creep to that door from my place on the stairs, avoiding the creaks where possible, just in case someone is awake in one of the other apartments. I am fearful someone may peek out and see me walking about this time of night so lightly clothed.

Each time I creep to the door, I lean into the door crack and implore with the same message, "Please let me in."

For two hours there are no results, no sound, no response. Panic rises within me. But I am determined to stay calm and compliant. I believe the door will be opened sooner if I remain submissive and remorseful.

Should I call my dad and have him come and get me? It will mean knocking on an apartment door scantily clothed. That feels like a big risk. I don't know the neighbors. It's too cold to walk to a pay phone, dressed as I am. I don't have a dime, and, besides, that feels like even a greater risk.

Will my dad come for me if I do call? Will he say, "You've made your bed, now lie in it?" He's an hour away. Surely my husband will let me in before he can get here. *Would I choose to go back home if my father did come?*

I'm afraid, desperate for relief from the punishment meted out by my husband. Tears escape down my cheeks though I am determined to be brave, strong, and relentlessly sorry. The sadness is deep. I've already experienced the emotional pain my new husband can inflict. Days spent when he would not speak to me because I was "too friendly" with another male classmate. And the time in a local café when a waitress with a well-endowed figure flirted, and he turned to me and said, "I feel like taking that scarf from around your neck and stuffing it in your bra."

I am a wife—I agreed to obey my husband. I promised to love, obey, and honor until death do us part, just hours ago. Besides, because of the pregnancy, how can I not stay? *Apologize and make things okay.* No matter how devastated I feel, I know I will stay, or if I leave, come back. I do not have the support I would need to leave, let alone stay away. It goes against what I had been taught—put the husband first no matter what. After all, my mother and all her sisters, my aunts, have experiences with their husbands worse than my experience right now. They have all stayed.

Knowing them, I can't imagine they even thought of leaving. *I should not think about it. Just stay patient. He'll let me in before long.*

My father and many of my nine uncles were heavy alcohol drinkers. That led to spending money meant for food and children going without. It meant nights sitting up waiting for husbands to return. A number of times I saw bruises on one of my aunts. I did not think of it as abuse—it was accepted in the context of the man being the head of the house and the wife being subservient. My mother openly blamed my aunt, her sister, for the abuse she suffered because, "She wouldn't keep her mouth shut." She meant that her sister should not say anything when her husband came home inebriated and violent.

I do not remember what I did that made my forty-eight-hour husband angry enough to lock me out in the hall dressed as I was. He must have forced me because on my own I wouldn't have been out in the hall in pajamas without a robe. Perhaps I left something in the bathroom and that angered him. I do know the act was insignificant. It may have been as insignificant as my laughing at something he did or said.

I remember with clarity sitting on those stairs, and I can still feel the chill. Not just the temperature, but the realization of where I was in my life. I felt hopeless. There was nothing I could do about my situation except wait—wait for my husband to decide I had been punished enough to let me into what was now my home. No more going back to the bedroom shared with my sister. No more safety burrowing under the covers and hugging someone who loved me no matter what.

I did not know the meaning of true, unconditional love in any other form. I had not experienced it nor was it modeled. I heard the wives in my family called mother and o'lady, instead of any endearment such as honey or babe. I have no memory of any family member demonstrating a devoted love towards their mate. My confused concept of love was so tied up in obedience and sex that I responded to abuse with guilt, sorrow, and sex—in that order.

I had fought off other sexual advances and pressure instigated by boyfriends—keeping myself for my future husband. Eventually, I succumbed to the pressure from Roger. I gave in. I felt ravaged the first time, because the physical and emotional pressure was so great. My "nos" were ignored. *It must be my fault. Was I a tease? Was I frigid like he said?* I went numb and gave in. I accepted that "he needed it," and I thought I loved him. When you love, you give. I could not discuss this experience with anyone or ask why it felt so bestial.

The romance magazines that my Aunt Jane had hidden under couch cushions described this act as sensual and fulfilling a need. *Was this making love?* I remember clearly when I said to myself, *I must love him.* I was sitting very close as he drove his 1951 Chevy with the gear-shift on the left side of the steering column where he had moved it to allow more freedom with his right hand. He laid this hand on my thigh with a gentle squeeze. I thought this was an expression of love. I also felt the response in my groin for the first time and thought, *I am in love.*

Once I gave in to "going all the way," the real thing, no more petting and backing away, I knew I would marry Roger. It did not take the pregnancy to convince me of that. We had set a date for the wedding before I found out I was pregnant.

I was a "good girl," and good girls did not have sex with anyone they were not married to. I already carried the guilt of giving-in. I chose not to live with the guilt that leaving this relationship and marrying another would bring. I did not believe I had another choice, even though I longed for one.

I had plans to attend college in the fall after graduation. Roger would not hear of my moving away, and since we were sexually involved, I subjected myself to his desires and gave up mine. Few dating options existed in the small country high school that Roger and I both attended.

Only twenty-five students in our graduating class and most had been in my classroom since kindergarten. Roger transferred from a one-room-school within the school district our eighth-grade year. He was a good student and had plans of his own to go to college. I started my senior year unattached and intended to stay that way. But girlfriends were going steady, and my closest friend had become pregnant, dropped out of school, and married. I was the single one and "three make a crowd." So, I dated Roger, spending most dates locked in his arms, and now was locked in as his wife but locked *out* of our apartment.

Sitting on those stairs, I wiped the tears and snot, rubbed the goose bumps on my arms and legs, and whispered, "I can't do this." Seconds later I defaulted to, *"I have to do this."* These words would be my mantra for the next twenty-two-years.

When Roger finally opened the door, I stepped into his arms as a penitent sinner come home. I did not berate. I did not condemn his actions. I did not speak words of change. In fact, this act of being locked out when I displeased him continued for the next sixteen years. It continued until I took a stand one night after sitting under a tree for hours. When the door opened at my knock, I looked into his eyes and said slowly with a lowered voice, "Hear what I am going to say to you because I mean every word. If you ever lock me out of my home again I **will** leave you." He never locked me out again.

Why did it take so long for me to demand better treatment? What if I had used those words the first time he locked me out? Would he have responded differently? Would he have believed me and stopped? I was clinging to the thought that he was fulfilling the role society gave to him—that of being "man of the house." In a society that believed the wife should "obey."

Years earlier, another incident should have clued me into the possibilities.

I interfered with his harsh discipline with our youngest daughter. He was making her eat food she did not like. She gagged and spit up. He put more food in her mouth. She gagged and spit up again. He tried to make her swallow what she spit up. This went on for several minutes until I stepped in and asked him to let me take her from his arms. His response was a swing of his arm that caught me in the mouth, bruising a lip, and forcing me against a wall. His doubled-up fist and glare told me he wanted to hit me. I looked into his eyes with determination, a mother protecting her young, and said, "Go ahead hit me because it is the last chance you will get. The girls and I are leaving."

Though I meant what I said, his repentance and begging led me to change that threat. I stayed, and he never hit me again. Emotional abuse continued. I longed for change but did not know how to make change. I vacillated. At times I was strong and vocal about my unhappiness. Like the time he came home from work and I had not picked up the kids' toys that were scattered across the living room floor. He looked at me and said with sarcasm, "What have you been doing all day?"

Instead of saying: "I babysat two other children with our four; I swept and mopped the kitchen floor; I prepared two meals for six children and did the dishes; I did two loads of laundry, and right now I am sewing on a dress for one of our daughters." Rather than justify, I said, "Damn you." He looked at me in shock. I did not usually use that kind of language.

At other times, I withdrew emotionally and became submissive. I made sure the house was clean and a meal ready to serve when he came home from work. If I did not accomplish these things, I apologized to him upon his arrival. The emotional ups and downs confused both of us. My determination to change how I related did not last. I felt guilty when I struck out in anger, and made it up to him in bed.

Clarissa Estes in her book, WOMEN WHO RUN WITH THE WOLVES, says, "in every woman there is a wild and natural creature named Wild Woman." When I read it, I thought back to this earlier time and realized that I was living with a Wild Woman inside. I was overly domesticated, fearful, and felt trapped. I do not blame Roger. I was living out the only life I had been taught was acceptable for a woman. That of serving men. I was doing my best to serve my husband and provide a clean house with meals on the table when he came home from work. I served him sexually and seldom said no to his advances—even when I was dead tired from caring for a farm and four children. I stayed with my man no matter how I felt or how he treated me. I knew something was wrong, but kept up the acceptable image given by family, society, and church, and did my best to live it.

Weeks before I made the decision to divorce Roger I made the statement to a counselor, "I will not divorce. I don't believe in it."

In 1982, just months before I asked for a divorce, I delivered a worship talk while employed by the Seventh-day Adventist Church as Dean of Women at a college on the West Coast. I was responsible for devotionals for the girls on campus who had to attend four worships a week. It is titled, "Why Marriage?" The talk began with a question: "In a world that is screaming free sex and live-in roommates, why should or would someone choose marriage?"

The description I gave of marriage was: "not the ceremony—you know with all the lace, flowers, and such. It is not the piece of paper that the state issues you at the time of marriage with the minister's and witnesses' signatures. What we are talking about is a commitment, a commitment to a person, to a relationship. This commitment says, 'I am committed to the other's best interest. I promise to love, honor, cherish, and be faithful to this person for the rest of our lives.'"

While in my marriage vows to Roger I had used the word "obey," I did not use it in this talk. My beliefs about marriage had changed, without my awareness. I had stopped "obeying my husband." But I was still enmeshed in the dogma of "once married, always married"—no matter what.

In the worship talk I said: "The main reason for this commitment made between man and woman is because of the neatest experience that God has given to man and that is procreation. Man and woman together can and do create a human being. What a special privilege God has given to us. He didn't need to. He could have done all the creating, but He has given us that ability in procreation."

In the talk, I asked and answered, "Why am I committed to marriage? Because I love this man and not only want to but have decided to spend eternity with him. Also, because from him I have unconditional love and respond to him with that same kind of love. I have given my life to him—that is the ultimate in loving—giving your life to the other. Because I love him, I want to give him my best and that is a commitment of eternal love."

My understanding of love was very limited and perhaps distorted. I was not experiencing love the way I described and I was not giving unconditional love either.

I believed those words even though I was not living them. The anguish I lived with brought me to an impasse. *Why can't I live what I believe? Why can't I make myself feel what I believe I should feel?* Heartache impelled me to seek solace through God's word, but solace eluded me. I prayed repeatedly, "I believe, help Thou my unbelief."

2

I WAS CONCEIVED IN the cold month of February 1942, in the back seat of my father's 1932 Ford. The month was privy to war time shells hitting the continental United States, for the first and only time, bombarding an oil field and refinery on the coast of California. As lights were shrouded throughout the country, my life began within the uterus of my mother in the middle of the mitten of Michigan.

My parents, Paul and Mildred, married on May 4. Later that year, on August 29, at the age of twenty-two, farm raised and auto factory tough, Dad entered active service in the Army. He left Michigan for Kansas to be trained at Fort Riley. By the time I emerged from my mother's womb on November 20, he was part of a fighting force that would propel him to European shores. One of few to hit the shores of Normandy Beach and survive, he drove a troop carrier ashore amidst the horror, and then advanced with his unit. He endured the demands of a grueling and gruesome thirteen months on Germany's frontlines, and came home a "shell-shocked" man.

The star that hung in the window of my paternal grandparents' house, like those hanging in windows all over the United States, was for him. Born the next-to-youngest son of five, he made it possible for his younger brother to stay home, safe from the perils of war, to care for the family farm. Dad was the only one drafted, while his three older brothers received deferments due to having children. Instead of experiencing the horrors of war, his older brothers worked together in one factory producing vehicles of war.

I was born Paula Jean Fisk in a small-town hospital—in farm country where roads were tree-lined and gravel—where everyone you met waved hello. Fields of corn and beans separated the pastures of Angus, Guernsey, Holstein, Jersey cattle, and horses that were still being used to plow fields and haul farm wagons.

The center of Michigan was made up of small farms, small towns, small schools, and small churches that were the axis of those communities. One-room schools with grades one through eight still functioned and some would for another dozen-years.

Generations of my ancestors came to this country from Ireland and England, some coming down through Canada. Both sets of grandparents were born in Michigan as well as others before them. Records show these lands to be occupied by relatives a hundred years before. My maternal grandparents, Allen and Lula Courser, lived in the house in which Grandpa was born. Grandma Lula's parents, Herbert and Millie Nicholson, lived in the next county just a few miles away. As their parents before them, both sets of grandparents were farmers eking out a living with milk cows and fields of beans, potatoes, and rye.

My legacy came from a family of farmers and factory workers. Both my maternal and paternal families were close-knit but sometimes fractured. Sister angry with sister. brothers fighting, and sons-in-law not speaking to other family members. But their need for each other kept them tied together. Sister helped sister at times of childbirth and illness. Brother and brothers-in-law helped plow, plant, build, and repair. My father was fifth born in his family and modeled his mother by caring for others.

Grandpa and Grandma Courser's white clapboard house stood atop a small hill with a two-story barn sunk into the rise of land to its right.

Behind the house, and to the left of a one car garage and the outhouse, stood the two-room house Mom and then a sister, Aunt Ernestine, occupied while their husbands were at war.

My paternal grandparents, Charles and Effie Fisk, also lived on an incline of land in a small two-story stone house with a corn crib and outhouse behind and to the right a low-ceilinged barn. The youngest son, Uncle Marion, and his family occupied a small cement block house close by. He provided a playmate when his daughter, Nita was born two months after me.

Twelve cousins of four sets of aunts and uncles would greet me from my dad's family. All lived within a sixty-mile radius. I was born the first granddaughter on my mom's side of the family to join Terry, a three year old. His sister, Patricia, joined us two months later. Two of my mom's five siblings, Uncle Jay and Aunt Martha, sixteen and fourteen respectively, still lived at home and became our playmates and babysitters.

Twenty-nine more cousins completed the families in the next fifteen years. This made for fun playmate gatherings at holidays and birthday celebrations.

The families of Fisk and Courser did not socialize or relate in any significant way. It was not distance that kept them apart for their farms were within five miles of each other. Differing religious beliefs may have influenced the separation or maybe it was Grandpa Allen's affair with Grandpa Charlie's sister, Great Aunt Bessie. Grandma told me about it after Grandpa's passing, as we sat in her sitting room next to the oil heating stove.

She said, "He came home early morning. I was doing the laundry in this very room. I looked him in the eye and said, 'It's me or her. Decide right now.'"

I could picture Aunt Bessie, short, heavy set, hair dyed dark and tight curls. I did not know her well, but I knew she spent a lot of time at a bar in one of the local towns. I could not picture Grandpa being with her. He too was short at 5'5", stout and with short auburn curly hair due to his Irish heritage, but I could not imagine him in a bar drinking or his being untrustworthy. I am thankful she told me after his passing, so I never looked at him as a betrayer. Other family secrets would be revealed as I became an adult. Like the maternal male cousin three years older being the result of a rape of Mom's sister by a cousin to her brother-n-law.

Both sets of grandparents were Christian but believed very differently about the practice of worship. Grandma Courser had recently joined the Seventh-day Adventist church who believed Saturday to be the Sabbath, so she went to church on Saturday. Grandpa and Grandma Fisk worshipped on Sunday in a small Church of God church a few miles from home. Grandma Courser and Grandpa Fisk were strong, dogmatic, religious individuals while their mates were not. Both Grandpa Courser and Grandma Fisk were soft spoken and passive. I remember these two as loving and caring but far less influential in my life.

At a time when none of my ten sets of aunts and uncles attended church or raised their children within a religious belief, my life would be dominated by Grandma Courser's religious beliefs.

Dad's absence during half of the first three years of my life left an indelible mark. I, like many others born during this time, lived with extended family. Caretaking was done by a host of family members. My care was further relegated to others when a brother, Lewis, was born fifteen months after me and four months before Dad was shipped to the European theatre. As a result, I remained firmly attached to extended family—grandparents, aunts, uncles, and cousins.

Mom moved from the small house on her parents' farm after a few months into a rented house on Bass Lake a few miles away from Grandma's proximity. We went to the farm often to help with gardening, canning, and field work if needed. Mom's influence in my life was diminished by the dominant role Grandma played, as Grandma was a strong matriarch. I can still hear her words, "Mildred, you need to….." While Mom's response was noncommittal to her mother, Grandma's words would dominate my life and cause havoc with my relationship with my father.

On October 17, 1945, at 9:12 a.m. a telegram was sent from New York to Michigan: "Arrived New York today be home few days telegram or telephone later love, Paul Fisk." Three days later Grandpa Fisk drove Mom, me, Lewis, and Grandma Fisk to the train station to bring Dad home. As a two-year-old I had kissed my father's picture each night before sleep, so I recognized him when he stepped off the train and eagerly went into his open arms.

I don't remember that day or anything about the next three years, but I sense that my experience was not as I expected. I spent the rest of my life trying to please Dad, always striving for a warm response to assure me of his love. Post-traumatic stress disorder was unnamed and of course, untreated. The word used to describe his short temper and emotional distance was "shell-shocked." The first time he sat down at a table with his parents after his return, his insensitive father asked, "How many of your buddies did you lose over there?" Dad stood up, walked outside and closed the physical and emotional door behind him.

His return brought a drastic change in my life. Someone other than Grandma became a very strong influence. Until they died, just months apart, I felt pulled between them—conflicted about which one to please. Grandma was religious and expected me to be, whereas Dad wanted nothing to do with religion. At times this caused unbearable conflict within me. I did my best to remain loyal to both and often felt twinges of agony when siding with the desires of one, while displeasing the other. For instance, while on a family trip with Grandpa and Grandma, Dad wanted me to go fishing with him on Saturday and Grandma hearing his request took me aside and told me, "We don't fish on the Sabbath."

3

I entered kindergarten in August before I turned five in November. Mom walked me to school that first day, up the stairs, first room to the right. She knocked at the big wooden door and tears sprang to my eyes, but I did not cry out. When the door opened, Mrs. Houghton's cheerful encouragement drew me into the classroom and dried my tears. A sister, Susan, was born just weeks before with colic and cried day and night. Lewis was only two-years old and he demanded Mom's attention too. I was the big sister, called "Sis" by my dad and "Sissy" by my brother. I tried to be the big helper. I stood on a chair and washed dishes. I rocked my sister. I played with my brother. My parents were still broken from the war, Dad short-tempered and Mom overwhelmed. I felt left out. The classroom became my favorite place.

The recent move from a rented farmhouse in the country to the small familiar town of less than four hundred allowed walking to school and to Dad's work place, the garage where he repaired cars. Both my parents had attended this very school, Dad graduated and Mom dropped out her junior year. Cousins had attended before me. A few were attending with me, and many more would follow.

A house on a corner lot two blocks north of the school had become our home. The two-story, three-bedroom house with living room and kitchen was small but more than adequate. The large room up the stairs from the living room was used only for household storage. A root cellar for food needing cooler temperatures, such as onions, potatoes, and canned goods, was entered by a door hidden in the floor of the kitchen. A two-seater outhouse a few feet out the back door provided for toilet needs. In a chicken wire pen to the left resided Blondie, a Cocker Spaniel, and Maisy, a Beagle, one raised for our pleasure and one for Dad's hunting. To the right of the large open grassy field behind the house were the backyards and back doors of neighbors.

The first summer in the house a circus came to town and set up cages and rides in the field. I heard about this upon my return from a one time visit to stay with a cousin of my dad's. The grass was laying flat in many large areas and there were holes where stakes had been driven. *Dad hadn't allowed me to stay with relatives when I asked to, so why was I sent away at this time?*

I learned at an early age not to question Dad with "Whys." He was a small man at five-foot seven inches and one hundred forty pounds, but he was strong, powerful, intense, and short-tempered. He used the phrase: "dynamite comes packed in small packages" to jokingly describe himself. He also often said, when asked questions or as a response to something he considered wrong, "Use your brain." Then sometimes added, "Not mine."

Though pictures show him before the war with plentiful dark hair, after the war he always kept a butch hair cut. I do not remember his belt landing on me, but for all my growing up years, when his hand reached toward it, I cringed. His tenderness was rare but manifested often enough for me to know he loved me. When Mom pulled my first loose tooth and I was teary, he fixed me a cup of one-third coffee and filled the rest with milk and sugar. I forgot the tooth loss and felt cared for. *Was this his first show of tenderness?* This act solidified coffee to be my choice for comfort from then to this day.

Mom was five-foot four and skinny until in later years when her lack of labor rounded out her body to plumpness. She was attractive but not beautiful, dressed plainly and wore no make-up except a rare touch of lipstick. She was mild mannered even when angry. Her threats of what Dad would do to me if I disobeyed were sufficient to maintain obedience.

Across the street sat Pete's shop. Sometimes I stopped on my way home from school to visit Pete in his small, tar-papered building filled with leather of every description and shoes and boots repaired or needing repair. The smell of leather and oil still reminds me of Pete, a small man bent over with years of applying his trade. He always welcomed me with a smile. A fondness grew within me that I am still aware of seventy years later. It was at his shop that I first made my stand for right when under the eaves of his shop roof neighborhood boys, the Wrisleys and Bennets, pulled baby birds from nests and wrung their necks while laughing and patting backs. My words, "Stop, don't do that, "didn't stop them. *Did I tell Pete? Did I tell Mom? Was it only me that felt the pain their killing was bringing to the mother birds as they flew above their heads with cries? Was I the only one who cared?*

Farther up the street toward the school, lived Old Frank, as called by some, in the dingy single floored apartment building. Mom, Lewis and I had lived in the adjoining apartment for a short time while Dad was at war. Old Frank wandered the streets ignored by some, feared by some, joked-of by some. I said "hi" whenever I saw him. *Maybe a friendship had developed while we lived next door?* One day he handed me a card addressed to my brother and me with weak handwriting typical of the elderly. The card expressed fondness though I do not remember the words.

Was this the start of my life pattern of cheering for the underdog and accepting people's differences?

On the left and opposite corner stood Grandma Foote's restaurant. Grandma Foote was my cousins' grandma, my Aunt Ernestine's mother-n-law. White haired, short, and plump she was perfect grandma material, always accepting my presence with a smile and hug unless her hands were in dough or waiting on customers. Our families frequented her home away from home, particularly on Saturday nights when the fathers would play cards and drink beer while the mothers gossiped, kept eyes on the children, and listened to music.

Included on Main Street was the post office, two hardware stores and two grocery stores at opposite ends. Hubbards' drug store was two whole blocks up the inclining street to the right and as far as my cousin and I were allowed to walk alone when we turned twelve. Our purchase was always a five-cent cherry-flavored coke. Those two blocks felt long and we felt grown-up.

My mom's youngest sister, Aunt Martha, lived with her husband and son a couple of blocks to the north of the house we lived in, and oldest sister, Aunt Ernestine, lived with her husband, son, and two daughters south the same distance. This was our town, as in "my family's." I felt I *belonged* here.

On my walk to and from school, I passed what appeared to me to be a large church. It was the tallest building in town with its steeple. My first and second grade class-rooms were upstairs in the back of the church. Many of the teachers and store owners in town attended this church. No one in my family did. We did not attend church—not any church. Only my grandparents attended church. *Why didn't we? Why didn't any of my ten aunts and uncles, children of my church-going grandparents, take their children to church?*

The words I heard most often of God were the swear words from my dad's and uncle's mouths as they played cards around our dining room table or when my dad was angry.

I don't remember a Sunday school at Grandpa's church, but I do remember his leading in song service up front where his voice bounced off the wooden seats, floor, rostrum and pulpit with such volume that I can still imagine it. Grandpa Fisk was a true patriarch. He stood ramrod straight and rose up in the air as though it made space for him. He was taller than his five sons and more verbose. I remember him as warm but self-absorbed. This showed most in his religious life. Going to church was going with Grandpa not with Grandma. Before standing up in church on Sundays, Grandpa always brought in the widows. Family rumor said that Grandpa took Grandma to church first and then drove to pick up widowed women to bring them to church. He brought Grandma to church first, but not to fill some duty, because Grandma only filled a pew. She took no part in church activities. She limited her involvement to church service on Sunday morning and prayer meetings mid-week.

Grandpa also picked up the offerings and took them to the back of the church. Years later, an older cousin told me that her father, the oldest of the five boys, had to leave school in his eighth grade so that he could work and pay off money Grandpa stole from the church.

Grandma Fisk was a slight, grey haired, quiet woman who embodied acceptance and love. I have few memories of her, but they are sweet ones. I know that she suffered abuse at the hands of Grandpa—evident in her withdrawal in his presence, and her display of a cheerful and playful nature when he wasn't around. She always welcomed us with a smile and an invitation to enjoy one of her molasses cookies. I felt loved by Grandma Fisk who never demanded that I cater to her desires. I still remember the words she used as she descended the stairs after tucking us in, on the rare times we spent the night, "Good night, sleep tight. Don't let the bedbugs bite." *She never spoke of religion or God, but perhaps she was closer to God and God's love than Grandpa or even Grandma Courser.*

The one time I remember going to church with Grandma Courser came after spending the Friday night before at her house. My cousin, Pat, and I slept in Grandma's bedroom. Grandma must have slept with Grandpa that night to make room for us. They usually slept apart. Grandpa's bedroom was across the dining room against the opposite wall of Grandma's. On the night that I remember, the rooms were not far enough away. Moments after settling into bed, the door opened, and with a stern but quiet voice Grandma said, "Girls, I want you to be quiet and go to sleep."

When we continued to giggle, Grandma's next entrance was much sterner. The voice that said, "I want you to be quiet and go to sleep. We need to get up early for church." was raised and curt with emotion. I felt the seriousness. I became quiet, restraining the giggles and turning my back to Pat. We soon fell asleep.

Clothed in dresses we did not often wear and with braids Grandma had firmly formed on our heads, we followed her out to the car the next morning and sat sedately in the back seat. The church was a half hour away over two-lane dirt roads, so we each took a window and with few words, watched the scenery pass by. Grandma's mother, Great Grandma Nicholson, lived on the edge of the town where the church was, so we stopped to pick her up. A cheery hello from Great Grandma Millie, as she plunked down in the passenger's seat, lent to a cheerier morning, and we brightened to this new adventure.

Grandma took us downstairs to Sabbath school—a class for children before the church service. It was fun. We sang songs, listened to Bible stories and colored in our Sabbath papers. After Sabbath School we were led upstairs to the Church service. It was not fun sitting quietly without moving and listening to a man talk upfront about things I did not understand. But, we did sit quietly between our two grandmas, drawing on small sheets of paper and sucking on wintergreen mint candies that Grandma Courser always carried in her purse.

The lunch at Great Grandma Millie's house after church was a simple meal of vegetables, bread, and pie. When lunch was finished, and dirty dishes were stacked in the sink to be washed after sundown, we were handed a blanket and told to find a cool spot in the shade under a yellow Spirea bush in the front yard. Our grandmothers would rest inside reading the church pamphlets and perhaps napping.

It was hot and muggy. As Pat and I lounged outside with our own

Sabbath School papers and in our Sabbath dresses, droplets of moisture formed along our hairlines. We were uncomfortable with the heat and speculated on ways to get cool. Could we convince Grandma to let us play with a water hose as we sometimes did at home? But wait, she already said we were to rest and not play. Into the second hour of our repose, Pat said, "Let's ask Grandma for ice cream." It seemed innocent enough. We discussed who would ask. Being the older, I relented and timidly knocked on the front door.

When Grandma Courser opened the door with a reluctant, "What?" I did not feel so brave but spit out, "We're hot. Can we go down the street to that little store and get ice cream?" Grandma's face flushed with disappointment, and the prominent wrinkles in her forehead squeezed closer together. Her voice sounded angry, "This is the Sabbath of the Lord. We do not work or play on the Sabbath, and we do not buy on the Sabbath. Why hasn't your mother taught you this?"

Grandma's look of obvious displeasure and her sharp reminder, "We don't buy on the Sabbath," caused Pat and me to look at each other with a question and a shrug. We did not know what to say. We returned to the blanket meekly, and Grandma closed the door. We remained subdued for the rest of the day.

We had no idea what Grandma's "keeping" meant. Keeping the Sabbath holy was paramount to her belief in the Adventist Church, and to her concept of something she called "salvation."

Now that I look back at the incident, I know that Grandma's anger was not directed at us as much as towards her daughters who obviously had not taught us what she considered to be very important. The belief in proper observance of the Sabbath stood between her granddaughters' righteous experience of heaven or their descent into hell. Buying on the Sabbath was a sin. Not only was it a sin, she believed that if Pat and I did not keep the rules around its sacredness, we could not go to heaven.

Much to Grandma's apparent dismay, Saturday was a town day for our mothers—a day we looked forward to because trips to town twenty miles away were rare. Saturday was a day for us to spend our allowances and get a treat of candy or ice cream.

I did not want to do anything to displease Grandma, but did not understand what she was telling us. Eventually, Pat and I became Sabbath keepers by our own choice and would teach our children the same. We, the oldest granddaughters, would be the only ones to adhere to Grandma's religious convictions and educate our children within the church educational system.

Grandmother Courser's dominance over the family was made obvious the summer before I turned thirteen, when after an extended illness, she sent word to all her children to come home on Sunday with their mates and children. Her concern for the salvation of her husband, children, and grandchildren must have weighed heavily on her mind. Her religious convictions made it clear: all were "lost." This was a genuine heart issue for Grandma that I understand much better today since having children and grandchildren of my own. It must have felt like she would be saying goodbye to all her family forever. She would be in heaven. They would not.

My recollection of this event is based upon what others told me or what I overheard others discussing. My family did not attend the Sunday gathering, since we had out-of-town visitors. Twenty-nine children, grandchildren and in-laws crowded into my grandparents' house that Sunday afternoon.

I wish I had been there. Grandma proclaimed that she had had a vision about the Second Coming of Jesus. The only thing I remember for certain about what I was told is that Grandpa was in the vision and not ready for the Second Coming because he had a cigarette in his hand. While I don't remember ever seeing Grandpa smoke cigarettes, I do know that if it was true, this would have caused Grandma much concern. Adding to this distress, each one of her sons and sons-in-law also smoked. In her belief, the smoking of cigarettes was a sin and another cause for the loss of salvation.

I have pondered that meeting many times. Criticisms of Grandma that permeated family talk about the meeting always disturbed me. I was Grandma's first born favored granddaughter and always her defender. Whenever my mother or aunts railed against her I defended her. I should have been at that family meeting.

I imagine Grandma meeting them at the door and peering out at stone faces containing a silent question: "What's this about?" And a desire: "Let's get this over with."

I envision them entering through the woodshed, holding onto the railing next to the slanted cellar door as they made their way into the house. I am confident that Grandpa must have sat in the living room, two rooms from the entrance door, reserving dignity that he may not have felt. I am confident in the belief that my three aunts, two uncles, and their mates were not happy about being there—not a one wanted to hear what Grandma had to say. I've wondered what brought them there. Probably obligation. They did not know it was about a "vision." They must have believed it to be a very important family announcement. For Grandma it was. For them it was not.

I also feel confident that my aunts came in and sat near their father—as his defense and his comfort. Surely Grandma sat in her light grey cloth covered, wooden armed, rocking chair between the telephone stand and the oil heating stove, in the dining room. As was her way, she would have implored the family to surround her, giving directions as to who should sit where—grandchildren on the floor.

I imagine her demand to Grandpa was, "Allen, I want you in here," No hesitancy, no embarrassment. Not on Grandma's part. I can hear Aunt Emogene or Aunt Martha say, "Ma, leave him be." I imagine he stayed in the living room—distressed but quiet.

The sons-in-law would be the most uneasy—especially after they heard Grandma say, "I had a vision and God told me to share it with my family." No one would have said anything, but disgust would be in their demeanor.

Grandma would have proclaimed this vision, not to reiterate her faith in God, but to admonish her family to accept that the vision was for them. Further, for them not only to accept the vision, but to accept God and salvation. This would have meant accepting the Seventh-day Adventist Church as the true church, and keeping the Sabbath Day holy, that they all might be saved.

Did she end in prayer for them? Were there tears of emotion? Maybe, but I cannot imagine them from Grandma. Tears? Maybe from daughters upset by their mother's declaration that they were all lost souls—especially Grandma's portrayal of their father.

How did it close if not in prayer—did she ask for conversion? I wish I had been there. I wish I knew. *Why? Would it help me understand my grandmother's influence on my life?* The vision did not appear to affect any life within the family in a positive way. All the children, my aunts and uncles, had greater loyalty to a non-judgmental father than a Bible-thumping mother.

I remember the house they lived in so well that I could draw a picture of it including the furniture. I remember the smell of earth in the cellar, damp and dark, where I helped Grandma cut seed potatoes. I remember even the little wren that appeared each spring to nest in the bird house next to the garden. I can still see the rows of flowers as I crossed into the garden to help pick green beans. But about God I remember the do's and don'ts. I do not remember even one conversation or experience that showed me that Grandma knew God as love until just before her death many years later.

4

MY EDUCATION IN the kindergarten, first and second grade was nurtured into me by Mrs. Houghton. I felt safe and cared for even when in the second grade my friend, Rosemary and I, wrote the spelling test words very faintly on the sheet of paper we were using for the test. Mrs. Houghton saw what we had done and brought it to the attention of the class. She expressed her disappointment but with such love that it did not feel like punishment. At her urging I said, "I'm sorry," with downcast eyes. I became a good speller from this experience and never once cheated at any time in future schooling.

In the Teacher's Reports that Mom preserved and passed on to me, Mrs. Houghton wrote, "She cooperates very well and the children all like her. Paua is a very good little student….never has any playground disagreements. I enjoy working with her very much." In the last report from second grade she wrote: "I would like a room full just like her."

The last day of school that year, Mrs. Houghton announced that she would no longer be teaching at the school. I can still relate to the deep sadness I felt. At the end of the day, she gave each of us a clipping of the large Impatiens plant in the classroom. With the clipping clutched in my hand, I walked very slowly up the slight hill to the post office corner before crossing main street toward home. As I walked, I cried. A cousin, Terry, three years older and usually inattentive to me, walked past, stopped, and asked, "What's wrong with you?" I tried to explain, "Mrs. Houghton, she," but only cried harder and louder. Shaking his head in disbelief that I could be so sad about a teacher, he walked away and left me trudging home. I remember so plainly my walk to the corner at the post office and yet have no other memory. *Did mom not notice the tears or the plant? Did she perhaps want Mrs. Houghton to be gone? Was Mrs. Houghton too special to me? What happened that I remember Terry's response but not Mom's?*

Third grade with Mrs. Sarver was a completely different story. I was sad every day for what seems like weeks into the school year. Day after day, Kathleen, a second cousin of mine, entered the classroom crying and was shut in a closet until she stopped. The classroom had a wooden floor and wooden desks, nothing to absorb the cries behind the closet door. I felt so sorry for her. There was nothing I could do. I couldn't focus on anything else but that closet until Kathleen was let out. *Was this the first time I wanted to help and couldn't? Did she tell her parents? Did I tell mine?* Probably not. Dad told us more than once, "You get in trouble at school, you get more trouble at home." Spanking was allowed. I guess being locked in a closet was too.

This classroom is where I became directionally challenged. Standing before the class, Mrs. Sarver said, "Raise your right hand," I raised the wrong hand. "Point to north," she requested. So nervous by now that I hardly knew up from down, I could not remember north. With a raised voice she admonished me in front of the class. Though I do not remember her words, I do remember the fear and sense of stupidity that sunk into me like dampness sinks into grass when the sun goes down. To this day, I return to that class room each time I have to determine directions as in north or south. In my mind I stand facing north, toward the front of the room, and then know east is to my right hand and the west to my left. I just did it again to make sure of where east and west are presently. Repeatedly, throughout my life I have turned the wrong direction while reading a map or listening to verbal directions. In the reports Mom preserved for me there is none from Mrs. Sarver. *I wonder?*

My journey to school changed to a bus ride my fourth-grade year and to Mrs. Beach as my teacher. Maybe due to the move and changes in my life, I do not remember this classroom but do know I did well as in the Teacher's Report, Mrs. Beach wrote, "Paula is a very sweet child. She has many friends and gets along with them well."

Fifth grade introduced me to delightful Mrs. Williams as a teacher. Pure white hair wound around her head in braids giving the sense of an angel. She taught my father when he was in the third grade and openly favored him. She told my mother a story of his response to her one day in class as she was correcting his spelling or reading, when he looked up at her and said, "I could just bite you." Always gentle, even in correction, I loved her, but she did not replace Mrs. Houghton in my heart. In the Teachers Report for that year Mrs. Williams wrote, "Her attitude toward those who do not do as well is always kindly and considerate."

The theme throughout these reports of my care for and kindness toward others mystifies me today. *Who modeled it for me? Who taught this acceptance and care of others that I carried at a young age?*

Our move to the country consisted of a purchased forty acres just a mile south of town on a narrow, dirt road lined with trees. Before our property on the north side of the road was a pasture where a neighbor pastured a herd of Angus with a mean, noisy bull that tormented us children with his bellowing and hoof pawing that left clouds of dust around his body. This on the days we walked the third mile home from the bus drop off or if we were making noise in the yard next to his fence. Half way on the third of mile from the two-lane pavement out of town stood a shack where Lester lived. He too frightened us through the years whenever he became intoxicated and shared all his anger through tirads of words exclaiming our audacity of building a house within eyesight of his run-down, tar-covered cabin. Thankfully, he only threatened our demise with words and would withdraw from Dad's appearance into silence until the next alcoholic binge.

Other neighbors were a half mile further to the east, the Johnstons, five kids in a dark and dreary basement on the south side and Kings on the north in another humble dwelling. This dirt road caused much angst in spring and winter as in the spring it became impassable with mud and in the winter with snow. My dad spent many hours digging ditches for the water to drain off the road in the spring and shoveling snow in the winter. We children, too, were solicited and taught how to combine the ruts with ditches to drain off the water from rain or melted snow.

Family provided the labor to build the first living space the summer before our move. Even Great Grandpa Nicholson, Mom's grandpa, was enlisted to build a lean-to porch on the side of the two-stall cement block garage that became our home. It provided a small but sufficient space with a living room and kitchen in one half and two bedrooms in the other. One bedroom allowed for the sharing of a metal bunk bed for my brother, Lewis, on top and my sister, Susan, and me on the bottom at opposite ends. Nails for hanging and wooden shelves provided for the few clothing items we had—mostly jeans and t-shirts.

The outhouse, at the bottom of the hill, was too far away to walk to in the dark so a porcelain pot covered with newspaper also set in our bedroom. The cigarette smoke from my dad's chain smoking, mixed with the smell of the pot, unwashed bodies, and garbage pail under the sink must have provided an offensive odor that I do not recall. I say unwashed bodies because I do not remember any bathing. We must have, *but how?*

Until the outside pump was brought inside as a small hand pump over a small sink, a pail of water with a dipper hanging on the side sat on a counter and was used for all, family or friends. Dirty water drained into a bucket also holding garbage beneath the sink in a cabinet. An oil stove sat in an opposite corner providing heat in the winter and a place for me to lean upon in the middle of the night with the many ear aches I suffered.

A large over-stuffed green chair was Dad's throne when he was home. Wooden straight back chairs provided other seating at the small wooden, drop-leaved table that sat in the middle of the kitchen. Mom's favorite piece of furniture appeared to be a buffet with doors and drawers and a flat top to display any special dishes she had acquired. The year I was ten a small black and white TV filled the second corner of the "living" room.

The property had been a residence once before, evidenced by the old poorly groomed apple orchard and cleared fields to the right and left of the slight hill the garage sat upon. The field to the left became a large garden that provided labor for Lewis and I. The larger field to the right provided summer crops of beans or cucumbers. Lewis and I spent hours in those fields first picking up stones and then pulling weeds. It is where I learned to drive a tractor. To Dad's dismay and sometimes anger, my confusion of turning right or left as he demanded, caused frustration for him and fear for me. Demands to step on the right or left brake also brought frustration and tears.

The summer the fields were planted of cucumbers, the first experience of diversity came into my life when Mexican laborers came to pick the cucumbers. We watched them from afar as demanded by Mom and Dad. They were not to be trusted. Though this was communicated by the adults, I did not feel afraid but curious. They did not speak English or I might have tried to sneak in a conversation.

A large oak tree stood guard over the slight rise to the property from the road and provided food for the many squirrels and chipmunks that occupied the property before and after our arrival. The first summer, I created a cemetery for placement of the little animals I found dead and those I did my best to nourish and care for but often failed to keep alive. I felt responsible for the little creatures—toads, birds, chipmunks, and squirrels. I often cried over their dying. Snakes occupied our property in large numbers. They were no real threat, but Mom passed on to us her hatred of snakes from an experience in her teens of swimming in a river where a water snake wound itself around her shoulders. She did not withdraw when she saw a snake but went for a shovel or hoe and did not rest until she had killed it. Lewis and I, too, hunted them in the tall grass around our property. We caught them, placed them in empty, plastic bread bags. At the end of the day we stoned them. Some days we would catch and kill a dozen or more. While intending to save the lives of small animals, I readily ended the lives of another creature no more dangerous. They also were helpful by eating the insects that destroyed garden crops and rodents that ate the chicken feed. Mom was intent on killing what she was afraid of—making it look like anger. As years passed I became aware of others, as well as within myself, that anger is a cover for fear and miscommunicates our need for safety. This response to fear was to become a focus as I grew in wisdom of "what is."

A small three cow barn, a chicken coup and dog pen completed our farm. Dad fenced half the property with barb wire and acquired a herd of a-half-dozen cows that provided milk, the chickens provided eggs and meat. The Beagle hounds were raised for hunting—Rhubarb, a multi-colored Beagle, was our favorite dog. Lewis and I were given the responsibility to herd the cows in at dusk to be milked. The pasture was heavily wooded so finding and herding became a wearisome task. Sometimes finding the cows and bringing them to the barn before dark also created danger. One of the trips through the woods part of the pasture I heard a blood curdling scream from my brother and rushed toward him as fast as dodging trees would allow. Dad also heard the scream, cleared the fence on his run, and arrived at Lewis before me. He was covered with angry stinging hornets whose nest he had accidently stepped upon. Dad's fast work of recovery and mom's nursing care restored Lewis.

Each spring Mom ordered chicks—hundreds of them. They grew into squawking, flapping, scratching hens and roosters that flew at and on us when we went into the pen to feed and water. A large, Leghorn rooster set free from the pen became guard of the hens and whenever we made our necessary trips to the outhouse attacked us with the spurs pointed toward flesh. Lewis and I fought back with kicks and sticks and we accompanied frightened Susan on her trips to the toilet.

While living in the garage, we received a visitor by the name of Mrs. Thomas. This visit was evidence of my grandma's desire for us to attend church. Mrs. Thomas was a Seventh-day Adventist and member of a church in a small town a few miles to the east. We did not attend with her, but she would stop by after church on Sabbath afternoons to drop off The Little Friend—a church paper for children. One Sabbath afternoon I saw her car enter the driveway and ran quickly into the house/garage to change the shorts I was wearing. Somehow, I believed I should not be wearing shorts and that she would judge me. I tore through the pile of jeans in the corner of the room until I found a pair with legs, pulled them on and only then went out to say hello. She was a sweet lady and today I can assure myself that she would not have judged me for having on jean shorts that Sabbath day. She had two sons that came with her. One was a year or two older than me and one a year younger. Though very little communication passed between us, one day the younger son handed me a note that read: "Roses are red and violets are blue, Sugar is sweet and so are you." *How could he know I was sweet?*

By the time I entered high school a cement block house had replaced the garage providing separate bedrooms. Susan and I shared one small bedroom. A double bed with an iron bedstead served our slumber where night after night I would convince Susan to give me a back rub and fake sleep not keeping the promise to give her one.

The year I turned thirteen the bathroom was completed with the only door inside the house. Curtains hung at the three bedroom doors. *Is this in itself an indicator of loose or non-existent boundaries?* Though Dad would not allow me to bathe and wash my hair more than once a week because he thought it was "wasting water," it did save us from trips down the hill. I didn't understand why we couldn't take more baths and snuck a few in when Dad was not at home. We had a well. There was no drought. The mentality of scarcity came from both parents. Their profound belief of lack carried over from the market crash of the 1930s, and then the scarcity during the second world war. The belief in scarcity has followed me throughout my life.

Only fifteen months apart, Lewis and I were often companions, leaving Susan in the house with Mom. We spent hours in the woods building stick and leaf cabins, exploring streams, playing in the snow and ice skating in the winter or collecting pelts on his trap line. We also worked in the garden and fields weeding and harvesting. However, I drove the tractor first and rode the planter for Dad because Lewis was smaller in build and not strong enough. He resented my strength and my working with Dad. I resented that I did outside work with Dad and was still responsible for inside work that he did not have to do. Dad did not allow for a boy to do a woman's job and Mom did not encourage it. *Why was it okay, not only in my family but many others, that a girl could work in the field and the barn but the boys of the family only worked outside?*

Lewis was a tease. He was able to bring me to anger quicker than anyone else in my life. He orchestrated a group of boys to gang up on me at school and pelt me with snowballs. He teased and hurt my dog and not the others. I was taller and stronger in build so could best him in most anything we did. Contention defined our relationship throughout our lives even though we were always available to one another's needs. Though I ousted him while young, he would prove he had a better mind and out educate me.

Lewis and I eventually attended the little Seventh-day Adventist Church that Mrs. Thomas introduced us to and became baptized members of that church. Neither of us realized at the time how profoundly this would affect our future lives. This little country church with my grandmother's urging propelled me into a religiously focused and conflicted life.

5

THE SPRING OF my Freshman year of high school, I was baptized and became a member of the Seventh-day Adventist Church. I was doing what I believed I should do. I did not realize what power this commitment would have in my life, let alone how it would dominate my experience of high school.

Before being submerged in water, a requirement to become a member, I agreed to twenty-seven doctrinal beliefs listed in the Certificate of Baptism. I have the original copy with my fourteen year old signature, dated 5/11/57. The beliefs include long statements of clarification after simple statements followed by Biblical texts upon which they are based. The first one,"The true and living God, the first person of the Godhead is our heavenly Father, and He by His Son, Christ Jesus, created all things," stayed an agreement for longer than many others of the twenty-seven, but would become an issue for me years later. The declaration of God being Father, became the premise for writing this book.

The fourteenth belief, "The seventh day of the week is the eternal sign of Christ's power as Creator, Redeemer, and is therefore the Lord's day, or the Christian Sabbath constituting the seal of the living God. It should be observed from sunset Friday to sunset Saturday," caused more discomfort in the years to come than any of the others. The rules for "observing" the

Sabbath were many and I was a rule keeper. For years this belief dominated my weeks—always being conscious of Sabbath preparation.

The twentieth belief, "The church is to come behind in no gift and the presence of the gift of the Spirit of prophecy is to be one of the identifying marks of the remnant church. Seventh-day Adventists recognize that this gift was manifested in the life and ministry of Ellen G. White," became a prominent part of my life. For years her books dominated my reading, along with the Bible. There are many compilations of her writings I did not appreciate because the heart of her writing was taken out. "Desire of Ages," "Ministry of Healing," and "Education" became favorites. "Desire of Ages", about the life of Jesus Christ, sits on my book-shelf today.

I also said "yes" to thirteen questions such as: "Do you believe in God the Father, in His Son Jesus Christ, and in the Holy Spirit; do you accept the death of Jesus Christ …as an atoning sacrifice for the sins of men; have you accepted Jesus Christ as your personal Savior; do you believe that the Bible is God's inspired Word; do you accept the Ten commandments as still binding; is it your purpose to keep this law including the fourth commandment; do you believe that your body is the temple of the Holy Spirit and that you are to honor God by abstaining from such things as alcoholic beverages, tobacco in all its forms, and from unclean foods; do you believe that the Seventh-day Adventist Church constitutes the remnant church; and do you desire to be accepted into its membership?"

All of the above agreed to by a fourteen year old bound for a life of conflicted devotion!

I have no memory of the baptism, the Minister who performed it, or who attended the Saturday morning services. My only memory is of later in the day when my family gathered in town for grocery shopping. As cousin, Pat, and I walked down the street, she asked, "Do you feel any different?"

I answered, "Not really."

The main struggle to keep the vows I made was to keep the Sabbath day, Saturday, holy as I had committed to do. This meant no work, no entertainment, no shopping, no watching TV, no listening to secular music, or reading anything but religious material. Since the Sabbath begins, as the Jewish Sabbath does, at sundown on Friday night, it also meant no attendance of sports or secular events on Friday night. While my friends' Friday nights were spent in all kinds of camaraderie, mine were spent at home trying not to watch TV but reading in my bedroom. As I have said, Grandma Courser was the prevailing influence in my religious upbringing, and I wanted to please her. I also wanted to please my father. When I decided to be baptized at the age of fourteen, my mother told me I had to ask my father for permission. Oh, the trembling of my heart! I knew my father would not like this decision, but I did not want to disappoint Grandma. Also, by now I had heard many sermons, attended baptisms, and been indoctrinated into the beliefs of the Seventh-day Adventist Church. I believed I needed to be baptized in order to be saved—to go to heaven when Jesus came.

I waited to approach the subject with Dad until he was in the garage working on his car. He was engaged, with the hood up and hands deep within the motor. Hearing me approach, he looked up and said, "Hi, Sis," using the name he called me since my siblings' birth. I hesitated, the greeting throwing me off but not diminishing my fear.

"Dad, I want to get baptized." My mouth was dry and my legs felt shaky. The words came out somewhat slurred from the tremendous fear I felt.

He looked up at me sternly and simply said, "You've made this decision now and I don't want any complaints later, hear?" Mom might have already told him that I would be coming to him with my request and he was prepared.

I understood this to mean he would not forbid the baptism. I nodded and turned with relief, but with tears brimming because my dad was unhappy with me.

My only memory of seventh and eighth grades is the trauma relating to body image such as being skinny to the point that male classmates would say, "Hey, Fisk, turn sideways and stick out your tongue. You look like a zipper." This said to point out that I had no breast.

I have no memory of the teachers that signed the Teacher's Reports that Mom preserved from the 7th grade. Mr. Mohre wrote "Paula is doing very nice work......she is very cooperative and easy to get along with ...... all in all she is doing fine. And Mrs. Otterbein wrote "It has been a real pleasure to know your daughter.....she is always so sincere in her efforts to do well....I feel that Paula is a real asset to any group to which she belongs." Such accolades do not relate to my feelings. *Why don't I have memories of these classes? Was it trauma at home or trauma from the teasing in the classroom? Was it what happened that I remembered years later on an airplane flight to see my father who was dying?*

> I sit on the green couch facing the TV. I am right next to Dad and he is rubbing the nubbin of my breast that is just beginning to form. His finger goes up and down over that spot. I sit in a frozen state. I want to move away but can't. I am so afraid of Dad's reaction. I act like I don't know what is happening. I move away so gradually, hoping he won't notice. Slowly, slowly I microinch my body away and finally stand. No response from Dad. Maybe he didn't know what he was doing. But Mom did know. As I leave the room, Mom is in the dining room I pass through and looks at me with disgust on her face. We say nothing. That is all I remember.

Moving from the woods-rat that I had been into the years of early teens had challenges. Clothing had not been an issue until now. A white nylon blouse that was easy to wash by hand and that dried quickly became my main attire along with the skirts mom made. The blouse was sheer and the fact that I was not wearing a bra but a sleeveless t-shirt at thirteen and fourteen brought the derision from male classmates. The day came that Mom took me to town and into Montgomery Wards to buy a bra that I still did not need. When we got home, I went quickly into the bedroom carrying my package, believing it was something to hide and be private. Later that night when I came into the living room, my dad started baaa-ing like a sheep. He and Lewis followed it up with laughter. I knew then the baaa-ing was supposed to be braa-ing to let me know they knew I was wearing my first bra.

The sensitivity to breast development was nothing compared to the trauma of menstruating! Putting rags between my legs. Big bulky rags that had to be washed out by hand. And hung on the clothesline outside for all to see. This embarrassment was lessened due to not having any neighbors close by. I endured the rags for months before I secretly, with babysitting money, bought my first sanitary napkins. Menstruation was not talked about amongst my friends. Mom nor my aunts talked about it either. *Why was causing me to feel dirty? Why was what was happening to my body such a secret?* I do not remember any conversation preparing for its appearance in my life. Its appearance affected how I related to others, including family. I was no longer a kid.

The first time that I found the sticky red stuff in my underpants, I thought there was something wrong. I hesitantly asked Mom, "What is this?"

She said simply, "It means you're a woman now." She told me I would have to wear the rags each month. She went on to tell me that when she started her period her mother, Grandma, had said, "Now you can have babies and if you get pregnant, don't come to me."

Once a month I pulled into a shell from the cramps and fear. Fear that others would know what was happening to my body. It wouldn't be until I gave birth that conversations about menstruating would become permissible or acceptable with Mom, aunts, and friends. Even then, it was spoken of behind closed doors. There were no advertisements of sanitary napkins or tampons, no Pamprin or Midol for cramps, no explanations, no allowances at home or school. This "curse" you experienced alone.

Thankfully, a Health Class was made available my junior year and Mrs. Sears taught us about our bodies, focusing on sex organs and their functions. She taught about intercourse and pregnancy but did not speak of prevention, as we were taught abstinence. The class provided me knowledge to pass on to Mom and aunts. When Mom, Aunt Martha, and I were discussing the class one day and how to prevent pregnancy after marriage, my mom said, "Well, before my tubes were tied, I just got up and peed." I looked at her, somewhat aghast, and said, "Mom, it's not the same hole. You don't pee out the same hole." Using the words of vagina, sperm, penis, scrotum, vulva, was not done in our family. Not even the word breasts, but instead boobs or knockers—always slang. Neither did we use the word menstruation. It was "my period", "the curse". *Why did I know more than my mother? Why couldn't we talk about it more? Why did it always feel like there was something bad about my body and its functions?*

Eventually, after learning about tampons from friends, I purchased them on my own. Mom was opposed to their use. She was afraid they "took" a girl's virginity. Of course the word virgin was never used either. One day while watching Dick Clark's "BandStand," she said with some rancor in her voice, "Just wait and see, one of those things will fall right out of a girl." I didn't say anything because she didn't know I was using them. I did not want her to question me. I could not have lied.

High school did bring some relief from junior high's hurtful experiences. I enjoyed it more. I tried to look attractive, or at least acceptable. The guys' teasing continued with jostling at the lockers and a fist to my shoulder sometimes causing soreness and swelling. *Love taps?* Most of the guys in my class had been in school with me since kindergarten. During the winter I saw more of them than my family. In fact, they were so much like family, they did not date me. This felt like rejection. A couple guys in the class ahead of me showed interest but I was not interested. Leo even took me home from his senior play where he played the part of an older man with grey hair that he had not washed out. When he left my dad said, "You're not dating someone that old."

The fact that I did not participate in activities on Friday night or Saturdays, left me lonely and longing. I was left out of many experiences, such as the time I was selected by an adult committee from the community to serve as Bean Queen during bean harvesting time. Though I was selected, Sally, as runner-up, rode the float in Saturday's parade and was announced as the Queen of the Bean Harvest. Being selected increased my self-worth and image, but I was hurt and frustrated when Mom told me I would not be able to participate. I went to my bedroom, cried in a pillow and reminded myself that only I had made the decision to be baptized. I had made a commitment to "keep the Sabbath holy." I remembered Dad's words and did not complain or mention my unhappiness.

Enter the picture, Roy. In the middle of my sophomore year he was introduced during a class and because we were assigned alphabetical seating, was given a seat next to me. My heart did a flip. He was different—not one of guys who were more like cousins or even brothers. He was kinda mysterious. *Where did he come from?* Later I would learn he was a foster son of longtime residents and was here to stay. I wanted to date him. I longed to date him. We flirted back and forth. At times I would think, *he really likes me.* Then he'd date someone else while he flirted with me. He'd ask me to write him a letter and when I did, read it to the guys in our class. They would make fun. He took me home from events a couple of times and we made out. But he never asked me out. I had no idea then how long that longing would last. I have dreams of Roy to this day. Dreams that I am always searching for him, trying to have a relationship, an attachment. It has never happened in my dreams either, the desire I felt so strong sixty years ago. *Why? How could that stay with me so long from a high school puppy love?*

Dating was relegated to local events when I became sixteen. Bill entered our classrooms my junior year and he too was mysterious, different, city bred. All the girls wanted his attention. Eventually, I won that attention and we went steady until his parents decided that he was too fond of a non-Catholic and insisted he break up with me. He was transferred to a Catholic high school to get him away from temptation.

One day at the lockers Roy said, "Roger, wants a date with you. You should accept." Roger was his closest friend. I was disappointed and felt the rejection. *Passing me off to his friend? His way of getting rid of thoughts of dating me and yet maintaining some contact?*

Roger and I started dating the spring of our Senior year, and the hands that wouldn't go away started pawing my body any chance made available. I did not like the feeling that my body was being owned by another, but thought it was the way it was supposed to be. It felt like the sacrifice for having a relationship like all my other friends. Being the one without a steady made me feel unwanted and left me out of gatherings of couples. By fall and before entering a business college twenty miles away from home, I was committed to the relationship and knew I would marry Roger. We decided to marry at the end of the first semester of college. We set the wedding date for January. Roger was attending and boarding at a University forty miles away from home and me. He hated it. He did not plan to return for the second semester.

By the end of November, days after my eighteenth birthday, I knew I was pregnant when I flew down the hallway one morning to vomit in the bathroom toilet. Mom heard me, came to the door, and said with tremor in her voice, "You're pregnant and it's all my fault." At the time I did not ask why she was blaming herself for something I had done, but later put together that she was pregnant with me when she married Dad and thought it gave me permission to do the same. She still clung to her own guilt of having had intercourse without marriage, and passed it on to me.

"First comes love. Then comes marriage. Then comes baby in the baby carriage."

6

DOCTOR HUGGET WAS grey haired and grandfatherly. His voice was mellow, low keyed. I was somewhat relieved but nothing can completely relieve the anxiety of laying on a hard, narrow table with your legs spread wide and feet planted above the table into cold, metal stirrups. My experience of having my vagina entered had been in cars or on couches discreetly and only by Roger.

Doctor Hugget, was introduced by the nurse who had taken vitals, and said, "Well, we are going to have to look into down here," as he moved to the end of the table and continued with, "You know what goes in has to come out."

Roger was not with me at this appointment. He did not ask questions about the appointment. It was not discussed. He went to work to support us and I focused on a house that was now a thirty-five by eight-foot trailer. I cooked, cleaned, and provided sex each night while my body grew a baby.

On July 15, six months and one day after our wedding, Trudy Jan, a eight-pound, five ounce baby girl was born. Though that birth was fifty-nine years ago, I remember the details, as most mothers do. Beyond the pain, and most of the time childbirth means pain, I remember the young man who stood at the end of the delivery table next to Dr. Hugget. Doctor explained that the young man, though not much older than me, was an intern and that he was going to give the shots I needed around my vaginia—though he didn't use that word. All at once I was on a merry-go-round and trying to get off. Later my mother told me the story. She sat with Roger in the waiting room after my departure to the delivery room. They heard screaming and made the comment that it must be the woman who had gone in after me.

Then the husband appeared and asked Roger, "Is that your wife screaming in there?"

An hour passed with the screams and me trying to get off the merry-go-round before I heard Dr. Hugget say, "You have given us a great scare young lady and now we need to get down to business and push this baby out."

My response was, "You told me I could watch. The mirror, where's the mirror?" My effort toward focusing on the mirror was lost as a contraction took over and I began to push, and push. And then finally, the mighty release that only those who have birthed can know. When the nurse held up the baby and said, "you have a daughter," my happiness was dulled by the novacaine gone wrong. Through the fog I suddenly realized they had rushed the baby away and that there was no crying. I became frightened and asked as strong as I could with a weakened voice, "Where's my baby? Why can't I see my baby?"

The attending nurse said she needed to give me a shot—not adding that it was to help shrink my uterus. I thought it was to put me to sleep because my baby was dead. I shook my head, saying, "No, no" She tried to reassure me that the baby was fine. I did not believe her. In between asking for my baby, I prayed, "Our Father in Heaven, our Father in heaven." It was as far as I could get with the Lord's Prayer. The nurse tried to calm me down and reassure me until I asked anxiously, "Do you have children?" She answered, "Yes, eight." I then asked, "How would you feel if one of them died?" I was determined my baby must be dead. She said she would feel awful but that my baby was not dead. While it seemed like hours, it was only minutes until Trudy was brought back to me to hold. Oh, the relief. Through tears, I saw that she was fine. Because of the seizure the cord had wrapped around her neck three times preventing ease in breathing, let alone crying. I was fine in a few days as the novacaine left my body. Years later I found out that the young man with the questioning face had put his needle into a blood vein instead of flesh.

Why were we as baby producers not educated about birth? There were no books available to me on birthing and my mother and aunts did not talk about it in my presence. Birthing at home with women around you who could help prepare and support had been done away with by this time. Roger had been birthed at home and my mother-in-law had encouraged me to do so. Grandma Courser was not a midwife but one who was called upon in the community to assist with the births of neighbors. Her children were born at home, but her grandchildren were not. So I didn't even consider it. Natural birth was discouraged. Even nursing the baby was discouraged and supplement bottles were given in the nurseries instead of helping a mother learn and accommodate the natural. *Why did women become so accepting of men's way of birthing and providing for an infant?* That is what had happened. Men were the educated and the only physicians. They decided birth was safer with needles, drugs, and hospitals.

In "Midwife's Tale," Martha Ballard's diary of 1785 to 1812, she recorded the deliveries and payments of births. She also recorded the names of those neighbors assisting with the birth. The record documents hundreds of deliveries with few deaths. A physician came into town and convinced others, *husbands?,* that she was not dependable and through trickery and threats, he took over her business. This happened all over the United States.

She also records with some of the births, the name of the Father. These names given while in "travail" were from unmarried women. Martha was charged by a 1786 "Act for the Punishment of Fornication, and for the Maintenance of Bastard Children" to get the name of the guilty person who impregnated the woman. Intercourse between unmarried persons was a crime. Laurel Thatcher Ulrich, author of A Midwife's Tale, writes, "Though trials for fornication were unusual, fornication was not. Between 1785 and 1797 Martha delivered 106 women of their first babies. Of these infants, forty or 38 percent were conceived out of wedlock."

I had been taught, and maintained the belief, that having sex before marriage was a sin. I carried the guilt of my act being a sin, but not a crime. *The guilt of sinning was heavy enough, but to be charged with a crime for bearing a child?* Most of the women mentioned in the diary, documented by Laurel's research, eventually married the Fathers. It was not the lack of love that prevented the couple marrying, but that of finance and having a place to live if they moved out of their individual parents' homes.

This act of having intercourse with someone you love, called "making love," is no longer a crime. It is still considered by most, especially conservative Christians, a sin. *Is it really a sin? Making love is a sin? Is it against God because the couple does not have a piece of paper from the state saying it is okay for them to have intercourse?* It would be many years after my first birth before I would question, discover and release the guilt.

Midwifery returned by 1999 when my youngest Granddaughter, Kara, was born and I had the joyous privilege of assisting with her birth in her parent's bedroom. Husbands were not allowed into the delivery room when my girls were born, but were allowed and encouraged to participate by the time Kara was born. Her father cut her umbilical cord. *Are families strengthened by the presence of family members during birth? Did the sterile conditions imposed by doctors and hospitals really save lives?*

Birthing became easier for me and less emotional due to knowing what to expect but was still drama filled. Two years and a month after Trudy's birth, Kimberly Sue arrived. She was followed by Lori Kay two years and six months later and Brenda Lynne two years and nine months after her.

Each of the births I remember clearly. Kimberly did not cry when born, but I accepted earlier than I did with Trudy's birth, that she was fat and breathless but doing fine. Lori's birth frightened us all including the doctor as she was born with meconium in her lungs and though weighing nine pounds, eleven ounces due to being three weeks late, she was immediately put into an incubator where she touched both ends. I left the hospital sadly not sure of her survival. Many prayers, ours and across the U.S. from family and friends, and four days later the doctor told me, "It is a miracle. Yesterday I did an x-ray and the lungs were still full, today the x-rays showed them clear." So Lori came home to join her two sisters in the little house we occupied on a college campus. At this time Roger was attending an Adventist college in southern Michigan and I was employed at the College Bookstore as an assistant to the Manager.

I don't know if Roger and I ever discussed it, but long ago I had decided I wanted six children. I wanted a boy first to take care of the sisters who would follow. Didn't get a boy the first birth so thought the second and then the third would surely be a boy. I was never disappointed once the girl was born, and Roger did not express disappointment either. Family sometimes made the statement, "Another girl?" with a voice pointing out failure on my part. Men were expected to want a boy to carry on his name that was now the wife's name, and women were expected to give a man an heir.

We did not use birth control after any of the births, as we were not in the frame of mind that we had completed our family. So when I became pregnant shortly after Lori's second birthday, I was pleased. I did not have thoughts of it being the last child I would birth but did think and hope for a boy once more. I also had no thoughts or fears of the process of birth. I did insist on not receiving novocaine or any other drug. I thought all the drama about birth was over. Then Brenda was born with hemolytic disease due to having a different blood type from mine—A positive with my 0 negative. I went home once more without a baby.

The doctor informed me before leaving the hospital, "If the count is not down tomorrow, we will have to change her blood." I did not ask for an explanation and one was not given. Later I learned that because my blood was O- and Brenda's was A+, as were her sisters', antibodies had built in the bloodstream causing the condition. I was strongly advised not to have any more children. The condition of hyperbilirubinemia with high levels of bilirubin can travel to the baby's brain and cause seizures and brain damage.

I was given a prescription for "the Pill," the first oral contraceptive, Enovid, a mix of hormones progesterone and estrogen. The first pill came out in 1960 just eight years before and was still being perfected. The Pill caused my body to believe I was pregnant so that it would not release any more eggs to be impregnated. It also caused me nausea and feelings of irritability. I didn't ask questions. *Why not?* I just accepted and did what I was told. There was no information available to me other than what the doctor said—no internet to look up information.

The last two births happened while Roger was in school and I was responsible for all at home and doing my best to help with income. I did not expect him to get up with the babies at night, or feed a bottle when I was tired. I did not expect him to wash the dishes or fix a meal. So he did not. I did it all. *It's my responsibility to care for the children and the home. I can do it. I have to do it.* I was still sitting on those stairs waiting to be let in or was it "let out?'

7

I HEARD THE SCREECH of brakes and crunch of metal. I stood mute! Moments before six-year-old Kim and eight-year-old Trudy, had departed the kitchen. They cheerfully jumped down the outside steps, with lunch boxes in hand, and their long hair flying in the wind as they ran.

I rushed out the door with my heart pounding and though it was early spring with frost on the ground, barefoot. As I rounded the corner of the house I saw a car with its grill smashed against the tree where my daughters had stood while waiting for the bus that would transport Kim to kindergarten. Trudy would walk across the road and down the street to a second grade classroom.

The car had failed to stop at the corner across from our house, and in an attempt to turn onto the road instead of into our yard, hit the tree. Thankfully, it happened moments after Kim's departure and Trudy's walk across the road. They were safe. I wiped away tears and whispered a prayer of thanks before reentering the kitchen where Lori played and Brenda sat in a highchair.

This incident confirmed my desire to move. The accident, and near tragedy, brought focus to what I had been feeling—fear that we were not living in a safe place for our children.

I was determined to take my children to the country. My need for safety had to do more with my yearning to raise children away from worldly influences than it did about the two-lane-highway. On a farm I could choose with whom they played, where they spent their time, as well as, teach them how to garden and prepare healthy food.

A year had passed since Roger's graduation from the university nearby. My five-year stint of employment to support the family so Roger could go to college, had taken its toll. We came to the small university the summer Kim turned two, and in the next five years I was pregnant two times while still employed—returning to work within a couple weeks of both births.

One day, in the fall of our fifth year, and before spring graduation, I sat at the kitchen table with my family to consume the meager meal I had prepared. I reached for the glass of water next to my plate and could not lift it. I knew something was drastically wrong. I stood up to go lie down and collapsed. Everything went black. Roger carried me to bed. I cried, rocking the bed with violent shakes while he called friends to come and pack for the children and me. We made a hurried three-hour trip to my parents' home.

Two weeks to convalesce at Mom and Dad's gave me the recovery time I needed to be able to resume the care of children and home until graduation. I never returned to my bookstore job. Instead I babysat ten children so that I could stay home with my four. While the pressures of a professional career were gone, my level of stress was not.

There were times when I lay prostrate on the couch not able to gather the strength to stand. Stand, I always did. The income I brought in from daycare was necessary to survive the months until graduation—a family of six had to eat.

Graduation finally came. The accumulation of five years of struggle now ended. I could quit providing the major income. Roger had a degree! Since he had majored in English with a psychology minor the plan was for him to teach at an Adventist school. Unfortunately, no offer came that he would seriously consider, let alone, accept. We had to move from college student housing and needed income, so he was employed by a friend as a construction worker.

A small, dark, beach house on Lake Michigan became our home. It was isolated from everyone, no neighbors, and a quarter mile from the beach. I sunk into depression.

Trudy, as a seven-year-old, took care of her siblings while I slept until noon. I would then drag myself out of bed to the façade of a functioning household before Roger came home from work. He could not understand why I was not happy living on the beach—did not understand why it was not a joy to carry a nine-month-old and maneuver a three, five and seven-year-old a half mile to have fun. This *fun* was often interrupted with diaper changes that meant traveling the quarter mile back that we had traveled minutes before. Low functioning as I was, I always forgot to bring something—like diapers or water to quench four children's thirst. A round trip would leave me too exhausted to return to the beach that day—disappointing the girls, who now added their grouchiness to my stupor.

Two months into the employment, Roger accidentally ran his thumb into a table saw blade and could no longer work construction. This forced him to find other work. He accepted a position as a social worker in the same county as the university he'd graduated from.

We had moved from the beach house into the house on the busy street for a school year. Now I was requesting and planning another move.

Roger was hesitant to pursue the purchase of property, for he was very reluctant to spend money. Savings gave him the feeling of security. My pleading and my parents' willingness to loan us a $5,000 down-payment produced the results I wanted. The first property we investigated, just sixteen miles from where we were living, was visible a half-mile down the two lane road as we approached. It consisted of ten acres on a hill, six miles from the closest small town, and just a few miles from a Seventh-day Adventist church and church school.

A small two-story farmhouse and an old two-story barn that leaned south, sat on top of the hill. A long drive, lined by plum trees on the right and cherry trees on the left, took us to the top of the hill where two large pine trees and five weeping willows surrounded the house. To me, it looked idyllic. As we turned into the drive, I said to Roger, "If you buy me this, I will love you forever."

It took more discussion, more begging and pleading, but the property became ours. I did love that farm. It was my dream—I could be all I dreamed of being. Even more so, I could do all I wanted to do. I could spend my days with my daughters, and be the housewife I thought I should be. I also thought that my being at home would please Roger and allow our home to be less permeated by tension and hassle.

The house was small for our family of six, but sufficient, with three bedrooms and a bath upstairs and one bath down. The kitchen was modern but small—allowing only two of us in the kitchen at a time. The small living area allowed for a dining room table with six chairs, an upright piano, and two wooden sitting pieces of furniture that Roger built. He installed a barrel, as a wood-burning stove, in the field-stone fireplace to heat the house in winter to save on fuel expense.

The large, old barn reminded me of days I had spent in Grandpa Courser's barn. I liked listening to its creaks and groans when the wind blew. The smell of hay was nostalgic—easing drudgery. Other than a play house for the girls, the barn housed the hay I helped pick up in the fields to provide for the horses I was given and those I boarded. A large half acre garden lay to the north of the house and a small chicken coop stood next to it. We acquired chickens, horses, rabbits, dogs, cats, and added Adventist friends who lived in the area.

I cleaned the house and barn, cooked, sewed, washed clothes, fed animals, picked fruit, canned vegetables, baked bread, fixed meals, and cared for four children. During the school months, I drove them to and from school three miles away. I also cleaned someone else's house one day a week, so I could have some spending money. Roger didn't think I needed cash. He asked, "What for?" and would not give me any except when I identified a need that he agreed with. It took a receipt to assure him I spent the money as we had agreed.

Often he came home at six o'clock in the evening still in well-pressed clothes and would brusquely express his dissatisfaction with what he perceived to be a dirty house, chores unfinished, or the lack of a prepared meal. I tried to accomplish this every day so that the evening would be cordial. But there were times when I just couldn't get it all done. Sometimes he would respond angrily. Like the time he was looking for something in a kitchen drawer, could not find it, and expressed his anger by pulling out the drawer, dumping its contents on the floor. I picked up the mess—angry but unwilling to express it, and unwilling to leave the mess until he picked it up.

One day, after living on the farm a couple of years, I went to a farm market a few miles away to pick up some things my garden did not provide. This was an unusual trip because Roger worked in a town twelve miles away, and brought home any needed groceries. As I milled around the crowd in the market, I came face to face with a friend who expressed her pleasure in seeing me with a hug. As we maneuvered around the tables holding the locally-grown fruits and vegetables, we continued to chat. She asked, "How are you? I haven't seen you in ages. What are you doing with yourself?"

I stumbled over words, trying to respond with intelligent comments. "Well, mostly I take care of home and children." I felt panicked by the feelings mounting inside. I felt "dumb." Stammering out, "I need to go, kids waiting," I made it to the car in time to burst into tears.

What is wrong with me? It was a friendly meeting and my response had nothing to do with the person I met. I thought about it all the way home and into the night. *I don't have confidence anymore. I don't believe in me. I'm a failure—as a mother and as a wife. Why can't I be happy doing the very things I said I wanted to do most?*

I could no longer put on a face, cover up the pain, or pretend that all was well. Those words I said on the stairs eight years ago came to me unbidden. *I can't do this. I have to do this.*

I was unhappy in part because I could never get everything done, so there was no sense of completion or accomplishment that lasted. There was always laundry, children and animals to feed, lessons to help with, baking to do, and on and on and on. There was the stimulation and satisfaction of Church activities—often someone to take food to or babysit for. Helping others brought some fulfillment. But I was isolated in a small Church community with strict expectations of what to eat, what to wear, and most of all, what to believe.

The small country Church portrayed ideals of conservatism. The "no's" were TV, movies, makeup, jewelry, novels, alcohol, caffeine, processed foods and meat. I believed we should, and Roger insisted we live as conservative Adventists. Baking whole wheat bread, making homemade sauces, soups, and dressings, and canning and freezing hundreds of quarts of fruit and vegetables gave me purpose and some sense of satisfaction. My children's lunch boxes contained homemade whole wheat bread made with no chemicals or sugar, covered with peanut butter for sandwiches, and fruit. Since we were vegetarians, I also made gluten from wheat to supplement dishes usually made with meat.

The girls attended the Church school where they were required to wear dresses or skirts. No jeans were allowed and if they wore slacks they had to be covered by a skirt or dress. Clothing was difficult to come by since clothing was not in Roger's budget. It would have been less expensive to provide pants and shirts, but rules were rules, and dresses it must be. Out of necessity, sewing clothing was added to my list of chores. Thankfully, two Grandmas and an aunt also sewed and provided clothing.

The focus within our home was on obedience to fundamentalism. I sought happiness by obeying the rules and teaching my children what the Church taught. I was so unhappy and constantly felt like there was something wrong with me. I went to Adventist counselors or therapists to seek understanding—to ask for help for what I sensed was not right. I persisted on talking only to Adventist counselors because of my fear that other counselors would deceive me or tell me that the problem was our lifestyle, or my belief in God.

My requests that Roger go with me fell on deaf ears. I believe now, that it was fear that kept him from going with me. At the time, however, I thought he believed that I was the problem.

I felt hopeless. I feared his displeasure. When he was unhappy or angry the girls learned early to follow my example and did everything to bring him back to a place of happiness or at least accord. We were extra pleasant to him. We made sure the house was clean, chores were done, piano practiced. Everything done to his satisfaction. That is except for the straightening of their fingers while playing the piano. Roger, though I expressed that the teacher said curved, insisted they needed to straighten their fingers.

Once we achieved peace, we tried our best not to do anything that would upset him. Sometimes, we accomplished this for days and sometimes just hours. The isolation of living in the country, and the Adventist school, church, and friends, kept us in close proximity as a family so the efforts made to make and keep peace were intense. *What if I say this? Should I tell him this? Or that? What if I can't? What if I don't? Why do I feel like I have to get permission?*

I sensed something deeper was happening and asked the counselors I sought out, "Why as young as they are, will my daughters not let their father undress them without calling for me?" This question plagued me! When we came home late at night and the girls had fallen asleep in the car to be carried in, they would open their eyes to see who was undressing them. If it was me they closed their eyes, if it was their father, they called for me. The responses I received from the counselors did not satisfy nor enlighten me. Was it just because our daughters were very modest? One counselor told me that there was such a thing as emotional incest and that maybe it was happening between the girls and their father. The counselor did not have any further insight into my dilemma. *What is happening in my home? What am I not getting? What am I missing? Why does something feel wrong?*

Years later when I read *The Feminine Mystique* by Betty Freidan, I was reminded of this time on the farm. She quotes a statement that had been reported to her: "I begin to feel I have no personality." I had lost my personality. I no longer held a prestigious position at a university, in fact, I worked on a farm. I had subjugated myself. No one did it to me. I thought it was my dream, and in some ways it was. At least it was my dream for my children. I felt guilty for all my remorseful feelings. I felt guilty for not being happy.

I was told by a Church member that my personality was too strong, that I needed to be more subdued. So I tried to be subdued. It only lasted as long as I was depressed. Sooner or later, I would talk too much or be too friendly, and Roger would withdraw or confront. When in Church groups—the only groups we were ever in—I tried to be quiet and demure. I thought this would be more representative of a Christian woman. But more importantly, I wanted my husband to be happy with me. The times I failed at being demur, Roger would let me know his displeasure, and home would become intolerable until I pleased him enough to get into his good graces again. I thought the Church, and therefore God, supported his way of thinking and being, and obviously didn't support mine. I did not believe that his reaction or actions, such as not speaking to me for hours or days, was supported by God, but I accepted that I was the problem. I did not want to be involved in any groups, and found reasons not to be. I usually used illness. Illness gave me an out. I increased the use of this *out* as the years passed.

I did not read *The Feminine Mystique* at this time. It was criticized by Church leaders, but another book, popular at the time, was acceptable since it emphasized Christian living. A Church member, and friend, Delores, encouraged me to read *Fascinating Womanhood.* It was apparent that Delores thought this book would help me accept my role as a wife. If I just followed some of the suggestions in the book, I could have a better relationship with my husband, and therefore become a better wife. It didn't enter my mind at the time that probably her husband was just nicer and more responsive to her than mine was to me.

The subtitle of *Fascinating Womanhood* reads: "How the Ideal Woman Awakens a Man's Deepest Love and Tenderness." This sounded good. I surely needed love and tenderness and failed miserably at awakening my husband's. I read the book.

In the book, Helen Andelin says, "If your husband doesn't love you, you are likely doing something to cool his affections, or have lost something that awakens his love. In most cases a man stops loving a woman after marriage because she stops doing things which arouse his feelings. When you regain your charming ways, love can be rekindled."

Irritation flooded me as I read the book. *What's wrong with me? Why do I feel angry? It's wrong to feel this way.*

I read, "When you apply the teachings of *Fascinating Womanhood*, in a miraculous way your husband's faults tend to disappear. Men have been so obnoxious that neither their wife nor anyone else could stand them, but when the wife lived *Fascinating Womanhood* the man became pleasant and agreeable." I tried to follow some of the suggestions, but they did not seem to work for me. Nothing I did succeeded in evoking love and appreciation from my husband. I viewed the problem as mine. So I sought help. Every Adventist counselor told me it was not me. They continued to say that it would be best for Roger to come to counseling with me, but of course, he would not.

The anger I felt was not acceptable even to me. Therefore, I could not express it. How could I explain why I was rankled by the idea of manipulating my husband into showing me love? Another friend I talked with about the book, responded lightly, "I can't believe that he's not responding if you are following the book's suggestions." She went on to describe what her husband responded to—humor.

So I tried being cute when he was angry. I made a joke to lighten the situation, and he was still angry. The book says, "Childlikeness is one of the most charming taught traits……Childlike anger is the cute, pert, saucy anger of a little child…A scene such as this invariably makes us smile with amusement….This is much the same feeling a woman inspires in a man when she expresses anger in a childlike way."

Roger did not find me cute, pert or saucy when I tried this. His yelling, turning his back while I expressed my feelings, and then not speaking to me for days, was not cute either. I felt more humiliated, less competent as a wife, and a failure in my pursuit to be the "ideal wife." In fact, I felt crushed. I couldn't talk to anyone. Anything I had to say sounded selfish. My husband was being himself—the spoiled youngest son. And I was being me—the oldest, outgoing daughter who always made things right. I did not know how to make *this* right.

Fascinating Womanhood goes on to say, "Although you owe your husband a generous amount of sex, he doesn't own your body." I "owe" my husband? She continues, "the most important thing to remember is his sensitive masculine pride." I did take responsibility for that, and it is one of the main reasons that I rarely said no to his sexual advances.

Wrap myself in cellophane and meet him at the door when he returns from work? Cook in the kitchen with just an apron on? I did not have to encourage sex. Roger insisted on having sex at least every other night as though it was his due for putting up with me. I remember too well the foot in the middle of my back and landing on a cold hard floor. I had said, "I'm too tired, not tonight."

Do men really have such sensitive egos that their wives need to continually build them up? Where does the line of manipulation begin and end? Are his feelings more important than mine? Even when I am suffering, am I supposed to be really careful to bring out the best in him, in order to get what I want?

Trying to understand who I was in relation to what I was being told I should be, continued to be a struggle. I felt powerless to change my demeaning circumstances. My underlying depression was kept from surfacing because I had too much to do to stop and contemplate my own needs. I was tired, and I was sad, but I believed I was responsible for the sadness and hard work was responsible for my tiredness. I just kept doing what I had to do to survive. My emotions were numbed by doing, by keeping busy. Sex became another task to complete before I could sleep.

A year before leaving the farm and while contemplating what was wrong with me, I read a magazine article regarding premenstrual tension. At the time two weeks out of every month I was very emotional. Screams and threats during the day left me feeling so sad and guilty that at night I crept into the girls' bedrooms after they were asleep. Often with tears streaming, I knelt and prayed for forgiveness asking God to help me be a better mother. Sometimes this act was repeated during the day when one minute I was yelling and the next moment crying and apologizing. The article I read described these emotional ups and downs as hormonal imbalance. It also spoke of hysterectomies being an answer to this malady.

Being the doer I am, I made an appointment to see a doctor. He asked, "How can I help you?"

I replied, "I want a hysterectomy." When asked why, I said, "Because if I don't get help, I am going to kill myself or one of my daughters." This statement got his attention. Description of my menstrual periods and the weeks before, convinced him of my need. I left his office with an operation date and with hope.

So it wasn't all Roger's fault that I was so unhappy. The surgery and estrogen pills that followed helped with the bouncing destructive emotions, but that ill-fated statement I made upon first look at the farm "…..I will love you forever" would continue to be tested, or in the language of the Old Testament, *weighed in the balance and found wanting.*

8

THE CHURCH DOMINATED my life, with Sabbath sermons playing a pivotal role in the domination. The small, conservative, Seventh-day Adventist Church I was a member of while living on the farm was personable and social. It was small enough that I knew each member and greeted them with a warm smile and often with a hug. Each Sabbath was an experience of camaraderie. When there was not a potluck at the church, my family was invited to others' homes, or we invited other members to eat lunch at our home. Church members often helped one another in need. Prayer sessions bonded the members and we assumed care and responsibility for each other.

One Sabbath as I sat in the hard wooden pew with a daughter on each side, listening intently to a sermon based on Proverbs 16:18 (NIV): "Pride goes before destruction, a haughty spirit before a fall," I inwardly flinched. Pride? *Am I prideful?* I was confident I was doing all the right things to please God. I kept the Sabbath holy to the best of my ability—cleaned the house and prepared food before sundown on Friday. I followed the requirements of church doctrine to a "jot and tittle." And I was proud of it. *That's it. I am Prideful.* I prayed then and there when we knelt, "God, forgive me for having pride in my life, please humble me."

A few weeks after the sermon and my prayer, an elder of the church, the highest official of this local Church, and a close friend of Roger's, started calling me during the daytime to ask a question or pass on some information. At first I presumed it was related to Church business as I was not only a member of the church, but also held the position of Sabbath School Superintendent, under his supervision as Head Elder.

I grew suspicious and uncomfortable when he called just to talk. Then he started expressing affection and appreciation on a personal level. I stopped the calls. I told him, "Please do not call me again. I am not interested in getting involved with you or anyone else."

A few weeks later, in the presence of Roger, he announced that he needed a secretary. Speaking more to Roger than to me, announced that he wanted me to consider the position. He taught at the Adventist University a few miles away and would accommodate any hours I needed if I would work for him. My response was, "I'll think about it." Later when we were alone I told Roger I did not want to go to work for the professor. I was surprised by his response as he said, "We need the money, and you should work for him."

Fear kept me from telling Roger why I did not want to take the position. I was afraid he'd be angry, blaming me for being too friendly. Besides, our relationship did not lend itself to that kind of honesty. So, I prayed and asked for a reason to not accept the offer of employment. Within days after this prayer, Roger was offered a social work position in another county a few hours away. We decided together that he should take the position and we would move. Whew, I was relieved! Then he came home after a couple days' orientation and announced that he had changed his mind. He had turned down the offer.

I felt angry, betrayed, and withdrew. Days later I went to work for the professor. He was solicitous of my affection—expressing appreciation for everything I did in the office. He never criticized. He first showed affection with a hand on the shoulder, then a hug. Even though I tried to remain dispassionate, I started to respond. Not to his caresses, but to the emotion brought out by kind treatment. He complimented me on how nice I looked each day even though the way I dressed was modest and reserved. I was flattered by the attention, more so because demonstrative appreciation had not been part of my experience.

I was greatly impressed that he did not get angry when I made a mistake, like the time I accidentally locked the keys in the office. I expected at least frustration. Roger would have berated me. The professor said, "It's not a big deal. What are you afraid of?"

I did not believe I could or would have an affair. I was committed to my family. I was in control. I was loyal and obedient to God's commandments. I was also needy. The appreciation and affection felt good. I relaxed with him, and let down barriers.

The professor invited me to attend a conference in another state. He told his wife and Roger that he needed me to help with an upcoming presentation. My uncomfortable feelings were way-laid by my desire to have the experience. It was the first time away from kids and husband in twelve years. I was captivated by the feeling of freedom. I borrowed clothes from a neighbor to appear attractive. It was my first time to fly commercially and to stay in a high-rise hotel with all the trimmings of glamour. It was an invigorating experience. I felt significant, respected, worthwhile—admired.

The second night we were at the conference the professor walked me back to my room after the evening meeting. Though uninvited, he entered my room and ignored my requests for him to leave. His affection was welcomed, but I didn't want to succumb to the pressure to go further into a sexual liaison so I resisted. No longer able to keep my eyes open, I climbed into my bed at three o'clock in the morning. As he followed, I remember this thought passing through my brain: *I have sex with Roger and feel no love from him, why not give sex to someone who I do feel love from?*

I had been *giving* sex for thirteen years. Making love was not in my repertoire. This experience, though with the professor felt more akin to making love than giving sex to my husband ever did. To be desired and not demanded was unfamiliar. So I set aside, for a few days, my commitment to my husband and to God, and relished the freedom from the box I had been living in. I did not allow myself to think—that would come later.

One night after the return home and while lying in bed with my husband, I could keep silent no longer. Roger was suspect of my despondency and asked with suspension, "What's wrong?"

A week had passed since the conference. I strove to keep control of emotions that were overwhelming me. Guilt assaulted me. I hesitated to answer when Roger followed the first question with a second, "Is it Ron?" He would know if I refused to respond, so I weakly answered "yes" to his next question, "Did you sleep together?"

He leapt from the bed saying, "I'm going to see him."

I thought Roger would kick me out. I did not think our marriage would be recoverable. He went to talk to Ron, his friend, and they made an agreement. I would stay with Roger, I would not return to work, and they would remain friends. Years later I realized it was because of his own guilt that he responded as kindly as he did.

I did not blame Ron. He was willing to leave his wife and his position at the university if I would go away with him—in fact he begged me to do so. I was not willing. I did not love him. I had responded to and awarded his affection. Now, I just wanted it over with and forgotten.

I carried the heavy burden of *lost sinner* for weeks. I plead forgiveness, "Please, God, forgive me and cleanse me that I may be whole again." I was sorry, so sorry, but my sorrow was not for the pain caused to my husband or for the pain caused to Ron's wife. Acute agony clung to me but it was because I had broken one of the Ten Commandments. *How could I fail so miserably?*

Asking for forgiveness was foremost in my mind—especially forgiveness from God. Hours spent on my knees pleading in prayer for forgiveness helped alleviate the pain and guilt. I had betrayed myself first of all. *How could I, who believed so strongly in the Ten Commandments let this happen?*

I was devastated, often repeating to myself, "This is hell, I am serving my time, and will not need to go there." I listened to the song "One Day At a Time" over and over again. I was humbled. *Could the affair be God's will, an answer to my prayer weeks before when I had asked to be humble? This became my belief.*

My betrayal of Roger and the need for his forgiveness held less intense emotion. I apologized to him and to the professor's wife, who was also in pain. She responded coldly. I also felt a great need to apologize to the church congregation, but did not. I knew it would not give me the cleansing and forgiveness I sought. I also did not want to humiliate Ron's family or mine.

Roger and I received counseling from a male counselor and minister of the university Church. We attended a weekend of Marriage Encounter where we made new vows, a new commitment. It was a honeymoon stage that we had not experienced previously. Our marriage survived, bound together by four other lives.

I did not feel or even put much thought into my betrayal of the two men getting together, staying friends, and deciding my future. Again, I was unaware of personal freedom, but succumbed instead to male domination in the situation—only seeing myself as a sinner.

Both of our families continued to attend the same church and remained as Church officers. No one knew except the four of us. We still appeared to the church congregation as friends because we spoke cordially with each other. I had not been as close with Ron's wife as Roger had been with Ron, so the diffidence in our relationship was not noticed. I felt shame, but forgiven, and tried to regain confidence and belief in my self-worth by putting on a smile and acting as though all was well.

My life was as well as it could be, given my belief system. Major changes in my life were on the way. They would challenge not only my beliefs but my very soul.

9

I SAT NEXT TO the principal of an Adventist boarding high school in the office of my new position at Food Systems Consultants. I transferred to this company after leaving employment with the professor. Ed and I were sorting out the equipment needed for a new cafeteria, when he stopped the conversation, turned to face me, and asked, "Would you consider accepting the position of Dean of Girls at the academy?" The Dean of Girls was responsible for administration of the girls' dormitory, as well as any issue that affected the female students on the boarding high school campus. I was pleasantly shocked and felt flattered, but thought, *Wow, such a prestigious position! Why would he ask me to fill a position like that?* Fear from the recent adulterous experience drove the question deeper—*is he coming on to me? Does he really think I could do something like that or is he just flattering me?*

Turning from the large catalog on the desk in front of me and with finger in place where I was describing the equipment he needed, I asked, "Why me? What makes you think I can do that?"

His response, "I'm impressed with your management skills, and I like the way you relate to the students here in the office," fulfilled my need to believe in my administrative abilities and not my ability to attract male attention. I thought, *right answer to my question!*

I was floored. The position of working with professionals in a college setting had done much to restore my self-esteem, but this was over the top. Administrators of Adventist high schools were respected and powerful influences on any campus they served. I had never dreamed of holding such an influential position within the Church.

The smile that spread across my face was erased by another thought, *there is no way Roger will allow me to take that kind of position.* I responded, "I'll ask my husband and get back with you in a couple of days."

I brought up the subject at the dinner table with the children present believing his response would be gentler in their presence. To my surprise, he listened as I explained the situation and the offer. He hesitated, looked down toward his plate in thought, and said, "Maybe you should consider it. I could take a year off and build that house I've always wanted to." Since we would live in a dormitory housing apartment, he could build and then sell the house to make up for the financial loss of his unemployment.

I was amazed that he was keen on this opportunity. I was not so amazed or surprised that he turned it into something favorable for him. I didn't care. It was an opportunity to provide a Christian education for Trudy who was entering high school. There would be less hassle than if we remained where we were.

I resolved to move—*away from past mistakes. A safe place for my daughters. God is leading in my life. The affair and forgiveness has better prepared me for this opportunity. I can do it.*

The academy occupied one-hundred and fifty acres of farmland, separated from a nearby community by a lake that bordered one side of the property. It had the appearance and feel of isolation, but was close enough to a major city to take advantage of shopping and entertainment. The campus was self-contained. The buildings for housing and administration nestled amongst large oak and pine trees that provided shade and concealment. The girls' dormitory was the largest building on the campus, accommodating a hundred students, dwarfing the chapel nearby.

I thought at first sight, as I had six years before when I first laid eyes on my farm, *this is idyllic.* Apprehension was subdued, but present. I had no college degree, most employees on campus did. I was hired based on the qualities recognized by the principal and those reiterated by my employer on the university campus. I would become a professional again. The opportunity felt admirable. Whenever doubts assaulted me I fought back with *I am capable, I'm a good Adventist.*

We followed the Church's dictates about diet, clothing, and amusement. I attended church faithfully and was in good standing. The Church, of course, did not know about my affair. I held various offices in the Church proving my abilities to communicate both one on one and from the pulpit. I faithfully spent time in Bible study and prayer on a daily basis. I also read the writings of Ellen White, who was known as the Prophet of the Church. I followed the admonitions in her writings. Close relationships I made with young women at the university gave me confidence. I felt comfortable with teenagers—male or female. I was a Mother of a teen and had a good relationship with her.

Leaving the farm was a monumental event for us as a family. A large moving van drove up the driveway on an August morning in 1975. I was eager with anticipation, ready to move on, to provide what I thought was best for my daughters.

There were eighty-nine teen-age girls in the dormitory that first year. Seven Resident Assistants, who were senior girls, helped manage the dormitory in the evenings. A woman Church member from the community stayed in the dorm for supervision every other weekend. Otherwise, it was my responsibility. The door to my apartment led from the hall where all residents passed. This meant if someone was unhappy, distressed, or needing assurance, it was this door she would knock on day or night!

I felt prepared to meet students' needs, and to meet parents. To assure them that their daughters would have competent care. To speak to the girls daily in worship. To handle disciplinary issues. To oversee the cleaning and maintenance of the dorm.

Before school started, a faculty retreat was held at the conference camp sixty miles away. My daughters and I attended and I was introduced as the new Dean of Girls. During the discussion of campus rules and discipline, I was disappointed by the amount of criticism of past and returning students. Comments, both by staff and faculty like, "We need to clamp down harder this year," "I sure hope he is not like his brother or he won't make it here," "I can't believe she was accepted back," were prevalent. This type of attitude towards what I saw as students' needs, disheartened me. I remained quiet, but inside my feelings vacillated between sadness and disgust.

Returning to my cabin from one of the meetings that had particularly displeased me, I found myself walking next to the principal and his wife. The principal asked me, "Well, what do you think so far?"

I answered truthfully, "Fine, except that I am disappointed with some of the criticism of the students from staff. It seems very negative to me." Before the principal could respond, his wife spoke up, "Just wait until you've been here a while and you'll be negative too."

I turned to look at her more directly and said, "If I get to the place of feeling critical and negative, I won't stay here," and walked on.

This conversation was indicative of what was to come. The principal's wife, Sara, and I would have other tension-filled conversations. The first time I experienced a committee with Sara, we were to review the girls' dresses which they intended to wear to the up-and-coming banquet. One of the girls had a ribbon with a brooch pinned to it and the ribbon tied around her neck. Sara spoke to the girl, "You cannot wear that around your neck."

Loreen was a self-assured girl from a prominent Adventist family. Without qualms, she questioned, "Why not?"

"Well, it's jewelry. You know you can't wear jewelry," was Sara's response.

Because it was my first experience on this type of committee, I inserted myself into the conversation gingerly, "Sara, I don't understand why this is considered jewelry. You wear scarves tied in different shapes around your neck. Why isn't that jewelry?"

She stuttered, "Because, because, my scarves all match my outfits."

I said, "I don't see the difference."

Her glare told me that *she* was the principal's wife. I acquiesced, and said, "Loreen, I don't understand either, but I think you better not wear the ribbon." Disgruntled, Loreen walked away. The subject was dropped, and she did not wear the ribbon to the banquet.

The rules for girls on campus stipulated modest dress. This was described in a handbook as no sleeveless tops, no shorts, no slacks to class, no noticeable makeup, and skirts below the knee. A lot of energy and time was spent on monitoring the students' dress—especially the girls' dress. Boys could wear shorts and sleeveless shirts, as well as jeans, to activities but the girls could not. I came to believe that the administration's intent was that if the girls maintained higher standards of dress and demeanor then the boys would not be tempted into misbehavior. In other words, keep the girls covered and cloistered, and the boys could be offered more freedom and be less apt to cause problems.

This supposed concept frustrated me further when male teachers came to me asking that I do more about keeping the girls in longer skirts as they were "bothered" by the girls' legs showing while they were trying to teach. I refused to measure hemlines as other deans were doing in other schools. I thought it to be demeaning for the student. I did address a length or lack of length that appeared immodest and at times demanded that skirts showing the thigh be changed. But my response to the teachers who spoke to me was, "I refuse to make the girls responsible for your 'bother.'"

Most of the rules on campus had been maintained in our home before coming to the academy. Sabbath was sacred. We did not read unbiblical mail or literature that day. I did as little cooking as possible and no housework—all was done on Friday before sundown. We attended Sabbath school and church unless we were ill. On the Sabbath my daughters did not play games that were not biblical in nature, and they stayed in the clothes worn to church to deter activities that were not considered appropriate for Sabbath. We did not participate in activities outside of church services on the Sabbath Day, no parties—not even birthdays.

I dressed modestly, wore no make-up, and did not listen to rock music. I did not use profanity, not even gosh. I required my daughters to refrain from the same. I knew my family could keep the rules, and they did so in my presence. Primary in my home, and now in my administration was my effort to keep and enforce the rules that governed our lives as Adventists.

There was great cultural diversity represented in the dorm, and yet, I was expected to treat the girls the same—in terms of rules and consequences. The girls came from wealthy homes and low-income homes. They came from the inner city and from farms. There were those who had attended public schools all their earlier elementary school years and those who had attended small church schools. Some were generational Adventists, and some didn't know what the word Adventist meant. There were girls whose behavior always pleased, and those with obnoxious behaviors that caused me constant consternation.

Thankfully, more than my aptitude for the rules, I came with the capacity for unconditional love and compassion—though I could not have defined it as such at the time. It was not behavior that determined my attitude toward an individual. My daughters had not yet put this capacity for unconditional love to the test as one would later, but the girls in the dorm and the faculty and staff often did.

The neediest, and therefore the ones with the most dysfunction, demanded and received more of my attention. I would have liked to spend more time with those who were pleasant, but there just was not enough time for me to spend quality time with ninety individuals. My desire to meet the needs of the girls was satisfied in part by the camaraderie I developed with the girls that served as resident assistants. They followed my direction and bidding. They helped and counseled others as I trained, supported, and relied on them. These girls helped to sustain me.

Students were required to sign an agreement of obedience to the campus rules when they applied to attend the academy. The first evening in the dorm they were oriented on acceptable dorm behavior. My compassion encouraged leniency for those who had not had the experience of keeping Adventist rules and I often said, "You did agree to keep these rules. You don't have to agree or even understand but you must adhere to the rules in order to stay here."

An effective response to misbehavior was, "You made a mistake, now let's right that mistake by not repeating it and by accepting the consequences of your behavior." Often this response surprised the girls being disciplined. They had expected harsh discipline, so their appreciation led to more open communication.

On the first Sabbath of the school year, the afternoon sundown service was to be held in a field that was also used as pasture. The students would sit on the ground in semi-circles for song service, boys on one side and girls on the other. Prayer, as the sun descended, would end the Sabbath day. The rule of no slacks on Sabbath was dismissed for this occasion by the principal after I pointed out the immodesty of girls sitting on the ground in skirts or dresses. However, when girls came to me to say they only had one good pair of slacks and did not want to ruin them, or to comment, "It is ridiculous to sit on the ground in good slacks. We think we should wear our jeans. What's the difference anyway, except for the cloth?" Some went on to inform me that the boys got to wear jeans and asked, "Why can't we?"

I listened. It made sense to wear jeans. A call to the principal to express my opinion gained permission for the girls to wear jeans. I made the announcement and most of the girls wore jeans that day to sit on the ground in the cow pasture. I wore dress slacks. A number of the faculty and faculty wives were furious and let me know within hours. A telephone call from one informed me, "It is just not proper. It is not allowed here. This is unacceptable Sabbath attire for young ladies."

A rule I used to help direct many decisions like the one about jeans versus slacks was: *Always say yes unless there is a clear reason to say no.* When a student came to me with a request, I first said to myself: *Is there a reason to say no? Is this unsafe? Is it immoral? Is it against Church doctrine?* I believed in modesty, and honesty in particular, so I built dorm rules and expectations on these two main principles.

The criticism I received often offered an opportunity to speak with some of the women who disliked what they considered was leniency, and eventually I was able to impress them with the differences it made in campus life and in the lives of students. Some of my worst critics eventually became friends and supporters.

One of the main critics was the farm director's wife who was traditional, conservative and obese. I visited with her often trying to soften her criticism. I still chuckle with a conversation we had. Ruby said, "You need to do something with those girls that waddle up on stage in those high heels to sing in the choir. I think you should measure the heels and say they can't be over an inch high."

I looked at her and said, "Ruby, I will measure the girls' heels when the principal starts measuring the staff and faculties' waists. I believe weight is more of a health issue than high heels." Needless to say, the conversation ended, and she did not pursue the idea.

The first months of the first year of administration I established a solid platform demonstrating that I cared about each girl and that I was approachable. Being approachable was extremely important if I was going to positively affect the lives of those in the dorm. I believed that I was a representative of God and desired my representation to be love. Being inundated with requests for appointments to talk privately, was evidence of success.

I spent numerous late-night hours listening to and responding to the agonies of teen hearts—agonies often created by fundamentalist religious adults. I asked myself, *how can these stories the girls are telling me be coming from Christian homes? Why are so many hurting? What can I really do to make a difference?*

10

MID-MORNING ONE DAY in the first year at the academy, I sat making notes at my desk that faced the hall door. I heard a sound and looked up to see a black face peeking around the door frame. Ada was a fifteen-year-old inner city student who had never come to my office. In fact, she had never looked me in the face or spoke other than a grunt when I addressed her. I spoke, "Come on in Ada."

She took a step in, facing me. The whites of her eyes, shiny with tears testified to her pain and fear. Her first words were, "I neva talked with a white lady afore." She said, "I need help," as tears slid down her cheeks. I moved from behind the desk, and gestured for her to sit as I sat down in a chair near her.

Three more times in the next five minutes she said, "I can't believe I talkin with a white lady." I listened intently to decipher the words that hesitantly and painfully left her mouth. She was pregnant. Her words were "I'm knocked up."

She said "Don't know what I'm gonna do." She had told no one except a friend, Maye, who was one of the resident assistants. Maye had encouraged her to speak with me. Her greatest concern was what it would do to her mother.

Her mother had no money—had "tried to raise me right. Now this.

Oh, how I tell her, how I tell her," came pouring out with the tears that slid down mixing with snot and dripping through the fingers pressed upon her face. I put aside my need to surround her with my arms. I knew this would be going too far for her comfort. She did let me place my hand on her arm with the words, "Ada, I will help you."

Head bowed and eyes toward her lap, she told of how her brother's friend had come to their house and said, "I wanna do it with you."

"I let him," she said. "He's the father. Have to be him."

I did not ask questions but let her spew out what would come. The brother's friend was a student at the academy. "Please don't tell em I told you."

I was not surprised by Ada's admission of her pregnancy, but the description of "I let him" was disconcerting. Her anguish pulled at my compassionate heart, and I felt no judgment.

Maye lived in the same neighborhood as Ada and attended the same Church. I had spent hours talking with Maye to understand the community and culture that was so different from mine. She was the first to tell me about an unreported date rape—hers. She also talked with me about Ada's wildness, and her concerns for Ada's mother who was trying desperately to do what she thought was best for her daughter though her resources were almost non-existent. Maye, herself was raised by a grandmother and did not know her father. I did not tell Maye about Ada's visit to my office but guessed that Ada would tell her she had come to speak with me and relay what I had told her.

I did not know the black community well enough to know who to ask to help this young woman, now a mother-to-be. I realized how I responded could destroy the very fragile fabric of this young woman's life. Therefore, I communicated with no one on campus for fear it would be treated as a disciplinary situation. I did not know what I should or could do, but I was determined to do whatever it took to help Ada come through this experience in the best way possible.

I told Ada, "I assure you this will not be handled as a discipline situation. You can trust me not to tell anyone within the campus, but I will have to tell someone if I am to help you. Right now I don't know who that someone is, but it will be someone who can help."

A few more words of reassurance and she left my office, appearing to believe what I had said. I knew that the Adventist Church had an adoption agency on the west coast and a couple of calls later, had located the phone number.

Ada came to my office, discreetly, while classmates were at work or recreation, to discuss how to tell her mother. I volunteered to talk to her mother, but Ada's response, "My mother neva come here," told me that Ada would be on her own in this regard.

I encouraged her to wait to talk to her mom until we had the answers for what to do next. I wanted to prevent the helplessness that the mother might feel and the response it might engender. Ada was suffering enough. A few telephone calls to the agency, and arrangements were made for Ada to fly to the west coast, have her baby, and leave it there for adoption. The agency would take care of all expenses. I talked with her mother on the phone after Ada had told her of the pregnancy. She was frightened but supportive of Ada's decision to go to the west coast, and she supported the adoption.

My communication to others on campus was to say that Ada was sick and not returning to school. The young man who had impregnated her was not approached as far as I know, though he might have known he was the father. The next six months Ada's life was on hold far from home and Devon, the father, was scot-free.

I decided not to approach the principal or dean of boys about the young man's involvement because I would then be coerced to tell Ada's story. Because sex without marriage is considered a sin within the Church, a student would be dismissed from school if knowledge of such an act were reported. My experience told me that the girl in such a situation was often treated with disdain. The old idiom of "it's the girl's fault" hung heavy with administrators on campus.

I longed to talk with the young man but believed that doing so would be seen as a betrayal by Ada, and as infringement by the dean of boys.

Days before Ada delivered, she called me. "Can I come back?" I said, "Yes, you can come back." When she returned to campus for the next school year, she allowed a hug and thanked me for all the help. She was restless—maybe some of the kids taunted her. I do not know what happened but Ada stayed only a few days and withdrew from school. She would only tell me, "It's too hard."

Life on the campus was "hard." Hard for me too. Counseling needs in the dorm were overwhelming. I spent many, many nights in the dorm until wee hours in the morning listening to someone pour out pain and fear while tears flowed—theirs and mine. The day in the life of a student was divided between work and school. The seniors and sophomores went to classes in the morning and to work in the afternoon. Therefore, the juniors and freshman went to work in the morning and classes in the afternoon. This meant it was rare to be able to counsel a student during the day. After dinner was recreation and early evenings were full of class activities. It was most often bed time when the knocks came on my office door, and the lines formed outside.

My own daughters felt neglected. Roger let me know he was angry because of the hours I spent in the dorm counseling students. I did my best to pray with each of my daughters before they went to sleep at night, but I often missed this appointment because of chaos or emergencies. I felt torn between being with my daughters and fulfilling the needs of the dorm students. Since responsibility was so ingrained in me by a demanding father, I succumbed to fulfilling the dorm needs first and those of daughters and husband second. I would hurry the time spent with them by saying, "I gotta go," and then leave with guilt on my shoulders like a heavy shawl that pulled my shoulders down and weighted my feet. Often I wiped tears from my eyes and took a deep breath before opening the door from my apartment into the dorm entry that led to my office.

I wanted to be there for my daughters. *I was just a few steps away, and they could come to the office anytime they wanted.* That is if they could push through the bodies waiting around my office door. I assuaged my guilt with self-talk: *I have to do this. The girls are better off on this Christian campus even if I'm not there when they need me. Being here protects them from worldly influences. I'm doing what God wants me to do.*

When I approached the principal to ask for the services of a counselor or therapist to attend to some of the dorm girls' needs, my hopes were dashed by an abrupt response of, "The conference officials would never allow someone to come on campus for counseling."

He did not need to, nor did he try, to explain the reasoning. I accredited the decision to the lack of interest or need for control of the Church officials who made decisions regarding campus life. It appeared to me that they sat in an elusive ivory tower unwilling to either address or acknowledge the grass root personal problems of the students. Furthermore, I believed that they did not want to alarm constituents who financially supported the school with words about embarrassing student or family problems. It was as if Adventist families were not supposed to have the problems I was observing. I was admonished not to obtain help outside the campus. In fact, subtly I was told it would be better not to talk about it with anyone. I was told, "Just do the best you can."

I was not a trained counselor and many of the girls living in the dormitory needed professional services. This was a time before the media educated us regarding incest, rape, bulimia, and anorexia. Labels and medications were not available for the disorders that we accept today as commonplace. I tried to treat with love those behaviors that should have been treated by therapists.

Attempting to meet the needs of the girls the best I could, I read all the material I could find about emotional wounds. I read about how to listen and how to confront. The library on campus met student needs but none of mine. Time to search at any local library was non-existent. I was on my own except for an organization managed by Adventist college deans that provided workshops and conferences. I attended every workshop I could and assimilated information from the presentations by other professionals within the Adventist Church.

I sought solace from Bible reading, and presented daily worship talks in the dorm chapel focusing on relationships and love. I agonized: *Where is the love?* The idea of God being Love was elusive and yet alluring. Eating at my soul was the desire to balance doctrine and rules with the depth of God's love. The Church's do's and don'ts started to pale by comparison as I focused on every biblical text I could find that emphasized love. This was made difficult by reading the King James Version of the Bible as it contains far fewer texts using the word *love* than the newer versions I read later. Many leaders in the Adventist Church, at that time, frowned upon the use of other versions, and I was conscientious about reading and presenting what was most acceptable. Verses demanding love such as Leviticus 19:18, "Thou shall not avenge, nor bear any grudge against the children of thy people, but thou shalt love thy neighbor as thyself: I am the Lord," also goes on to read, "Ye shall keep my statutes......" I interpreted each verse as another demand for obedience.

"If ye love me, keep my commandments," as in St. John 14:15, and "This is my commandment, that ye love one another, as I have loved you," in 15:12, combines love with obedience. I used the text of 1 John 4:7-8 in worship talks to implore the girls to love one another. But still I perceived these texts as demands and did not understand how to communicate this love in relation to demands for obedience emphasized by the Church.

The binary belief system of sin versus grace, preached by others on campus, kept me, as well as the students, confused. Unacceptable behaviors like provocative dress, make-up, wearing of jewelry, and the use of tobacco, alcohol or drugs, were designated as sin. The non-confession of sin would keep one from heaven. *God is love and forgiveness? Jesus saves us from our sins? Grace is free?*

I accepted keeping the Ten Commandments with what I believed to be God's endorsement. I tried to live sin-free and had failed. Now I questioned, *Is God a God of love? How do I show these girls the love of God when condemnation of behavior is what they experience?*

And then someone recommended I read the book *Love* by Leo Buscaglia. This book more than any other literature, influenced my comprehension of love. I read with tears flowing down my cheeks, and the voice inside saying, *yes, yes, this is it.* In the introduction of the book Buscaglia tells the story of a young woman student of his who committed suicide. He ends the story by declaring, "I simply wondered what I might have done; if I could have, even momentarily, helped."

Every day I faced the question: "What can I do?" I did not want to look back and ask, "What should I have done differently?" I longed to give the message of God's love to the girls who sat in chapel seats each night listening to my attempt to explain God and tell them how to live their lives. And even more, it was my desire to give this message to my own daughters.

Buscaglia wrote, "In discussing love, it would be well to consider the following premises:

> To give love you must possess love.
> To teach love you must comprehend love.
> To study love you must live in love.
> To recognize love you must be receptive to love.
> To trust love you must be convinced of love.
> To yield to love you must be vulnerable to love.

I read these words with longing. I felt so unworthy of love. *How could I love enough? How was I to inspire in others the love of God and self if I did not know God's love or know how to give love?*

In the last paragraph of the book, Buscaglia quotes Father William

Du Bay, "The most human thing we have to do in life is to learn to speak our honest convictions and feelings and live with the consequences. This is the first requirement of love, and it makes us vulnerable to other people who may ridicule us. But our vulnerability is the only thing we can give to other people."

As I absorbed the essence of love I strove to put it into practice in how I related to the girls in the dorm, and to my own daughters. Even if I didn't know how to preach love, I was convinced I could show love.

The administration was set up as a disciplinary system—some infractions would send a student home on probation or dismissal. I believed this was harmful to the self-worth of most students who experienced it, and I did my best to handle situations of misbehavior quietly without taking it to the discipline committee. I knew Jackie was smoking in the chapel in front of an open window, but I also knew she was in a lot of pain and in survival mode. I also knew Mary was having sex with a boyfriend, but knew that discipline was not the answer for her conflicted emotions and committment.

Theron waited outside my office many nights and sometimes during the day. She did not ask for anything, she appeared and stayed. She was a loner. Sadness cloaked her shoulders and at times she flung the cloak aside displaying a deep anger. Her family was steeped in the kind of conservative Adventism that did not allow for the teens in the household to make choices of their own. This caused her to withdraw, deceive, and not ask for help when needed. Her mother's dominance in the family was portrayed by her straight spine and the slump of the father's shoulders. The relationship between mother and daughter was antagonistic. This was disconcerting, but I was even more concerned that the father did not seem to be engaged with his daughter at all. Mom made all the decisions and Theron rebelled.

Theron's life was also complicated by the lack of financial provision brought on by the inclusion of seven cousins into their family—the children of her mother's sister. As the oldest daughter, she also carried major responsibility for the care of younger siblings and cousins.

One morning at 2 a.m. as she was leaving my office, she turned to face me after a good-night hug and said, "How can you love me?"

Taken aback, I first stumbled with words, "Ah, I think, I believe…" And then it came to me. I said, "Theron I love you because God loves you. It is not me that is able. It is God loving you through me." Tears sprang to her eyes, she turned and left.

I spent many hours with Theron, and while she and I developed a workable relationship, she did not succeed on campus. She failed classes and also failed to cooperate with teacher's requests for appropriate behavior. She was not allowed to return the next year. I encouraged her mother to insist Theron see a counselor and told her that if Theron saw a counselor consistently for the next year I would help ensure that she would be accepted back into the academy.

Theron did see a counselor once a month for the next school year as she attended public school. It was obvious to me she had deep emotional scars. I suspected some abuse at home—within a family that was highly praised by the church they attended. Though her mother told me, and Theron admitted that she never spoke in the counselor's office, she did fulfill the letter of the law by going to the counselor each month as required. I fulfilled my promise to see that she was back in the dorm the next year. She returned her junior year and succeeded in graduating from the academy her senior year. Though we had many sessions and I gave many hugs and lots of encouragement, Theron was unable to divulge the root of her unhappiness and depression until years later. By her senior year she was less of a loner, and more cooperative with teachers and administration. Theron went on to graduate, not only from the academy but from an Adventist college. She became a Dean of Girls at one of the SDA academies and later served as an administrator in state social services.

We kept in touch through the years and she was able to express the pain of the sexual molestation she experienced from her mother's brother. Though she also shared this with her mother, the uncle was allowed to be in the home and invited to family events. She confronted the uncle and his denial was accepted by her mother. This continued to create pain in Theron's life until her untimely death at fifty. She never married nor had children of her own. Through the years she cared financially and emotionally for nieces and nephews and received the love she deserved. To me, Theron's story represents the destructive results of incest to the very core of a person. Incest creates and leaves scars that are often irreversible.

11

KRISTINE CAME FROM conservative Adventist heritage. Her paternal grandparents were well known at the Adventist university campus where her uncle was a professor. Her father was the black sheep of the family. When Kristine came to the academy, she had been kicked out of her home by an abusive mother. At the time, her father, an emotionally distant man and long haul truck driver, was on the road and no help to Kristine.

Her paternal grandmother discovered she was living on the street and made arrangements for her to come to the academy. Kristine spoke as little as possible and refused to participate in any activities on campus. Within the first six weeks she had skipped every chapel and most of the worships that she was required to attend. Plus, she skipped forty-plus classes. The report of skipped classes alone could cause her to be expelled.

I pleaded with the principal and the discipline committee to keep her on campus, and insisted she have appointments with me to talk. She appeared at appointed times, but talked very little. Eventually, I learned that her mother's abuse had driven her to the street, and there she had been raped. She would not allow me to touch her. She resisted any comforting hug with her eyes of pain.

The resident assistants complained that I was allowing her to get away with ignoring the dorm rules and regulations. They wondered aloud why I protected her, especially, when she would not answer her door at night for check in. This did prove to be a mistake. When the report came to my desk that she had not responded to bed-check two nights in a row, I knew I needed to attend to Kristine. I knocked on her door the second morning and opened it with a key. She was out of bed but appeared dazed. "What day is this?" she asked.

"This is Wednesday," I responded.

"But, but, what happened to Tuesday?"

"Kris, you tell me what happened."

She was frightened and willing to talk. She told me that she had taken some pills because she was so depressed. She said she had done this before but just "not so many."

I turned, walked out the door as I said, "Get dressed and come to my office." I breathed a prayer on the way back down the hall, "Thank you God she did not die." And I contemplated: *I've protected her to a fault. I have to correct this.*

When she appeared at my office door a few minutes later still shaken and weak but willing to listen, I said, "Kristine this has really frightened me. It must not happen again. If you ever take pills again I will call an ambulance and they will take you to the hospital. If you continue this, I will not be able to keep you here, you will have to leave."

It did not happen again. Kristine took major steps toward healing in the months after this incident. We developed a close relationship that has lasted past her graduation from the academy. She attended an Adventist University still supported by Grandma, and was eventually employed by the Adventist Church as an elementary school teacher. This brought happiness and pride to her grandmother who had supported her financially though absent emotionally. My protection of Kristine could have been disastrous. Though tough love became a part of my vocabulary and understanding, I was still reluctant to administer the tough part.

The knocks on my office, as well as my home door, came with demands for my intervention. Students called for me even when they weren't supposed—when I was off duty. I had set up an open door policy. I was their advocate, their Mother or Father depending upon whether they needed nurturing or strength. I thought I had to be all things for them—that I was the savior.

My administrative load was especially heavy because expectations for the girls were higher than for the boys. There were two boys' deans since there were two small dorms with forty boys each, providing more coverage of duties. Many girls came to my office in tears because teachers sent them to the dorm to change from skirts deemed too short; necklines too low; or because of makeup and jewelry. I felt protective of the girls. It seemed to me that they were criticized and penalized just for being teens, for exhibiting naturally expected behavior as young women.

Denise was especially prone to spend time in my office for offences regarding dress. She was tall, long legged, blonde, and beautiful. The male teachers in particular complained that she dressed provocatively. With a knock on my office door, she would appear sometimes angry and spewing words, "I hate Mr. Wilson. He's out to get me. No one else in that class gets sent to change but me!"

Other times, she would come with tears smearing the makeup she was sent to remove. Counseling hours spent with Denise revealed that her makeup and provocative dress was not to attract, it was to cover the pain inside that she did not know how to express. One of the resident assistants told me that she heard her in the bathroom vomiting. I approached her and asked, "Denise are you sick?"

She answered, "No, I'm fine, just an upset stomach." The second and third times, she responded the same until I suggested that she make an appointment with the doctor. Then I was told by more than one person that they saw her picking food out of the garbage can. This I could not believe and thought it an expression of their jealousy.

I knew nothing about bulimia at this time—had not even heard of it. I knew Denise was in trouble, but could only listen to her and watch her tears, as she divulged sexual experiences with older men. The help Denise needed was out of my league and I was not allowed to solicit help. Her parents were well-known within the Conference of Seventh-day Adventists and well respected in the Church they attended. I did not know how to approach them. Denise begged me not to. I did my best to support and encourage her to heal from whatever pain was in her life. I did not reveal to the administration what I knew about her dysfunction for fear of getting her sent home.

I handled many infractions of the girls this way. The one thing I would not tolerate and made very clear to the girls was dishonesty. I often said, "You be honest with me and I will do whatever I can to help you. If you lie to me I cannot help you."

This was especially true when it came to illegal drugs. I believed drugs were often used to cover pain and there was a lot of pain in the dorm full of teenage girls making bad choices. If I found someone had sneaked drugs into the dorm, I sent them home and rarely supported their return. I was determined that the girls in the dorm would not be subjected to the dangers of drug use on my watch. I was conflicted regarding the use of illegal drugs such as marajuana. I did not agree with it being illegal and felt all the money being spent on convictions and incarcerations could be better spent helping those who were addicted or self medicating. I supported the selling of any drug—tobacco and alcohol too—as illegal to minors. However, I did not support the use of drugs as illegal because I felt that most were using to self-medicate. I especially disliked the idea of millions of dollars spent to arrest those using instead of spending the money to treat them. It would be twenty to thirty years before marajuana was legalized for medicinal use, and even longer before recognition was brought to the mistake of incarceration instead of treatment.

When girls used prescription drugs or over the counter drugs to either self-medicate or make a suicide attempt, I created it as a cry for help. I remember sitting in my office more than once when one of the resident assistants brought a girl to me who had taken pills and now was afraid of what would happen. I called the doctor that treated the students or the emergency room staff in a hospital ten miles away and reported what had been taken and how many. Sometimes it meant a hurried trip to the hospital, and sometimes I used Ipecac Syrup as instructed by physicians. I then sat with the girls, often holding hands with a cold cloth to their head as they moaned, groaned, and vomited. The syrup not only eliminated the drug in their stomach but caused them to feel so ill that they often promised, "I'll never do it again, I promise, I'll never do it again." Teenage girls' emotions, fragile as they are, often lead to self-abuse. I did my best to protect them from themselves, but also from the dictum of administration that would have sent them home.

Martie was someone I was forced to send home even though I cried over her departure. She, too, was part of a well-known family within the Adventist community. Her grandfather had been a minister, and in denominational administration. When Martie entered the dorm her twin sister was in a mental ward due to suicide attempts. The family believed the sister was demon possessed, and when she was released from the hospital, invited ministers of the Church to facilitate exorcism.

At first Martie appeared to be very stable. Her parents spoke of how proud they were of her "good behavior." But then, late one night a few weeks after her arrival, she appeared at my office door with a very strange look. I knew she had just hung up from a telephone call as the community phone was outside my office, and I had heard the desk monitor call her to the phone. I invited her in with, "What's wrong," as I rose to meet her across the room.

Her face showed terror. "I just got a call from my grandmother," stumbled out of her mouth as I neared her enough to put my arm around her shoulders and pull her to a chair. She looked like she might faint.

"Tell me why that's upsetting you," I responded.

The next words from her mouth caused me to feel like I might faint, "Because my grandmother is dead." She started to cry and shake. A few hours later Martie was deposited in bed and told to see me the next morning as I would excuse her classes. This was only the beginning of late nights with Martie. Over the next two weeks, she demonstrated the same characteristics her sister was being treated for. Other faculty got involved. One of the music teachers who gave her voice lessons, experienced her departure from reality—heard voices from her that did not sound like her. He set up a session late at night for an exorcism and invited me.

The second time an exorcism was administered, the principal heard of it. He came to my office the next morning, and with anger told me, "She has to go." I knew we could not continue with late night sessions and other students being involved, but I did not believe the answer was to expel Martie. I did not have a choice.

He said, "I want her gone today."

I told him, "Then I am the one who will take her." I took her home. I felt very discouraged. Driving home by myself, thoughts plagued me. *Why can't we keep her at school? Why does it have to look like punishment for a sin? Or crime? Doesn't love and caring heal even this? What could I do differently? How can I help make a difference? I thought love was the answer. Shouldn't we be able to portray more love?*

The most difficult situations to deal with had to do with sex. The subject was taboo. I wanted to address issues of sex from a positive point of view, but emphasis from Church teachings was that of abstinence, sin, and secrecy. I questioned for myself, that I might pass on to the students, how to relate to the act of what we call "love making" and sexual intercourse. *Is it just for the making of babies? What does "making love" mean? Is it really just for married couples? Is it a sin when two people love each other but aren't married? It's still "making love." How do I stress abstinence and still help?*

A student would be expelled for any sexual activity on campus. Even holding hands was not permitted, and if observed by staff would lead to placement on "social." If placed on "social" the students could not be with or near each other under any circumstances for a determined length of time—sometimes for weeks. Get caught making out and you could be suspended. Expelled if nudity or intercourse was involved.

There were rumors of girls being intimate with each other—the word used was "lezzies." I did not know how to approach the subject, so I did not. The Church taught that lesbians and homosexuals were sinners and condemned. Disclosure would lead to expulsion. Though I did believe that homosexuality was a sin at this time, I did not want to take the chance of having to send someone home if I found out that their sexual orientation was other than heterosexual—the only acceptable one.

I received a call late one night from a young, recently married, male faculty. "Can I come over to talk with you after the students are in bed?"

I said, "Of course," and stayed later than usual to sneak him into my office to talk. He was nervous and hesitant. We had built a trusting relationship through other dialogues in regard to students. We agreed there was excessive criticism by some staff of normal teen behaviors. Our discussions had allowed for mutual respect and trust.

After testifying to his belief that there was no one else he could talk to, he described the difficulty in his sexual relations with his wife. In agony he poured out rage against himself and why he couldn't change how he felt. He wanted to make the marriage work. He loved his wife. He wanted to stay in the Adventist school system. But, he was afraid that he was a homosexual. He knew that if he confessed his fears he would be fired and unable to find employment elsewhere. He said he was from a proud Adventist family and would be disowned with any confession of homosexuality.

All I could do was listen and reassure Ted that God loved him just as he was. In my attempt to encourage this sobbing man sitting before me, I said, "Maybe it's your wife. She is not a very demonstrative person. She is quiet and meek. Maybe if she was more passionate she could turn you on."

He looked up at me and said, "Don't blame this on her. It's not her. It's me."

Our conversation ended with my promise to pray for his release from pain, but I had no advice or assurance. I did not know what to think or believe about the issue. I was not convinced that the Church was wrong. I was striving to understand what the agony I ascertained in this man meant. Everyone I knew at the time said that being gay was a choice. But, if it was a choice to be or not to be homosexual, why was he making the choice to bring so much pain into his life? I could sense the pain—it was genuine.

If it is not a choice they must be born this way. How could it be a sin if you were born this way?

I was, eventually, convinced the students I listened to, as well as the faculty member, were not choosing this experience. I felt unsafe and could not share the questions and conclusions I had with anyone. I kept my beliefs to myself and did my best to support, with loving acceptance, the students who came to me.

Lily, a girl whose paternal grandparents I knew well because they had been members of the same Church I attended before coming to the academy, sat in my office numerous times with heart rending tales of molestation by her maternal grandfather, as well as three of her four brothers. Though I knew this family prior to taking the position at the academy, I did not believe there was anything I could do about what had happened but listen and hug. I never once thought of calling the police. The awareness within the Church and community was nonexistent and unacceptable. I am convinced that even had I called the police and reported the molestations and abuse, nothing would have been done. The girl and I would have been the ones questioned and shut down.

I found out years later, that during this time, my own daughter was unwilling to come and reveal to me what she was experiencing. Trudy worked for one of the dean of boys and spent afternoons in one of the boys' dorms to accomplish secretarial duties. A senior boy started coming to the office on a regular basis. First it was just a friendly chat, but then one day as she was climbing the stairs to the office, Tyler appeared at the top of the stairs naked. She did not report it. A few days later he came to the office door in a robe and facing her he opened it to reveal his nudity and his erection. Trudy did not report it. His nude appearances increased until Trudy realized she had to do something because it was frightening her. She spoke to the Dean. Tyler was expelled from school and not allowed to take part in the graduation ceremonies. The incident was not brought to the discipline committee. Though I knew Tyler was removed from campus and not allowed to march in the ceremonies, I did not know why. *I wonder if the dean of boys didn't tell me, because he was protecting Tyler? What would I have done if I had known? Was talking about sex so taboo within the Church and culture that daughters were afraid to even come to Mothers?*

There would be other times that my daughters would experience harassment, abuse and even rape, yet not share it with me or others until years into adulthood. *My daughters knew others came to me to share these tragic events, why couldn't they?*

Since I could not bring professionals on campus to help the students, I decided to present what I could through video presentations. I convinced the administration to allow me to present a video once a week on a sensitive topic such as addictions to the student body. One of the videos regarded alcoholism and how it affected the family. I stood in the back of the chapel, as usual, to keep an eye on the students. As I stood there listening and watching this demonstration of families in crisis due to an alcoholic in the family, sadness engulfed me. Tears stung my eyes. I felt like running out. I restrained the emotion.

Later in my office after the last girl had spit out her anguish, and was comforted, I sat at my desk in my own anguish examining the cracks the movie had revealed. *Why do I feel so sad, so afraid, so confused? We're a Christian family. Roger doesn't drink alcohol.* I came to the conclusion that while I did not live with an alcoholic, our home and the relationships within it, were functioning akin to what I had seen on that screen. Especially noticeable was how carefree and present the girls were when Roger was away and how tense and isolated they were when he was at home. Once more I was made aware that the students I was counseling were not the only ones who had troubled homes. I did not know what to do. I could not move away or out. Through the years as I learned more about addictions I understood that Roger's addiction to sex was creating in our home what alcoholism caused in others.

My marriage remained unhappy. It was a constant struggle to balance the dorm needs with family needs. Roger had completed and sold the house he was eager to build but income from the sale was eaten up by expenses. He built the house too good for the market. He was hired by the administration, first, as an assistant to the dean of boys and taught a class or two. Then the third year at the academy, he accepted the position of Business Manager and served in this position until our departure.

For fifteen years Roger continued locking me out of my home when he was displeased. Sometimes when I drug myself home to drop into bed for a few hours' sleep I found the door locked. I did not carry a key because keys were a nuisance to carry everywhere I needed to be within four floors of the dorm and many walks to and fro across campus. I, also, was concerned about leaving the keys somewhere available for a student to pick up.

Roger's lock out was often because I had not left my office when I said I would, or when he thought I should. Though I spoke to girls often about not accepting abuse, I still accepted his abuse. To this day, I do not understand why it took me so long to remember that when I stood up to Roger about hitting me, he had stopped.

Late one evening when I returned from a run, I found the apartment door locked, again. I sat under a tree in the dark so that no one would see me and contemplated what to do. I decided I had had enough. Something had to change. I remembered the personal power I felt when I told him I was leaving the second time he hit me while living on the farm.

Why hadn't I learned then that it was more about what I allowed and accepted than what he did? He sought power because he felt powerless. He would treat me however I demanded.

I went to the door and knocked loudly. Anger allowed me to take the chance that someone in the dorm would hear. Roger unlocked the door and turned to go back to our bedroom. I said, "Wait. You are going to want to hear what I have to say." He turned back to face me.

I took a couple steps toward him. Looking straight in his eyes, I said, "You better listen to what I am going to say because I mean every word. If you ever lock me out of my home again, I will leave you." He never locked me out again.

By the fifth year as Dean of Girls, I was a successful administrator. The dorm was organized and clean, unlike the first couple of years. The resident assistants were the best ever, and provided me more relief from duty. Trudy was away at college, and the dorm apartment had been completely remodeled allowing each daughter to have her own bedroom. I felt good about what I had accomplished. I received respect and accolades from students, parents, and faculty.

The relationship with Roger remained the sore spot in my life. The demand for sex was tearing me apart. It felt as though I was trying to please a naughty son. When Roger turned to me in bed, I tried to accommodate. But I felt nausea and disgust especially when he whimpered like a child not getting what he felt he needed. Afterward giving in, I left the bed in tears and anguish. I questioned, *what is wrong with me?* The old words of *I can't do this* and *I have to do this,* tortured me.

I accepted the responsibility for change and sought a counselor. Dr. Julia Williams was a pleasant, grandmotherly, woman who taught psychology at the Adventist University three hours away. The sessions helped me sort out how to move forward with my marriage. In one of the sessions, Dr. Williams told me, "You need to end the marriage. I do not believe the marriage can be saved. If you persist in the marriage it could destroy you emotionally."

I could not accept this counsel. The three-hour ride home lent to soul searching. *I don't believe in divorce. How can I possibly go through a divorce in the position I'm in. Besides, the Church doesn't allow for divorce for reasons other than adultery. I'll lose my job if I divorce. I can't do it. I have to stay. If it just wasn't for the sex I could pretend all is well. I can keep a face on for others. Just not for me or him.*

The organization within the Seventh-day Adventist Church for housing administrators of colleges and academies held yearly conferences on one of the college campuses. I attended a number of the conferences, made a number of friends, and became acquainted with administrators from other institutions.

While at a conference in the spring of 1981, I was approached by the Dean of Women of a west coast college. She asked me to consider taking the position as Assistant Dean of Women on her campus. I was interested. It was a flattering offer. *Me with no degree, an administrator on a college campus?*

On my way back to campus from the conference I entertained the idea that maybe this was what I needed to end the marriage. I could accept this position, divorce Roger, and go to the west coast as a single woman.

However, when I told Roger of the offer he was so excited about the opportunities it offered, I couldn't bring myself to tell him I wanted to go without him. I saw Dr. Williams one more time before leaving. She expressed, strongly, that she believed I needed to accept the position and tell Roger I was going without him. She said that she would meet with the two of us and help me tell him since I felt I could not do it. Though I wanted to believe divorce was okay—I could not. I did not take her up on her offer.

Leaving the dorm girls was emotional. Many tears were shed by me and those who would return to the dorm next year without my presence. Leaving Trudy behind and settled in her own apartment was even more heart rendering. I would be a long ways away.

My experience at the academy produced growth and maturity not only for the girls I counseled, but for me as well. I would never be the same after the experiences that had opened my eyes and thoughts to so many issues and concerns.

I started to question my devotion to and belief in the Church. *Why are the conservative, rule abiding, parents the unloving ones? And why are the liberal, rule breaking, parents the ones that appear more loving?* This seems so minor now, but then the experience with parents and administrator's interaction with students is what truly influenced my question.

How do religion and love go together?

This question stayed with me for the next leg of my journey. It was the beginning of my questioning the Church. Though my mother and grandmother did not like my moving to the west coast, they were very proud I was "moving up in the Church." They did not realize that "moving up" would facilitate my "moving out."

12

On July 2, 1981, I left my parents' home in the Midwest with my sister, niece, and Brenda, to travel west to the alluring opportunity awaiting me as Assistant Dean of Women at a Seventh-day Adventist College. As I pulled out of their driveway, tears stung my eyes and threatened to reveal to my sister that I was not as brave as I pretended. My father, always the mechanic, had walked around my car several times checking the tires, and oil levels—putting off the inevitable. He kept control of emotions as I hugged him, but I felt his sadness. We were two of a kind—doers. Tears slid down Mom's cheeks though she remained stoic. She would miss her grandchildren.

It was a delightful trip for me as I drove toward the setting sun, often traveling the Lewis and Clark Trail. I loved the opportunity to be with my sister without our husbands dictating travel arrangements. We caught up on years of our lives on that trip without revealing true emotions and concerns about our marriages, for in the back seat sat our two twelve-year-old daughters. I did not share with her that I was contemplating the possibility of Roger not moving with me, but the freedom in that thought was invigorating enough now that I had put distance between us.

I was longing for change—change that would allow me to feel safe with who I perceived myself to be. Personal power and independence in thought and action were urging their way into my being. However, the thoughts of the past also nudged, *I can't be independent. I am supposed to sacrifice for the marriage. Needs of others come first. I am being very selfish to think of moving into this new opportunity without Roger.*

The freshmen and sophomore dorm provided an apartment for my family on the ground floor of the three-story building. Across from the front door of our apartment was the entry to the high-rise dorm of seven floors that provided for upperclassmen, and graduate students.

My office on the second floor and near the front entry of the freshmen and sophomore dorm provided a window to look over much of the small campus. The large elm trees, old brick buildings with columned entries, vibrant green grass, and many flower gardens in full bloom, gave the appearance of gracious academia.

It was another secluded campus, self-contained with provision for all needs, even medical. Administration for the women's dorms was provided by a Dean of Women, Associate Dean of Women, and two Assistant Deans of Women. I filled the role of one of the assistants. My experience as Assistant Bookstore Manager at an Adventist University, while Roger studied and received a degree, had prepared me for some of the differences between high school and college administration. But it did not prepare me for the freedom of lifestyle choices within the institution of higher learning. This was made evident to me the first day of my arrival when I knocked on the Dean of Women's apartment door and saw Pepsi bottles sitting on the floor next to the door. Caffeine consumption was considered unacceptable within the Church and indulging in it was considered a sin by many Church members. At the academy a student was disciplined for bringing it into the dormitory. Teachers would have been reprimanded if they were caught drinking it. At least this was my belief and the sight of the caffeine drink in open sight of anyone passing this door unnerved me. *What else do they allow here?*

Two weeks after my arrival, a meeting for all the deans, led by the

Dean of Students, allowed me to express some of my dismay with the dichotomy of the administration on campus. Dr. White was one year from retirement, had been Dean of Students for numerous years, and of the old-school of thought. In this first meeting in preparation for the new school year a question was asked of him by one of the Dean of Men, "What do we do if a student comes with a late night pass that says he is going to be out late because of studying with a friend off campus, and I know that he, in fact, is planning to attend a movie?"

Movies were taboo and this taboo was described in dorm rules as conduct that could be disciplined. A short discussion followed with other described scenarios that led to Dr. White's answer to the question: "You should sign the slip if it reads that he is studying off campus."

Another dean asked, "What if it says he's going to a movie?"

"You shouldn't sign it," he said.

I was aghast! Moving forward in my chair I quickly raised my hand and asked, "Did I hear you correctly? If a student writes a pass that she's studying off campus, and I know she's going to a movie I should okay this, and yet if she writes the truth, that she is going to a movie I should not?"

A slight nod gave me permission to continue. "I don't understand this. The Bible says nothing of movie attendance, but it says a lot about lying. I refuse to sign a pass that is a lie."

He looked a little stricken and asked, "What *will* you do?"

I expounded, "I will address the student, saying that I know she intends to go to a movie, that I don't agree but hope that she is making a choice of an acceptable movie." Movies were shown on campus to the student body. It was the movie theatre attendance that was not acceptable. I reiterated: "I will not sign an agreement that condones a lie."

It was my desire to be seen as trustworthy, dependable, and honest by the students. I intended to build trust by directness, kindness, and respect. I believed it important to be honest and to keep my word—I wanted to teach by example. When I had to correct a behavior, I did my best to do it with kindness, a smile when possible, and with firmness that created respect.

Students, more often than I wished, told me of detrimental experiences with administrators of the academies they attended and with administrators on this campus. The experiences were described sometimes by a simple "I was lied to."

As I was acquainting myself with the differences between being an academy dean and those of a college dean, I was also for the first time, acquainting myself with independence without an authority figure like my father or my husband had been for the last thirty-five years. Guilt and the assumed pointed finger of God, would not relent. The convictions that divorce was not an option for me pounded like a hammer driving a stake through my heart. I could not tell Roger not to come. I could not contemplate divorce. Instead, I evoked a promise from Roger that he would look for work immediately to help support the family, and not enroll in classes as I suspected he desired.

He drove across the country in our green Ford van with sixteen-year-old daughter, Lori. It was a trip she abhorred due to the fact that their relationship was fractious. He would not rent a motel room but insisted she crawl into the back of the van amongst boxes to sleep when he stopped for the night. He slept in the back seat. I met their arrival with cheer, trying to believe that I could make things be okay in this new setting.

Within days, instead of looking for work Roger enrolled in classes offered to spouses of those employed by the university. And, I settled uncomfortably into being the bread-winner, while he judged my performance as wife and mother. He, again, became especially irate when I did not return to the apartment at a time he thought I should. He did not lock the door, as he had while at the academy—besides I carried keys this time. Telephone calls to my office demanding my return to the apartment were frequent. The fact that I did not respond favorably to his demands heightened his annoyance, foreshadowing my vacillation between guilt and animosity. I could not attend to his needs, the dorm's needs, and mine. So I continued to focus on dorm needs and ignored his and mine.

College administration was easier with shared responsibilities. Hours were more defined, and technically, I did not have to spend as much time in the dorm. But I saw the needs and like always, felt the tug to help. I could see neediness in downcast eyes and stressed facial features. Being available to help, I thought, was my calling. This, again, led to frequent late night counseling sessions. It was these Roger objected to. I just thought I was doing my job—being responsible. I was *doing* and he wanted more of me *being* with family.

I stayed away from Roger as much as possible. Our daughters were victims of this avoidance. The dormitory responsibilities provided distraction from the ever-widening chasm between us. Our inability to have honest open communication continued to undermine any hope of having a healthy relationship. Instead of understanding his needs and facilitating communication, I withdrew and focused on my unhappiness. Roger was not totally to blame. I too needed to take responsibility for my feelings and actions. We both came from families that did not participate in open communication, and therefore we lacked the skills that led to communication and understanding.

At the academy my office had been flooded with girls asking for help or describing how someone else needed help. This was not the case at the college level. There were a number of reasons—students asserting their independence, the lack of time, but even more often because administration was not trusted. I did not yearn for a repeat of a schedule like that at the academy, but made myself available by being in my office when the young women returned to the dormitory at door lock. Yes, entrance doors were locked at curfew.

I was far from the academy and into the big league at the college level. I was still making decisions regarding young women's lives. Still making some the administration did not know about, and I believed, would not support. The incident with Tami was one of them.

Tami, a freshman from Virginia, was troubled. She had a pretty face and solid physical body that was covered most of the time with jeans and sweatshirts unbecoming to her beauty. She rarely spoke, and when she did, it was harsh and often critical. She met me in the hall one day with, "How's come that bitch keeps knocking on my door?" This question was to ask why Marta, the other Assistant Dean, was knocking on her door to get her to turn down her music.

The college girls could have radios and stereos in their dorm room, no TVs, but they were not to be heard in the hall. This was a major factor in contact with Tami. Her attempt to drown her pain with loud music, years before headphones, led to the kind of contact with us that she did not want. She slunk in and out of the dorm, and I spoke to her frequently about loud music, staying out past curfew, and non-attendance at worship. I had to catch her as she came into the dorm or was going out—making an appointment was difficult. I always spoke kindly and did my best to encourage her without condemning. I asked whatever questions she would answer. "Where did you go to school? Do you have siblings? How many? What do you like to do when you are not studying?"

Eventually, she did come in to say "hi" when she saw me in my office, and sometimes we just chatted. There seemed to be more she wanted to say or ask, but she remained aloof and hesitant in her communication.

Then late one night while sitting in my office I received a call, "I need you." I recognized the voice, though I don't know how, as it was slurred. "Tami, is this you?"

Again, came, "I need you."

I said, "I will be there. I am coming." I picked up my master key, and hurried to her room. I knocked on the door, and waited. I heard scuffling inside, but no answer. Hesitantly and with much trepidation, I placed my key in the lock and opened the door. Tami was crawling around on the floor—growling like an animal. The room was in shambles. The phone was on the floor next to her and off the hook. I spoke, "Tami I am here."

She responded with, "Get out, I don't want you," in a gruff voice that did not sound like her—even more harsh and caustic than her normal response to confrontation.

I kept talking to her but she did not sound or appear like the Tami I knew. She kept up the demands that I leave, and I kept up my response, "Tami wants me here." Eventually, I sat down on the floor next to her and said gently but firmly, "Tami, say the name Jesus." No response. "Tami, please say Jesus."

A growl.

"Jesus, just Jesus. Please say Jesus."

Her responses of a growled "No, get out," did not deter me. I kept prompting until very softly I heard the word escape her lips, "Jesus."

The word was barely out of her lips when she seemed to wake up. She jerked up, looked at me and said, without the growl, "Why are you here?"

"You called me," I responded.

She questioned, "I did?"

After a few more assurances that my presence had been requested, I retreated. Tami told me she was okay and would clean up her room by herself. I did not know what more to do for her and did not approach the subject of this experience at a later date. However, this was not the end of my adventure with Tami.

One Saturday in the early evening a few weeks later, she entered my office, held before me a crumpled paper sack and asked, "If I leave this with you for safe keeping, will you return it to me when I ask for it?"

I responded, "Yes, it's your property, and I will return it to you when you ask."

I asked, "What is it?" A nod of her head indicated to look inside the sack.

The gun lying in the bottom of the sack looked like a toy. I removed it gingerly, holding it between my thumb and first finger. It felt like a toy but the obvious fact that the chamber was filled with bullets assured me it was not a toy. This fact unnerved me. Tami looked me in the eyes, which was unusual for her, and said, "I've got some thinking to do and I'm not sure I'm safe with it." She turned, slipped out of my office, and left the dorm through the front door.

I was raised with guns and did target shooting with my dad and uncles, but I was still very uncomfortable with this life-threatening item in my hand. I placed it back into the sack and quickly worked my way down stairs to my apartment where I asked Roger to remove the bullets. This done, I returned with gun and bullets in the bag, to my office to take care of other responsibilities.

An hour before door-lock, Tami again appeared in my office. Her declaration that she came for the gun was short and curt, "I want it."

I handed her the sack, she looked inside and picked out the gun. She looked up with a glare, prepared to scold me when she noticed the gun was no longer loaded. I stopped the words from her when I pointed toward the sack and said, "In there." She turned and left my office. I watched from my office window as she walked determinedly down the sidewalk. A whispered, "God watch over her," escaped my lips.

Those words stayed on my lips for the next couple of hours as I met girls checking into the dorm for the night, and answered questions about upcoming events. And then for a couple more hours I met with girls who had not made curfew, and had to see a dean with excuses. Into these early morning hours my eyes strayed toward the front door praying that the next girl to enter would be Tami. It never was.

I did not leave the dorm when my shift was over. I sat in my office praying. Sometimes I walked the halls to stay awake, and often checked Tami's empty room just in case she had, somehow, sneaked back into the dorm. My faith in God's ability to keep Tami safe remained, but my anxiety grew as the hours passed. I would soon have to wake up the Head Dean, Nila, and report what I had done. This would not be received sympathetically. Tami's parents were influential. Her father was a physician, and was treated with great respect by Church and college officials. By five a.m. my anxieties overshadowed my exhaustion, and I fell on my knees pleading once more that God return Tami to the dorm safely.

Six a.m. came and I had to face my supervisor. I walked slowly down the hall, heart in my throat and tears not far from spilling. I knocked and waited, knocked again. Nila was surprised to see me standing at the door this time of morning because after a night on duty I would usually be sound-a-sleep in bed.

She asked, "What are you doing here?"

Nervously, I responded, "I have a confession. I did something that I now wish I hadn't done, but it seemed right at the time." I told her my story with the tears now brimming and passing through the barrier of composure that I sought.

Nila was shocked but pleasant, anxiety spewed from her eyes and voice. "We must do something. Are you sure she did not return?"

"I'm sure she hasn't. I just checked her room for the tenth time."

A deep breath and then she responded, "The first thing to do is call the parents, and then we'll call security." Her next sentence was such a relief that I wanted to hug her, "I'll call the parents and take it from here. You go get some sleep and let me know if you hear anything."

I went to my apartment but could not sleep. In fact, I could not do anything but pray, "Please, God, bring Tami back safely, soon."

I had left a message with the desk monitors on duty through the night, to call me if they heard anything of Tami. Doors were unlocked at 7 o'clock. At 7:30 a.m. the desk called. "Tami just walked in and went to her room."

I called Nila to tell her before going to Tami's room. She told me, "I talked with her parents moments ago. They are furious, and of course worried. They cannot believe their daughter has a gun, and especially, can't believe you returned it to her."

Then she said adamantly, "I will call the parents back and tell them she is safe. You go to her room and you get that gun."

Feeling anxious I walked upstairs to Tami's room. When she opened the door she portrayed an air of bravado and said, "What do you want?"

Strong words came to mind, like, *what do I want? You're asking me what do I want after the night I just went through?* Instead of spewing, I calmly said, "Tami, I have been very worried. We need to talk about last night." She turned away from me, walked to the other side of the room, and stumbled out with, "Well, yah I'm not sure about last night." The words kept stumbling slowly—"depressed and angry.....went down to the river." She ended the jumbled speech with, "I don't know why I am here. Don't know why I'm back. I was going to use the gun, but I just couldn't. I gave up and came back, don't know why."

I wanted to reach out and hug her. Instead, I took a deep breath, looked into Tami's face and said, "I know why you are here. I prayed for you all night. I asked God to not allow you to harm yourself, and to return you to the dorm, safely. My prayers were answered."

"Really?" she asked without enthusiasm.

"Tami, I have to have the gun," I stated with determination. I explained that her parents had been contacted and were irate about my allowing her to keep the gun. She relented and handed it to me.

I went on to suggest to Tami that she withdraw from school. I spoke of her unhappiness, her unwillingness to keep curfew, poor grades, and overall poor attitude. I did not tell her that I felt sure she would be dismissed from school for being out all night without a leave, let alone for carrying a gun on campus.

Tami said, "Right now I just need to sleep." I made an appointment to talk with her later in the day and left her room to get some sleep myself before facing Nila again to decide on Tami's future—and mine.

When I next met with Nila, she informed me that Tami's father was demanding that the gun be sent to him and not returned to Tami. My response was, "I will not do that. She is nineteen years old, an adult. This father has already caused damage to this young woman through his dominance and control in her life. The gun is hers, and I will return it to her when she asks." At first Nila was hesitant to agree with me, but eventually affirmed my determination and supported my resolution to return the gun to Tami.

The next afternoon Tami came to see me at my apartment to announce she was leaving school. She was not going home, but moving to California to another school. Arrangements had been made. She asked for her gun and I handed it to her. We said goodbye with a hug, and I asked that she keep in touch with me.

Tami did keep in touch with me through the next twenty years, and many times included in the notes she sent, were words of appreciation. She felt that my response to her not only saved her life, but also facilitated the self-worth she needed to move on to success in her life. She became a registered nurse, and serves one of the school systems in the state of California.

I'm convinced that Tami's struggle with life was due to a low self-image. I am not sure why she valued herself so little. *Was it perpetuated by the control her father demonstrated in her life? Or was it some type of abuse she had experienced and could not talk about?* She was third in a family of four beautiful, talented, and "good" daughters. The report from Tami that the two oldest were more beautiful, talented, and smarter, in my opinion was not true. I saw their pictures, and I knew that Tami was as beautiful. She also went on to prove that she was just as smart. Tami's role of being the "bad girl" in the family had done much damage to her psyche and to her relationship with her parents. The unfavorable relationship with Dad, as well as the lack of support from her mother, perpetuated destructive relationships with others, and near destruction to herself by self-medicating with drugs and promiscuous sex.

This was a scenario I saw often with the young women I counseled.

13

"Mr. Manley, it is such a pleasure to meet you. Anna talks so much about you." He stood before me with an extended hand that was hard and calloused, appearing as the characteristic cowboy—lean and straight, except for the bowed legs. He wore a Stetson and pointed brown leather boots. He raised cattle and worked horses, and "rode the range" his entire life. Smiling, I shook his hand and expressed my admiration for the care he and his deceased wife had given this young lady who had come into their home as an infant foster child. Now she was a freshmen student in the dormitory I supervised.

Later after getting to know Anna better, I wished I could take those words back.

I met Anna the first day after settling my office. She stood five foot one inch, plump, and black, with short kinky braids circling her head. I remember in particular her giggle. Later I found this to be a cover for a deep well of sadness. She appeared younger than nineteen. First thoughts were that she must be visiting a sister or friend. Five days later I was introduced to Anna again in a profound way.

As I sat in the college church the following Sabbath my eyes were in my lap, or maybe closed, when the special music was introduced. The most beautiful voice met my ears, and I glanced up to see Anna standing at the podium. I was overwhelmed by the voice that came from this childlike person. There was much more to Anna than first appeared. She was to become involved with my life in ways I could not have imagined at the time.

Late at night in the dorm she was noisy with her giggles in the halls, and with loud music blasting from her room. It became obvious later that Anna's reluctance to go to her room at night was because she was afraid instead of defiant. She did not know how to ask for help. She refused to discuss what was disturbing her, and when approached with the idea, refused counseling. She became belligerent when confronted with the negative behaviors and then giggled instead of allowing herself to cry.

She held fear and a very sad story close to her chest.

I was on vacation when I received a call informing me that she had cut her wrists in a suicide attempt. Responding to suicide attempts was part of the job as a dean of women. I had learned that most were cries for help and not a serious attempt. However, I responded to those cries seriously. Therefore, my communication the second time someone attempted suicide was, usually, "I cannot be responsible for your safety. Nor can I place others on my staff in that position. If you make any other suicide attempt you will be asked to leave the college."

I requested that Anna be given this communication from me.

The second time Anna was found in her room inebriated, I knew intervention was necessary. The college, like the Church, had a policy of zero tolerance for alcohol use. Usually, a student caught with alcohol or inebriated was terminated. Joy, a college counselor, and I put together a program to determine if the student in question had an alcohol problem. The student would be assigned a therapist, if and when the tests identified a problem. If they would not accept this counseling, their attendance at the college would be terminated. It was our attempt to help students instead of just dismissing them.

After Anna took the test, Joy was assigned as her therapist. Though she continued to demand attention from the dorm staff which caused continual strife, she did remain in counseling and attended assigned classes. I supported her stay at the college.

Eventually, Anna revealed to me that at the time I was rewarding Mr. Manley with praise for what he had done for her, he was demanding that she sleep with him whenever she came home. She had replaced the foster mother who died two years earlier. This family was praised by everyone who knew them. After all, they had fostered dozens of children. The family were Seventh-day Adventist Christian and not only supported and applauded by their local Church, but by state and local social work officials, as well.

I felt deep sadness for Anna. And I felt anger. *How could this happen? Causing unbelievable pain upon a child and at the same time get accolades from unsuspecting fellow Christians and officials! How does a man sit in church each week with this on his conscience? Why didn't social services pick up on what was happening? Why didn't church members?* Mr. Manley died before I had this information. I hope that I would have confronted him myself if he had not. But I'm not sure.

Poetry written by Anna was horrendously revealing of physical abuse at the hands of the foster mother, as well as, sexual abuse by the Father and older brother. She described herself as a small five-year-old girl laid down and raped by an older brother so strong and so demanding that she submitted dispassionately. Anna spent years in and out of mental wards to prevent suicide, and years and thousands of dollars from government funds for therapy.

The abuse caused havoc in her life and on her body. She now lives in pain. At middle-age, both knees and a hip have been replaced. The accolades for this Christian family who took her into their home as an infant have perpetuated even greater suffering in her heart. *Why didn't someone see what was happening to this child? Was it because they followed the rules of the Church—their outward appearance while sitting in church each Sabbath covering the malicious hidden behaviors?*

14

THE SECOND SCHOOL year at the college, I was promoted to Associate Dean of Women and moved my office to the seven-story upper class dorm I would supervise. The building was across a courtyard from our apartment making it more convenient to me and available to family. Roger took a position working for the local Adventist hospital. A part time position eventually became full time. He added very little to budgeted expenses and claimed he wasn't making enough money to do so. I later found out he had started a savings account in his name only. The tension between us remained unresolvable and tension grew between Roger and the girls. Kim was finishing high school and taking courses at the college. Lori was a sophomore at the Adventist academy a few blocks from the apartment and Brenda an eighth grader in the local Adventist elementary school. I was not as involved in their lives as a Mother probably should have been, but at the same time, put no pressure on them to perform in ways to please me. I trusted and had no need of controlling. Roger's inability to have control over their coming and going caused him angst. He needed structure to feel secure. The girls and I were unwilling to succumb to his pressure. His arguments with the girls about where they could and could not go caused them to come to me with complaints and at times anger and tears. My absence from the home and Brenda's being the youngest, and at home more, placed her in the position of answering to her father. She would ask if she could go to a friend's house and he would most often say no. She would ask to go to the park where she could meet a friend, and he would most often say no. So she started lying about where she was going and with whom. On the side, she often told me where she was and who she was with, in case I needed her. She told me she was lying to her father. Eventually, she would lie to me.

Roger's needs permeated our existence. I recognize now that my reserve and removal of myself from him, exasperated his emotions and he took them out on the girls. Especially his lack of trust. He wasn't wrong in what he wanted our family to be and do. It was the demands, the questions, the judgments, that caused the tension. I was at fault by not questioning, not confronting, not engaging.

I just plain did not want to be with Roger. I did not like him. I did not like me with him. He insisted that he and I attend the Village Seventh-day Adventist Church instead of the college church. He pressured the girls to do the same, causing more reason for argument as they wanted to attend where their friends did. It was a simple request. I relinquished my desires to be with associates and students and went to church with him. A small effort to keep peace. Trying to keep peace and trying to eliminate feelings of guilt by giving into such a small request, did not eliminate the tension. I felt at times as though I was living a charade in the middle of a bubble. Part of the tension for me was the fact that we were surrounded by student living. I did not want evidence of our dysfunction as a family to seep out into their midst. The less power over family that Roger felt, the more he tried to take.

When I think back, it is difficult to point out what was wrong. I only know that over and over again, these phrases passed through my mind while I worked and while I tried to sleep. *I cannot live the way I am living. I am weary, weary of the façade I live. Weary of getting up each day, putting on a smile and stuffing the tears. I don't believe in divorce. I'm in a fish bowl for all to see and glare, gloat, and most of all condemn.*

For months, for years, this dialogue, this way of living, tore me apart emotionally. I knew I had to make a decision. The turmoil in our apartment kept us all in a fractured state of being. I felt bound to dictates of the Church and my own beliefs. By distancing from my feelings, I distanced from my family—my husband and daughters.

I look back on this experience now, and wish I had believed enough in myself to know that I did not have to live this way. I wish I could have said, "This relationship is not serving me well. The marriage is over." Simply put, it was enough to believe in myself and recognize that my needs were not being met, but I was not there yet. I wish I could have given myself permission to not to have to prove anything to anyone but myself.

And then one night my need to make a decision was confirmed. I tried to be inconspicuous as I slipped into bed, but he reached for me. I recoiled. He sought. The words stumbled out between the gasps of my attempt to stay in control, "I can't. I can't do this anymore." Thoughts of *I have to, I have to,* assaulted me.

As I stepped out one side of the bed, he slid out of the other and met me at the end. In his anger, he spat at me the words, "You must. The Bible says that wives should submit." And he spewed, "Your body belongs to your husband," quoting 1 Corinthians 7:4 as he had quoted Ephesians 5:22 before it.

These were words from the Bible that I knew and believed. I had tried to live by them as I submitted to my husband's desires. But the unconscious recoil of my body just moments before told the real story. I did not allow the tears forming in his eyes to affect my decision—I said, "I cannot," and moved out into the hall and to a dorm room for a sleepless night.

I was bursting apart with sadness and despair. *Why can't I? I must, but I just can't.* The fault was not with me but with the belief that a marriage certificate is what makes sex obligatory. The sex felt incestuous. I did not have that word in my vocabulary at the time, but giving into sex with him was like pleasing a begging child. And then it felt violating, when he became angry and demanding.

A visiting psychologist, Dr. Schmidt, accepted my request for an appointment the next day after the confrontation. I poured out to him my remorse from the night before. I told him how much I had hurt my husband but just could not go on anymore with the façade of the marriage. I described Roger's reactions to my response and told him what he had said. Confessing that for years I had given in and 'submitted' to Roger's tears, I requested help.

He emphasized, "You question your ability to love, but you demonstrate love with your request for help." He further stated that he wanted to talk with my husband before another appointment with me the next day. I beseeched Roger to meet with this man to see if he could help us. He relented to the appointment. I thought: *he must be desperate to get me back in our bed.*

The next afternoon when I again met with Dr. Schmidt, he revealed a secret key to the liberation from my agony and remorse. He asked, "Why do you think your husband cries?"

"Because I am hurting him," was my response.

Then from his mouth came these unbelievable words: "Paula, I asked Roger why he cries and do you know what he told me?" Of course, I did not and shook my head loosening the tears formed in my eyes to scatter unchecked down my cheeks. "He told me he cries because it gets him what he wants."

I'm sure my heart stopped. *He admitted he cries to get what he wants! He uses this to get sex from me? To a stranger he admits this?* This revelation was more than I could absorb at the moment. I sat and let it sink in. *He knows what he is doing. He is manipulating me to use me for his pleasure. That is love making? That is what I'm supposed to give in to?*

I looked into Dr. Schmidt's face and asked, "He knows what he is doing?"

"Yes, he knows. It is the only way he knows to hold on to what he wants—you."

My remorse transformed into anger. For years I had accepted the responsibility that when he cried I was hurting him. I gave in to his wants and needs. Now he had admitted that he was doing it to get his way. We had to talk. I went to our apartment, and when he entered I confronted, "We need to talk and talk straight, no manipulation."

He started in, "You have control issues. You always have to be in charge."

I heard all the things I had done and not done to create a relationship with him. I listened as he erupted with all the wrongs he could think of. The allegations deteriorated to "never and always."

I finally said, "I am not going to listen to this anymore. I have nothing to say."

He responded, "You always say I don't share my feelings and now I'm telling you my feelings and you don't want to listen."

Before I turned to go, I said, "In all you have said in the last hour, you have not once used a feeling word." The door closed behind me as I escaped to my office where I agonized over the loss of a relationship I never really had.

I made an appointment with my regular counselor, Elder Bradford, the minister of the College Church who had a doctorate degree in marriage counseling. After I told Elder Bradford of my experience with Roger and Dr. Schmidt, he asked, "What would you do if you knew nothing was going to change?"

Slightly shaking my head side to side, I choked out, "I can't live this way."

When there was no response, I lifted my eyes to his, and as he held my gaze, he said, "I'm telling you that nothing is going to change." He told me he had met with Roger just days earlier in an attempt to encourage him to come for counseling and Roger had refused his overture.

For me all hope was gone. I realized within seconds that I had been holding on to the marriage and my sanity with the belief that I could change or he would change. If hope was gone, I had nothing to hold *me* together, let alone the marriage.

With hope for the marriage gone, I clung fervently to the permission and strength this man of God and minister of the Church could give me to end it. I not only needed another man to tell me what was acceptable to the Church, but also what I should do.

So I sat in Elder Bradford's office for two more hours, and, between crying jags, I wrote Roger a letter telling him I wanted a divorce. Hurt for me, and empathy for him, still wells up within me as I think of the next few days and my effort to get Roger to accept that I meant what I said. Since we lived within the dormitory provided by my employment, he had to move out. It took more assistance from Elder Bradford to encourage Roger's departure by helping him move out his things.

Oh how I struggled, even with the support and encouragement of two counselors who were also ministers. I remember vividly an afternoon when I came from my office to the apartment and found Roger there. He asked to talk. I sat next to him on the couch in the living room—far enough away to allow space but still too close for comfort. He asked that I reconsider, "I'll make the changes you need. Just tell me what you want from me." The pleading was with tears. I felt no anger. I felt pulled into the old pattern of giving in to his portrayal of pain.

He moved toward me, and I moved away not feeling sure of what to do. A Biblical chronicle flashed into my mind. It came clearly with only my silent request for help. It was Abraham's story and it was as if God was speaking: *Abraham did not believe, as his neighbors did, that he should sacrifice a son. Abraham heard God's voice and obeyed even though he did not believe.* I concluded that God was telling me that a divorce was what I needed to do whether I believed in divorce or not. I sensed God's unspoken request for me to trust as Abraham had trusted. Hesitantly but with conviction, I demanded that Roger leave and not enter the apartment again.

Making the decision and holding on to what I believed as God's admonition, did not make the transition easy, but simply possible. I was still struggling with what I believed the Church would say when one day as I walked across campus I came face to face with Elder Parker, Educational Director for the General Conference of Seventh-day Adventists. I had met him years before. I respected and liked him. Having had the opportunity to hear him speak in public a number of times, led me to make the remark, more than once, that sitting in a lecture of his gave me the feeling of sitting at the feet of Jesus.

He asked me, "How are things going for you?" An innocent question but immediate tears communicated to him that things were not going well. I told him my struggle. The words he spoke gave me further hope and peace, "Now, Paula, let me assure you, when the brethren tell you that you cannot divorce without the Biblical grounds of adultery, you should not let them convince you." He went on to say, "I have studied this subject extensively of late, and am convinced that what has happened within your marriage is in the truest sense, a divorce. Because your husband has treated you as described, he has committed adultery of the heart. You are already divorced." My tears then flowed from relief and happiness. Again, God had answered my prayers and led me into revelation.

I clung to those words from this godly man for the next few weeks, and maintained the stance that divorce was the only way for me to proceed with my life. He later wrote me a note imploring me to stay on as Dean of Women and to further beseech Elder Bradford to support me in my decision of divorce with the administration of the college.

I made an appointment with a female lawyer. Her statements of, "We can get you more," left me void of desire to win and left her frustrated with my non-desire. I just wanted it over with. "I want nothing from him and will share half and half," I said, over and over again, until she accepted that she was not going to get me to agree to "getting more." What I did require was that he pay off the balance of tuition after the deduction from my employment for Brenda's education. Since it was a denominational sponsored school, three-quarters of the tuition was paid for by my employer. I agreed to share our assets half and half.

Roger refused to cooperate with lawyers or the judge. He told me, "I will not be part of the divorce." Therefore, he did not sign any papers or show up to any court appointments. I was relieved when he did not show up—I did not want to fight.

My desire that both of us be at peace was hard won, and took a number of years. When we met at child initiated events we nodded or spoke hello, but never had a conversation. It saddens me that we were never able to come to a place in our lives that we could communicate some form of acceptance. Had I known the future, I want to believe that I would have made a stronger effort to communicate with him and bring closure. My peace and closure in regard to this relationship took place alone.

15

On September 25, 1983, my first day of college registration as Head Dean of Women, I turned from my desk and the student sitting next to it, to see Elder Bradford standing in the doorway. I thought he had come to check on me to see how I was managing this very hectic day. As the student silently left, I chatted brightly with him, sharing the progress of the morning until I noticed a difference in his facial expression and stopped.

He spoke, "Paula, this is not a pleasant visit. I just got off the phone with your brother. Your father died a few minutes ago."

Tears came to my eyes and I slapped the palm of my hand on the desk. "Damn this job!" escaped my lips. What I really meant was, *Damn the sense of responsibility that kept me here when I should have been there.*

My mother had called the day before, "Sis, your dad is not doing well. I think you should come home."

I told her I could not leave yet, "Mom, I have to be here on registration day. I am responsible. They're depending on me." She needed my support but did not ask for herself. *Would I have heard her? Why didn't I realize the pain she was experiencing and want to be there to support her.* Mom was so dependent upon Dad. Always she asked for his opinion and permission for anything she did. I never thought about how she was going to live without Dad. I only thought of me.

All summer I had thoughts about this day, *What if Dad gets worse? What if I have to leave?* I prayed, *Please don't let it be then. Please let me get through that weekend, the most important weekend of my career.*

Lewis called me earlier in the morning imploring, "Sis, I think you should come." As a college professor in another Seventh-day Adventist College, he knew what registration day meant for me. He had supported my decision to stay at my post for one more day. My parting comment was, "Keep him alive, I'll come tomorrow."

That decision was now sour within, and I sobbed, "I should have gone, I should have gone. I don't want to see him in a casket." And then I stammered, "It's his fault, he, he, he made me so responsible."

The eighteen months of attending to Dad's dying caused me extreme agony. I had spent many days and dollars traveling between the west-coast and Midwest to be with him, and hours mourning his dying. Now my agony was acute and enduring—he was gone.

This anguish of loss was exacerbated by Grandma Courser's illness and death just months before. She had become ill and hospitalized just days after news reached me that my father had prostate cancer. I flew home to spend a week caring for her in my parent's home. This provided an opportunity to demonstrate my care not only for her, but also for my father.

After the week I returned to campus and my responsibilities, spent and reeling with feelings of remorsefulness. I felt afloat—like a ship without a rudder. These two individuals had determined the direction of my life in a complex dance of allegiance, and now I felt the need to be with them and care for them. But I could not, due to the encumbrances of my responsibilities at the college.

Traveling to and from home provided one more visit with Grandma before her death. We did not talk of God's love, but a conversation did lend to talking about God's rules. She told me with a grin that she had eaten bacon while in the hospital—a sin designated by the Church. She went on to say, "I was hungry and that was on the plate so I just picked it up and ate it."

She continued, "God forgives us, right?"

In my mind this was a huge step in spiritual growth and acceptance of God's love. This conversation, though banal, brought me peace. It was the closest I ever came to hearing her speak of God being a God of love. It was also the last time I saw Grandma.

After her death, my heart's focus turned toward Dad. Weeks before the announcement of his death, I spent two nights with him in the hospital. Both arms were broken, yet uncast because the prostate cancer had metastasized to his bones. The breaks threatened to puncture his flesh as he flailed his arms and railed about the work he needed to do. He threatened my demise for my inept ability to get the work done. Yelling, "Get over here and hand me a wrench, damn it. I'm gonna kick your hind end if you don't get with it."

In his mind he was still the mechanic and in his garage. He repeatedly demanded that I "fix" this and "hold" that.

Trying to calm him, I started to sing a hymn. He calmed. With eyes closed, he lay back in the bed, his lips moving. I leaned closer. He was singing, "I walk with Him, and talk with Him." I had never heard my father sing, and did not know he knew the hymn, "In the Garden."

I imagined him on Grandma Fisk's knee as she sang this song to her child. She would have known it well, and I am sure that is where he learned it. I sang with him as my heart bled.

I had no previous spiritual experience with my father, but he represented God to me. Many times I used him as an example to express my understanding of God, "I love my father, and I know he loves me, but I move when he says move, and I do not ever want to displease him." As the Bible admonishes, I both feared and loved my father.

He portrayed to me a dichotomy of emotions—at times tender when I was hurt, but then angry and demanding about little things like spilled milk or a forgotten chore. His intolerance of questions and a perceived breach in my behavior often led to verbal outbursts and sometimes unwarranted punishment.

I have no memory of his physical abuse of me. But when his hands moved toward his waist and the buckle on his belt, stifling fear entered my body. I do not believe I ever consciously disobeyed my dad. I was afraid of his response and I wanted to please him in everything I did. I'm sure I made mistakes. I spilled milk, fought with my brother, and disrespected my mother, but never with the intention of disobedience. My fear of his responses continued into adulthood.

He mellowed through the years, becoming approachable, especially with his six grandchildren. When we visited and he came home from his mechanic's garage, he sought out each child with a pinch, ruffle of hair, or verbal remark to acknowledge them. He did not hug, kiss, or hold. But he did become more tolerant. One time I disciplined Trudy, who sassed me. I sent her to the living room to sit by herself until I told her she could get up.

While I intended that she sit there the rest of the afternoon, within five minutes Dad said, "Let her up."

I turned to him, shocked, and said, "Dad if I had done what she just did when I was her age, I wouldn't be able to sit down." He responded with a smile and another, "Let her up." I let her up.

Dad never said, "I love you." I never heard those words, or anything similar, from him. He disciplined me, took care of my needs, and protected me. He was there if I called upon him. He never complained about helping me, and I never felt as though I was a burden. He even came to my aid when I was in conflict with my mother, though he would not allow any expression of disrespect for her irrational demands.

What I heard, way too often, from my father regarding God was the cuss words that colored the air in my presence! It wasn't until I was married and had children that I asked, with much trepidation, "Dad, do you have to use that language to express your anger? Can't you keep God's name out of it around the kids?"

I barely got the words out of my mouth when my father said, "You mind your goddamn business!!" So I swallowed my frustration, but I do believe he respected the request for my children not to hear God's name used as a cuss word. I never heard him use the words in their presence after this incident.

I felt his pleasure when I acted responsibly. This is what led to my absence while he lay on his deathbed.

Elder Bradford stayed by with support the afternoon he came to tell me of Dad's death, and guided me through the purchase of airline tickets for myself and my daughters. He knew about the conflicted love for my father, and he knew about the anguish his death was causing me.

I was on a plane by evening. My daughters would follow the next day. The funeral, where it was, who spoke, what was said, remains a blur. I do remember sitting beside the grave, having to say good-bye for the last time, and the sobs that rent my body. It felt as though I was burying part of me and that I would not be able to recover. In a two-year period I had lost the three most important relationships in my life: my husband, my grandmother, and my father.

These deaths, Grandma Courser's and Dad's, gave me the freedom to question what I did not feel safe to question, due to loyalty, while they were alive. *Are men really in charge? Am I supposed to be submissive? Is God a god of love, or of law? What about obedience? How does obedience to law fit with grace? If I don't keep the Sabbath holy, am I lost? Is the Adventist Church the only true church? I used to be so clear on my beliefs. I want to be. Why can't I stop questioning?*

16

THE DIVORCE WAS final, and I was moving on with my life, or was I? Ever since I heard that Roger had been seen with another woman, I was obsessed with observing this for myself. I waited outside his place of employment and watched as he left the building in conversation with a woman. I felt anguish and remorse and did not understand why. I felt driven by a force that I could not control, and questioned my decision over and over again. *Am I being punished for getting the divorce? Am I wrong? Should I have given him another chance? If he could make someone else happy could he have made me happy? Is my unhappiness my own fault?*

A few nights after my stake out at Roger's place of employment, I went to the college athletic field where I had heard he walked the track with a woman. I stayed in the dark, around the edges of the field, behind trees and bushes, trying to get close enough to hear what Roger and the woman were saying. I kept looking around to make sure that I was not seen. It could have been very embarrassing for the Dean of Women to be caught sneaking around in the dark. When they appeared to be leaving, I hid where I would not be seen and waited. They left in separate cars. Not satisfied, I walked a couple of blocks to Roger's apartment building to see if they rendezvoused there.

I did not understand the desperation coursing through me. *What was I doing? Why do I care if he is with another woman? I chose not to be with him. I divorced him. I don't want to be married to him. Why do I feel so deficient, like a loser?* While chastising myself, I walked hesitantly into the parking lot and looked to make sure that her car was not parked there. Trusting that she had not accompanied him to his apartment, I walked quietly up the steps and stood before his door. I felt disengaged with my true self. I could not help it, I had to find out. *Was I the loser?* A war raged inside, tormenting me. *Should I, should I not, knock? Why should I? Why shouldn't I? What will I say? Why am I doing this?* I couldn't bring myself to walk away so I knocked.

The look on his face when he opened the door was pure shock. As I quickly stepped inside and closed the door so no one could see me from outside, I started mumbling through choked tears, "I saw you.....with her.....walking." I watched his eyes to see if I could see his betrayal. *Would he deny it, showing guilt? Why do I feel like he should have guilt?* These thoughts flashed through my mind as he took a step toward me saying, "Paula, she is just a friend from work. That is all she is."

He put his arms around me as I sobbed. I started to relax into those arms, but then I felt the passion of his loins. I twisted and pulled out of his arms. Turning toward the door I lamented, "I'm sorry. I shouldn't be here. This won't work.....I'm sorry."

I wanted so much to be held, to cry in strong masculine arms. But now I knew it could not be Roger's. Those few seconds in his arms had brought back immediate nausea and revulsion when I felt his desire for sex instead of lending me comfort.

The walk back to my apartment allowed further reflection with no answers, so I called a friend, Joy. As a therapist she was always able to help me sort out my feelings. She asked, as usual, "What are you afraid of?"

I answered directly, "I'm afraid that the failure of my marriage was my fault."

Still hampered by the feelings of failure, a few days later I called Elder

Bradford. I told him what had transpired with my stalking Roger and I asked, "What's wrong with me?"

"It sounds like you are afraid that if Roger starts seeing someone then the fault in the marriage might be yours," he responded. "You wanted to believe you could fix the relationship and since you did not fix the relationship, you feel like a failure. His being with someone else makes it look like he may be successful in a relationship while you are not." He assured me that I had the qualities to build a new relationship when the time came, and he encouraged me to give myself time to recover from the devastation I felt.

For weeks my heart continued to ache. At night in my bed alone I felt the physical pain and at times wondered if it could mean I was having a heart attack. *When will this end? When will I feel better? Will I spend my life this way? Will I ever trust again? Love again?* I wanted to feel loved. I had never really felt loved. I did not realize at the time that what I really needed was to love myself. It would take years for this realization to take place. In the meantime, I focused on work and my daughters.

Trudy was happily married, Kim was dating a college student who would graduate a year ahead of her, and Lori was dating a local guy who had grown up in the valley and graduated from the academy she was attending. I was a part of those relationships as the guys spent time at our apartment. I was happy for their ripening love, but felt my loss even more when the couples were around.

At the time of the divorce, Brenda asked to attend a boarding academy cross-country in North Carolina. A friend, whose mother had been one of the assistant deans with me at the academy and now Dean of Girls at this academy, asked her to come spend the school year with her. Brenda had a room in the dormitory, but would spend many hours with the family, so I was comfortable with the decision. She was receiving a lot of pressure from her dad to be with him, though living with me. She carried the belief that she was responsible for his happiness. So while she would rather be with friends, she gave into his requests unhappily. I thought that living away at this time might be best for her. It gave her supervised freedom from the stresses at home.

The assurance of God's love at this time would have helped me to develop love for myself, but while I assured the girls I counseled that God loved them, I did not feel this love and was not sure of it for myself. And I did not communicate or show it well to my daughters. They did not attend the dorm worships I gave that shared my belief in God's love.

The mandatory worship schedule for the dorm girls gave me a platform to talk about God and Church beliefs, but the counseling I did one-on-one about worship attendance provided a more personal dialogue. I received a weekly report of attendance to dorm and campus worship activities and made appointments with those who had not met the requirements. The questions I asked often brought the conversation to a question of their faith in God's love. Most had attended Adventist schools all their lives, as my daughters had, and attendance in the schools indoctrinated them regarding Adventist beliefs about God and salvation. As often as I could, I ended these conversations with a statement relative to their salvation or asked a question about their assurance of salvation. Over and over again, and with their tears sometimes interfering, I was told, "I don't believe I am saved." When I asked, "Why not?" they often responded with the statement, "I'm not good enough." Or, "I don't keep the Sabbath holy." Or, "Because I don't live as God wants me to."

When I talked about faith and the assurance of Jesus' sacrifice on the cross being enough and that all they had to do was *believe*, I often faltered. I used the words I had been taught to use, but my conviction was not strong. I was questioning these beliefs myself. *If keeping the Sabbath holy assured me of salvation, how did I then have faith that Jesus had redeemed me through his blood?* I was getting further from the belief of obedience and closer to accepting God's love, but this belief had not yet firmly jelled.

Disillusion continued to permeate my life. I wanted to believe what the Church taught. I wanted to feel safe and secure and not question. My greatest longing was to experience the unconditional love of God. I wanted that experience to be within the structure of Grandma's Church. I could not find it.

I continued to question the concept of love and what it really meant to love God, or love and be loved, unconditionally. Somehow, I **knew** how important it was but it felt fleeting like catching feathers in the wind. I would **feel** love and then not. *If love is unconditional, I should always feel loving, shouldn't I? Yet I didn't love Roger enough to stay in a marriage with him? Was that love I felt twenty two years ago when I said "I do?" I loved Dad, but I also feared him. So is that the same as loving God? To love God you fear Him?* And then, *Am I afraid of love? Do I need to prove I can love unconditionally to prove I love God?*

17

MOMENTOUS DOESN'T BEGIN to describe my five years at the college. Experiences had rocked the foundation of my beliefs—divorce and deaths. The two most influential persons in my life were no longer alive, though their words and admonitions still infiltrated my thinking. My ex-husband remained in the community, but we rarely spoke, and even then only regarding one of the girls.

Difficult and sad years turned to joy as my family grew. Trudy had married the first December after our move to the college. Roger and I returned to the Midwest as husband and wife to stand proud together for that wedding. She gave birth to Erik William three years later, four months before Lori's and Kim's weddings, a week apart. With determination, I had sat next to Roger so as to present a family united for their weddings. Sadness threatened to overwhelm me, but I kept smiling. We both did our best to help make it a delightful experience for the girls.

Brenda lived with me but attended school at an Adventist boarding academy three hours away. She had come home after her boarding school experience across the country to attend the academy that Lori was attending blocks from the apartment. However, before the school year began, she asked to attend a boarding academy again, one closer to home. Though I preferred she be at home, I gave in to her desires believing she needed to get away from her father's insistence she spend time with him. Years later I found out that it was not the reason for her departure. Once again a daughter did not share with me the abuse and pain she was experiencing. *Why was I so unapproachable to my own daughters? Why didn't I see the pain? Was I too taken up with me? My dysfunction? My own pain?*

Since the summer of the girls' weddings I had adjusted to life as a single woman, and enjoyed spending time with them and their mates. Still ambiguous about intimate relationships, I was hesitant to take a chance with dating. I turned down any invitations. I did not feel secure enough with my ability to date and remain dispassionate. I was more afraid of rejecting than being rejected. I had not experienced being left, only leaving. Being pursued by a couple of married men enhanced distrustful feelings and caused even more apprehension in trusting men.

My reluctance to date was motivated by fear of intimacy. Years later I would determine that "intimacy" was in-to-me-see, but at this time in my life it meant sex. I felt very hesitant to face what I considered a dilemma—would every man expect it? Would I be placed in the position to continually have to experience displeasure with my "nos?" As Dean of Girls and now Dean of Women, I was often placed in a position to counsel regarding this subject of sex and making love. I was conflicted in my own beliefs. Having sex a sin? Making love without a marriage certificate, a sin? Didn't want to deal with it in my life. So I kept male companionship, and even friendship, at a distance. In the future, maybe.

Some friends and acquaintances encouraged me to date, while others discouraged me from being near their husbands and no longer invited me to their homes. An obvious one was the Dean of Men's wife, Elizabeth.

Donna, who had resided in the dorm I administered while in the Midwest, followed me to the college and was employed as the dean's secretary in the men's dormitory. She visited me one day and hesitantly told me that the dean's wife had come to the office, closed the door, and announced that she had a favor to ask. When Donna assured her she would be happy to fulfill a favor for her, she said, "If there is ever a time that you notice Paula calling my husband or that they are having meetings, please promise to tell me." *Frustratingly unbelievable!*

I was not surprised by Donna's revelation, as Elizabeth always seemed uncomfortable whenever I took her husband aside to discuss college business while in her presence. Though I felt angry, I was able to laugh at what Donna was telling me. Elizabeth's husband was short, stocky and balding. I told Donna, "If I was to pursue a married man, it would not be hers. You can assure her that you will tell her if you see or hear anything."

Being single was not lonelier for me than being married to Roger because we had not socialized as a couple at the college. The friends I made were mine and not ours. However, even though I did not know what it would look like, I fantasized about being loved and cared for by someone who would offer an opportunity to socialize with other friends. I began to long for the idea of a couple. I didn't really know how this would work with my perceived ideal of freedom. My questions were, *What will or could coupling look like? Would I promise to obey again? Will I be able to trust?*

I had no concrete thoughts or beliefs about marriage other than what I had been given as a young woman. Obedience and "til death do part" still picked at my thinking. I did not like the idea of men being in charge. I didn't like that on campus all the major decisions appeared to be made by men. Men pastors, men administrators, men in at the Union level, and only men at the worldwide conference level. *Did it also mean men were the head of the house? If or when I remarry will I lose the position in my home I now hold?* I made the decisions. I had my own credit card now. I bought my own new car. *Will I be giving this up if I remarry?*

One day, as we were chatting, Bill, the Associate Dean of Men, approached me with the topic of Loren. Though small, the organization for Deans within the Adventist Church was spread across the United States. Everyone within the organization was at least acquainted. He said, "Hey,

I hear that Loren's getting a divorce. I think you two would make a good couple. You oughta check it out." *I think I will!*

Loren was tall, dark, and handsome. I liked that. He had been employed as a Dean of Boys at an academy in the state next to where I served as Dean of Girls for five years. We attended the same training conferences—even served on some of the same committees. His family had been in my home when one of the conferences was held on the campus where I served. So, I knew his wife and two children, Amy and Scott. I saw the respect he showed to his wife and the tender attentiveness he gave his children. He and his family had moved to the east coast when he accepted a position as Dean of Men at an Adventist college a couple years after I moved to the west coast to serve as Dean of Women.

I liked Loren. We were often in agreement in the committees we served together. More importantly, we were able to disagree amiably. I perceived in him strength and a caring of others when he talked about the young men in his dorm. He had the qualities of "tough and tender" that I was attracted to in a man. I did see him as somewhat withdrawn and maybe even arrogant. Later, I found this to be the protection he wrapped around himself. I also found some of my own wrappings of protection.

The conversation with Bill aroused my interest. I called Loren. Months of phone conversations while he was on the east coast and I on the west, allowed for hours spent sharing our feelings, beliefs, and desires. These conversations led us to a place of trust and a desire to pursue an intimate relationship. Both of us were coming from the place of painful broken relationships that had left scars we were yet to acknowledge. We believed in our ability to love freely and to love well. For the first time I talked with a man about intimacy—in-to-me-see. And we talked about sex! We came to a mutual belief that "making love" was not tied to a marriage certificate given by the state but to a commitment of love and devotion to each other

We had a lot to learn. *We agree on so much. Does that make it safer to disagree? Surely, we can work through anything that will come up. Will my girls love him as I do? Will his children accept me? We can work it out.*

Loren had resigned from his position at the college at the time of his divorce. He received an offer from a gentleman he had been working with to design residential treatment homes for at-risk and/or adjudicated youth. When the offer fell through because of lack of financial security, Loren decided to move to be near me. He and I were to the point in our relationship to consider commitment but felt we needed to be closer in proximity to make sure.

The college I served was the only one in the Adventist system that had a social work degree program that could help facilitate the development of his dream. I completely supported his dream of group homes or treatment centers for troubled teens. I too had regretted not being able to help kids who were in trouble. The program we talked about and wanted to develop would serve those who were not acceptable, not only in the academies we serve, but the public educational system as well. We could do it together. We could do it here with the support of the social work department and a friend that agreed to financial backing.

I knew marriage to Loren, or anyone, could be an issue with college administrators. The letter of hire dated May 1, 1981 read in part "...the following statements are understood and agreed upon as conditions of employment: A commitment to supporting the basic tenets of the Seventh-day Adventist Church coupled with an active endeavor to conduct your life in a manner which reflects a consistency and harmony with the church's policies and doctrines."

I also knew that Church policy statements were unsupportive of divorce. I had heard from others that the college chaplain believed that my position with the college should have been terminated at the time of my divorce. Remarrying was even more serious and unacceptable by the Church. Written doctrine stated, "Regarding divorce, Jesus taught that the person who divorces a spouse, except for fornication, and marries another, commits adultery." Adultery would be considered a reason, not only for terminating my position with the college but censorship by the Church.

Loren moved into a small apartment in the town adjoining the college campus, the fall that would prove to be my last one at the college. He kept a low profile on campus, visiting the Social Work Department only. But word soon got out that I was dating the man with whom I had been seen.

Upon arriving in my office one morning, the secretary said, "You are supposed to call Dr. Anderson's office for an appointment." Dr. Anderson was a new president of the college, and not the one who had hired me. We had been introduced only two weeks before.

I made the appointment. It did not go well. He had received information that I was dating. "Is this a true report?"

My, "Yes, I am," proceeded a conversation of concern. He needed to, "discuss your situation with a committee and the Union president." And further, "If you are considering marriage it will need to be dealt with." This implied to me that I would be disciplined. I told him that I did not appreciate an academic committee discussing my private and social life and that I would resign, "immediately if you prefer." His assurance that he did not want me to resign left me cold so I responded, "Then I will resign at the end of the quarter." I left his office shaking with anger. I felt betrayed and condemned by close colleagues who had reported my dating. I felt certain that the Dean of Men, pushed by his wife who had asked his secretary to report my contact with her husband, had done the reporting. The chaplain who had stated, at the time of the divorce that I should be terminated, was retired so it wasn't him. *Does it matter what others think? Is it with malice? Or religiosity? Or making favor with the new President?* I decided it didn't really matter and dropped any thought of confrontation or defense.

The Dean of Students, my immediate supervisor, did not want me to resign, my associate dean did not want me to resign, my assistant deans did not want me to resign. So I reconsidered. I also called the gentleman who had counseled me about the appropriateness of my divorce, Dr.

Parker, who was now Educational Secretary of the General Conference of Seventh-day Adventist worldwide. He counseled me to not resign and to write a letter to the president stating not only this, but my feelings about how I was being treated.

I wrote the letter stating, "Sir, please be advised that I plan to remain as the Dean of Women through the remainder of this academic school year." Further, I stated, "...I have strong convictions in regard to interpretations and statements made by anyone as to my marital status!" Then I wrote, "While I was married to a man who, on occasion, did not support the family financially and, who was, on occasion abusive to me and the children, no one of this institution or of the Seventh-day Adventist Church confronted him regarding 'consequences' should he continue to mistreat his family. How unfair that such an individual can maintain reputation and membership within the community and church. Yet, I must now be denied personal happiness because certain people want to dictate, interpret, and judge 'my' previous marriage and resulting divorce."

I went on to state what was dear to my heart, "It is interesting that others have told me that I should find someone to love and care for me. Yet, you suggest that I have no right to pursue such love and happiness within the realm of marriage. I believe that I do have the right to the pursuit of happiness - even in marriage. I do not believe that we are serving the kind of God who would make us live with a 'mistake' made at an early age. I do not believe that our God would make that kind of judgment call and I have not received counsel from individuals on this campus or in the Church that says I am wrong. Further, I do not believe it to be a 'caring' church nor institution that makes those kinds of statements, judgments, or mandates concerning its members and employees."

I did ask if any action taken would be an academic decision by the college or by the Church. In closing I stated that "your expectation is mixing my professional life with that of my personal life," and that "This expectation certainly can, in no legal way, be levied because of professional incompetence, negligence, or ill-reputation. Because of this, I am asking for a statement from the Church leadership. I would like to know how I will be dealt with as I pursue my personal life in a way I consider to be ordained by God - the right to the pursuit of happiness."

I sent a copy of my letter to Dr. Parker along with a small letter telling him that I was resigning as Dean of Women effective at the end of this school year. I wrote, "I do plan to pursue happiness as I see best for me at this time!" He returned the letter I wrote with a hand written note upon the back, stating, "Insist on the order of clarifications and advisements. It is your Pastor who must step forward in your behalf to speak for the Church (with or without consultation with his superiors). The Church through its clergy cannot in private counseling with you affirm your right to happiness, and then publicly through your Church employer deny you this. The Church must speak with one mouth - & its representative to you is your pastor, not your employer, in this matter." I appreciated his sentiments and support, but I was done. My pastor had supported me—he'd helped me write the letter asking for the divorce. I felt confident he supported my marriage. *So why doesn't Elder Bradford support me with maintaining my position? Is he afraid of administration? Afraid that he shouldn't have supported me?* He had not voiced support for remarriage but did not make statements against it when I had said, "No one, not even you, stepped in to help me when I was experiencing abuse from my husband. So if I find someone to love me and decide to marry, no one should step in then. The church won't keep me from remarrying if I choose to."

In President Anderson's return letter he wrote, "I appreciate your frustration over unfair expectations and accusations, and I want to assure you that ....I spoke only for the college and not the Church. Unfortunately, all of us here at the college, because of the special role we play, find our private lives and our professional lives overlapping whether we want them to or not. I would not presume to judge your motives or your standing with God, whatever you might decide to do in the future about remarriage. But as you yourself are only too aware, your role as Dean of Women moves the issue into a different arena, an arena where I have a clear responsibility to protect not just your interests but the interests of the entire college community." And he said, "I sympathize with you in your situation…..I am looking forward to continuing to work with you for whatever length of time you may be our Dean of Women."

My return letter stated, "Thank you for your response to my letter. I appreciate what you had to say and your support of me. Please accept my resignation as Dean of Women at the end of this school year. I feel very good about my ten years of deaning and the five years spent at the college. However, because of future plans deaning is a career that I am choosing to leave."

It was done. I quit trying to prove my points of contention. I finished the school year peacefully, supported by administration and staff. I left in good standing with the students I served and the assistants serving with me. I was happily looking forward to a new chance at marriage. *I feel love and loved. I don't need more than that. It will make all things possible.*

I was satisfied. The Church, and/or someone within it, wasn't.

18

THE COURTYARD NEXT to my apartment, which was surrounded on three sides by the dormitory, provided an ideal setting for a wedding. My daughters insisted on what they called, "a real wedding." They orchestrated a wedding reception decorated with lighted candles placed in the fountain and tables spread with mints, nuts, cake and punch. Rows of folding chairs created an aisle for me to walk down as I entered behind my two-year-old grandson, Erik. As the Bible boy, he walked up the aisle and handed the Bible to his step-great-aunt and uncle. The wedding was a family affair with Loren's sister and brother-in-law, he, an ordained minister of the Adventist Church, performing the ceremony. Loren's brother, David, stood as his groomsmen and my sister, Susan, was my bridesmaid. Brenda and Amy stood at the guestbook table. Trudy, Kim, and Lori, sang my favorite song, *The Rose.* Anna, the girl who took my breath away the first Sabbath of my tenure with the college, had become a part of our family and blessed the ceremony by singing *Evergreen.* I was a happy bride but a nervous one, uncomfortable in the spotlight. I felt excited about blending our children into one happy family. Though I did not have a clear view of what that would look like, I just knew I could make it work.

Remembering the controversy this wedding had and could cause, I was delighted that most of the ministerial staff of the college church honored me with attendance at the wedding. This, as much as the half of a Valium someone had given me, took away my fears of someone coming to the wedding to cause discord.

I had no doubts on this day nor any fears of the future, even though it was the last day I served as Dean of Women and had no income. I was ready to move on. I had complete trust in my decision to pursue love instead of career. I didn't know how life-changing it would be, but had confidence in myself to be able to handle whatever came in the future.

Amy and Scott had visited Loren a few weeks after his move to be near me. Though they had met me years before, they had no memory of me or my children. Scott remained aloof throughout the time we were together, but Amy and I fell in love. I had been excited with the possibility of having a son, and did not expect the connection Amy and I developed very quickly. Scott's aloofness mirrored my first experiences with Loren. Again, I would learn later, he, too, wrapped himself in a blanket of protection.

Loren and I left our moms, siblings, and children to get better acquainted after the reception and drove north for a two-night honeymoon four hours away. It was a beautiful experience for me. Now I knew what love making felt like. I even felt adored. Words Loren would continue to use throughout our marriage, "I adore you."

From the short honeymoon, we returned to the house a couple miles from campus that we had rented and partially settled before the wedding. And we moved ahead with the plans made with my now ex-associate dean's husband, Gary, to complete arrangements for the development of a treatment center, or group home as it was called at the time. Gary had the plot picked out a few blocks off campus and the plans to build were in place. We were to have one more meeting with the local Board of Commissioners a couple days after our return. The Mayor, chairman of the board, told us, "It's just a procedure. The board may give you some conditions you have to meet but the vote will move you ahead with your plans."

When we got to the meeting, we were shocked to see a number of local citizens there. It never entered our minds that people living on and around this Christian campus would be unfavorable to a group home for troubled kids. After we shared our desired plan, others shared their concerns and fears. The vote was taken by the town board and our plan/application was denied. It echoed what we had continually experienced in the academies we served of "kicking" kids out for unacceptable behavior. We were devastated. We were angry. I felt betrayed. *Did the same people who wanted me disciplined or removed from campus orchestrate this too? Was I being punished?*

We broke our rental agreement. Packed our bags and our furnishings. Rented a truck we couldn't afford. Rented an apartment with my last paycheck and moved two hundred and fifty miles away from the disappointment. We took our plans with us, on paper, and in files that we intended to use soon. We had confidence in our love for each other. This alone sustained us. *How different would life have looked if we had known how many times in the future we would pack up and leave disappointed? Would our love and determination have sustained us? Would we have had the courage to move on?*

Within a few weeks, Loren was hired as a case manager at a day-treatment center and we settled into the joy of just being together. Togetherness was what I wanted most. I felt loved and appreciated even though stress and disappointment hung over us like wet blankets. The main difference in this marriage and the one of the past, was the expression of love and appreciation. At times we both struggled with unspoken feelings of failure and depression. Loren would distance himself from me. Sometimes it took a day or two before reassurance of love was expressed, causing me angst. During this time saying, "I love you, I adore you," were words I needed. He needed them too. I did my best to express my feelings of love in other ways, but at times fell back to the practice of pleasing in bed to change his mood or demeanor.

We had rented a two bedroom apartment providing a home for Brenda when she was not at the boarding academy. We searched for employment, willing anything that could give us the income we needed.

I received a call from Elder Bradford within the first month of our marriage. "Paula a committee has been formed to discuss your status with the Church due to your marrying without biblical grounds for the divorce." He went on to say, "You are invited to come speak to this committee if you want."

I responded, "I will not be coming to meet with your committee. I have discussed my divorce and remarriage all I am going to discuss with anyone. Your little ole committee can do whatever it wants with my membership to your church." Further I stated, "I don't need a membership in a church. My relationship is with God. Not the Church." Though I sounded caustic, it was a cordial conversation. We were friends. He was doing his duty and I was speaking my piece. He ended the conversation saying he would call me with the committee's decision. A couple weeks later he called to tell me that the committee had voted to place me on probation for six months.

I asked, "And what will get me off probation?"

He stumbled with words as he said, "Well, well, I guess if your marriage is stable, and happy."

"Jerald, (using his first name instead of Pastor) are you telling me that the very thing that got me on censorship will get me off censorship?"

He answered, simply, "I guess you could say that."

I further asked,"How will you know if my marriage is stable and happy."

He didn't know how to answer that question so ended the conversation, "You will receive a notice at the end of the censorship in six months." Sure enough, I received a notice six months later that I was no longer on probation. I really didn't care. Membership in any church no longer meant anything to me. *Same people wanting me punished or disciplined? Same criticism from men about how I was choosing to conduct my life?*

I only cared about my relationship with Loren and our children. Our children were scattered across half of the United States and we both missed our kids. Guilt about our happiness away from them kept us from enjoying our life together as completely as I would have liked. This was especially true for Loren, Amy's and Scott's absence was torturous. We lacked the money to buy tickets for them to come visit. Telephone calls ended in sobs and promises.

Loren was hired by a day-treatment facility across town. We were so thankful to have income just in time to pay rent. Six weeks into Loren's employment as a case worker, I received a call from Susie, a friend I worked with before going to the academy. We had kept in touch and she knew that we were intending to open group homes. She heard the result of our attempts to build one in the college community. She and her husband had a counseling and consulting center a few hours away. She asked, "Would you and Loren be interested in taking over our center? We are moving. You could manage the center and move forward with your plans for a group home too." Move ahead with our dream. Of course I wanted that. But we had just moved. Loren had a job that paid the rent.

However, it didn't take much discussion to come to the conclusion that we did want to take over the counseling center and proceed with the group home plans. Besides, it would take us back closer to Kim and Lori and their husbands. Adding to this pull was the fact that Lori was expecting a baby and I was delighted to be grandma to a grandchild who was closer. Trudy now had two boys, three year old Erik and nine month old Brendan. I loved being Grandma but did not get to see them often enough for them to know me. Living an hour away from Lori would satisfy some of that desire.

Loren painfully gave notice at work. It was difficult to leave the kids and the relationships he had built with them. The director was rightfully irritated but our desire to do what we had planned was stronger than our sense of duty to this program. The sense of guilt was assuaged with the idea of doing what we felt we were supposed to do.

We rented a truck and started packing. Lori and her husband, Jon, came to help us pack and load the truck. They were delighted we were moving back closer to them. We went to bed late the night before the move, but with determination to arise early and have the move completed in one day. Seven o'clock in the morning, Loren's phone rang. It was Larry, Susie's husband who said, "Sorry to tell you this, but I've changed my mind. I am not ready to give up my center. We aren't moving." Devastating news!

"But we have the truck. I spent money I don't have to rent the truck," came out of Loren's mouth.

Only, "Sorry," came out of Larry's. Now we were stuck in an apartment we couldn't afford and no money to move. We emoted for a while, said goodbye to Lori and Jon, and closed the door on another dead end. We managed somehow to move forward looking for employment again. We had our ups and downs. We believed all was well and then we didn't. *Why is this happening?* I returned to the questioning, *Are we being punished? For divorcing? For leaving Adventist education?*

I remember one particular difficult day before we found employment. I said, "We have to get out of this apartment."

Loren said, "Let's go play a round of tennis. We'll get exercise, at least."

We drove to a complex with courts, entered a court and started volleying. I could not return his serves. He was a much better player trying his best to slow down his serves and send them directly to me. Still I could hit nothing. Disgruntled and near tears, I walked off the court and to the car. He followed me, and we went home. After sitting silent on the couch for some time, I spurted out, "I'm such a failure. Can't even hit a stupid little ball." As tears started to flow down my cheeks, I thought, *this is stupid. What am I doing feeling sorry for myself because I can't hit a ball?* I looked over at Loren. He looked at me and we burst out laughing. Laughter, belief in our abilities, and faith in God's care for us, got us through the next couple of weeks before Loren was hired by an Adventist-owned retirement living organization as Regional Manager. We could pay the rent. We could buy airline tickets to have Amy and Scott fly out for Christmas, even if it was spring break before they could come. We had a delightful time. Brenda was home on break and we spent time getting to know each other better as a family. The three kids got along great, though there came a time when Amy felt this older step-sister was taking away her brother. Bonding as a family wasn't as easy as I thought it would be. I wanted my daughters to have a Father that they could appreciate and even admire. I wanted that to be Loren. Blending families is work. We didn't realize how much work.

We settled into living and accepting that the security of income was more important than pursuing our dream. I was hired as manager of a nearby retirement community owned by the same company that hired Loren. We found a delightful house to rent and eight months after moving into the apartment, moved to a house that would accommodate Brenda and the other children when they visited. We were close enough to Lori that I could be with her when she gave birth. It all felt so homey. I was getting to be the mother and grandmother I wanted to be. There were rough spots, especially between Loren and Brenda, who was now living with us and working at a nursing home nearby. This brought strain to Loren and my relationship as I took the role of caretaker and he played the role of disciplinarian. I thought he was too hard. He thought I was too easy. This would continue to be a contention for us for many years to come. He lived the "tough love" I agreed with, but didn't practice.

And then it happened again! Ten months after renting the house and three weeks after attending the birth of Lori's daughter Lindsee, we received notice that the company that employed both of us had sold. We could stay employed by the new company but it would mean a move to Texas. "No, I will not move to Texas. It's too far away." Needless to say, I cried. I was once more crushed with the overwhelming feelings that we must be doing something wrong. *How can this keep happening? God, where are you?* The word punishment still came to mind over and over. We had not been attending church regularly, well hardly at all. We tried to attend but it felt so fake. So much like pretending. I went to bed each night with the words on my lips, "I am sorry if I am failing. Please show me the right way, how you want me to live." *Was God showing me by all these losses? All this moving? Having to leave my children?*

Within the month, Loren contacted another Adventist owned company with assisted living facilities and was hired as Regional Manager. When you are desperate for employment, without any income, any hire comes as a welcome and blessing. This is how we felt even though it meant that we had to move thousands of miles away from our kids. Far away from my new baby granddaughter, Lindsee, whom I had looked forward to getting to know and be with since being unable to be with Trudy's boys. Right before we moved, Kim went through a divorce and moved to California to live with her uncle Lewis, my brother. Our immediate family of children and grandchildren was now to be separated into six states. Brenda had a boyfriend she did not want to leave and moved in with his parents. It was difficult to leave her. I was sad and afraid for her, but I was also relieved. There would be less tension in our home. I could focus only on pleasing Loren and alleviating tension caused by his and Brenda's relationship. At least for a while. It would return again and again.

Three months later, a transfer. Yes, only three months later, during which Loren had a two week bout of bronchitis and a frightening five day stay in the hospital with Hepatitis B. He was transferred to a new office. The office was over a thousand miles away. A new office meant a new home. This move was joyous. We were ready to leave this place but even more so the joy was because the office and therefore our home, was near Scott and Amy. Near enough for them to be in our home on a regular basis. And near enough that my daughters and families could visit.

19

WE LIKED LIVING in Colorado. Liked the sunny skies and out of doors activities. We especially liked that Amy and Scott were living nearby. We were able to spend time with them and attend school events. Buying a house was satisfying and exciting. Only one more week we would sign the final papers. Then the earth dropped out underneath us. The president of the assisted living company we worked for walked into Loren's office and announced that the Colorado division was being closed. We were unemployed, again. Devastated, again.

Church attendance had been minimal. We attended when Scott or Amy invited us. We went once in a while to a Church closer but always left dissatisfied and asking ourselves, *why attend if we feel disturbed?*

I had my ears pierced. After all my years of telling girls they could not wear jewelry, I now had on my body proof that I was no longer a conservative Adventist. That's what I believed and thought others would too. The week before the piercing, I had attended church with a breast pin that had upon it fifteen to twenty tiny pearls nestled within the gold circle. This was acceptable and I felt no angst wearing it. I was afraid to go to church as long as I had earrings in. I was afraid of the judgment. I knew within me that wearing the earrings did not matter to God. I couldn't explain why or how I knew. I could not explain why I was afraid of the criticism of the Church that no longer had any authority in my life.

We were without employment again! Discouraged and fleetingly confident, we struggled with the unavailability of income and our seemingly inability to do anything about it. We still wanted to do what we both knew we did best, work with kids. Preferably high school kids. We didn't plan to go back to boarding academy employment, didn't even think it possible. Our dream of having group homes still hung in the back of everything we thought, but we had no resources. We couldn't see a way forward.

Everything changed when we received a call from the former Vice-President of Student Affairs under whom I served as Dean of Women. He was now Educational Secretary of one of the west coast Adventist conferences and needed to fill a principal's position before school started in two months. He knew Loren due to their connections with the Adventist Student Personnel Association and our marriage. On the phone, he said, "I have a great need and I know you two can fill it. Will you come, take a look and consider this position?"

God's answer to our prayers? Or His way of getting us back to being a part of the Church? It does answer our need for employment. We have asked for doors to open. We need to check it out.

We flew to the west coast for a visit to the campus, a beautiful place in the country with a covered bridge over a river that provided the only entrance—unique and isolating. A profusion of greenery surrounded the campus. The center of campus had open park-like features, with a covered circular walk and side-walks projecting to most of the buildings. The covered walk enabled students to travel from dormitories to classrooms, cafeteria, and gymnasium during the frequent rains. It also enabled them to knock on the front door of the principal's home without getting wet as the house we would occupy was on the circle of the covered walk-way.

We prayed in earnest for direction. We had no other offer for employment and were desperate for income. We were drawn to the income but also believed that this was an opportunity to make a difference in a system we loved, due to the students we had served in the past. We also disliked the way the system treated these very kids in the name of religion. Accepting the position meant we would once more be placed in a position to buttress a system we did not entirely support. *We can make a difference. We can change the way campuses have been run. We can show a different, better way. Together we can do this.*

I wasn't sure that I believed in Adventism anymore. Answers to the questions that plagued me when I left employment by the Church were still vague. If I was going to be employed by the Church again it would be to make a genuine difference in the lives of the students by demonstrating the love of God. We decided that Loren's position as the principal would allow us to have a greater impact on what happened on campus than we did as dormitory deans. The leaders who had interviewed and hired us spoke of change and rejuvenation—changing the paradigm. We were ready to be a part of that. We accepted the position.

"Making a difference" would prove to be extremely difficult and unrewarding. The Church conference constituency consisted of a number of conservative congregations with many members who wanted "status quo" or a less altruistic administration at their school.

Our first meetings with campus administration were enlightening beyond our expectations. There was a division on campus—an evident split between conservatives and liberals. The conservatives let us know immediately who needed to go and who needed to stay. They gave names of those employees and some students. The liberals were more hesitant to talk. They had already experienced prejudicial decisions made against them and waited to see who we were. Were we liberal or conservative—did I wear jewelry? Did we eat meat? Did we drink colas? Did we eat in a restaurant on Sabbath? Did we support and agree with Ellen White's writings? And so forth. It did not take long before it became evident to all that we were liberal. Liberal most of all because we did not judge others who were believed to be liberal.

I had taken off my wedding ring and wore no jewelry. I did not want to start off with consternation on the part of the conservatives. Some of the staff and faculty in the liberal camp wore simple wedding bands. So when I put my wedding ring back on, we were identified as liberal.

One of the most telling examples of our liberality came when we accompanied two of the faculty to a small restaurant-bar six miles up the river. Loren was a connoisseur of restaurants, and going to this little "unacceptable" place gave him an outlet he needed. The restaurant serving food and the bar serving liquor, were in the same building so going there was greatly frowned upon by the conservatives.

I was hired by the board as Dean of Students overseeing the dormitory deans and Discipline Committee. I also taught a Peer Counseling Class. One of the chapters in the syllabus I developed for class was focused on self-identity and self-worth. I had experienced through the years that low self-esteem was rampant with the young women I counseled. In the syllabus and class, I spoke of breaking the cycle of low self-esteem by emphasizing positive steps to raise self-worth.

"The place to begin," I said, "is that you are made in God's image. Jesus came to die on the cross for you alone. You are the son or daughter of the most-high God. All things are possible with God."

And I emphasized: "God's love is unconditional."

One day after delivering this lesson to the class, I received a call from the school nurse who was one of the conservative staff. Her daughter was in the class. She said, "I understand that you are teaching the students about self-esteem?" I replied hesitantly because I feared this woman's power with the conference officials and knew from others' experience that she would take her issues to the top.

I said, "Yes."

She went on, "Well, I'd like to know why you are teaching that."

Faltering, I said, "I think the students need it. I see a lot of students with low self-esteem." Her voice rose slightly, she said, "They have low self-esteem because they have sin in their lives. What you need to do is teach them to stop sinning. Forgiveness of sin will give them self-esteem that comes from the blood Jesus shed for us."

I did not know what to say. I was aghast. I felt attacked. I stumbled out, "I think they need to know about the unconditional love of God."

Her proclamation, "Jesus' blood is that unconditional love," left me with no argument or desire to argue. I clamped my mouth shut to keep from saying anything more and ended the conversation with, "I will see to it that you get a copy of my syllabus," in answer to her request. I hung up unnerved.

Why didn't I say more? Why not tell her I disagree with her? Why didn't I tell her that day after day I sat in my office listening to stories of abuse from dysfunctional Adventist households that created low self-esteem, and that one of the stories was from her own daughter?

I didn't say more because I feared she would twist anything I said into non-support of the Church and we could lose our positions at the school. I knew that she could add a word, leave out a word, and convince others that we were too liberal in our beliefs to be at this school. At that point I wanted to stay on that campus. I still believed we could make changes to enhance the educational and spiritual experience of the students. I knew that in order to stay I would have to be careful what I said in class and with some of the counselees that sought me out in my office. I would be especially careful of what I said to her daughter.

The call about Hannah's murder came the first week of the second school year. Jane, the principal's secretary, called and said softly, "Paula, you need to come to the office. Loren wants to talk with you."

I nodded to Jane as I entered her office, walked through it and into Loren's. One look of his face as he looked up caused me to ask, "What?" Before he could answer, I asked with urgency, "What is wrong?"

"I just got a call from the conference office telling me that they received word from a local minister that Hannah Fredericks was murdered yesterday."

Dropping into a near-by chair I spit out, "Murdered, how?" Agonizingly, slowly he told me the story while I held my breath trying to keep sobs from escaping.

"On the street? Alone? Why? What was she doing there?" The words tumbled out between gasps.

Had she returned, Hannah would have been a member of the senior class that was at a camp forty miles away for a retreat called Senior Survival. This retreat was formed each year at the first of the school year by class sponsors and the campus pastor, to facilitate bonding within the senior class.

As Dean of Students, I was the one who needed to deliver the horrid news of Hannah's murder to this group of seniors.

Hannah was petite, dark-haired, and cute. Her bubbly personality hid the darker struggle within. She was well liked by classmates and faculty. Though rebellious at times and often questioning rules, her cheerful and devil-may-care attitude way-laid most anyone's displeasure or dislike of her.

As I drove toward the camp I tried to formulate how to announce the tragedy. *What do I say first? I have bad news? No, not that. I'm sorry to tell you? No, too cliche. How am I going to talk without sobbing?* Unable to come to grips with what to say, I prayed. *God, please give me the strength and composure to announce what I need to. Give me the words. Help me say the right things.*

As the students gathered around, including, Amy, who now lived with us, I sat silent. Formulating in my mind how to speak these words of horror, I continued to pray silently for the right words. Each student and adult came with obvious questions displayed on their faces, since I was not expected to be a part of this assemblage. They knew something serious must have brought me here.

I diverted my eyes from her friends. I needed to keep my composure.

I began, "Just an hour ago I received some information that I feel is important to pass on to all of you. The news came to campus," still hesitant to say it, I searched for words that would shock the least. Starting over, "For those who were not here last year, there was a young lady by the name of Hannah who was a member of this class. She did not return this year." And then after a deep breath to keep control, I said, "I received news this morning that Hannah has been murdered."

The sound of sobs and screams kept me from continuing, while others were asking, "How? What happened?" After gaining composure, I went on to explain as best I could what I did know, and assured the students I would know more by the time they returned to campus in a couple days. The next few hours were spent hugging and praying with students, including Amy.

The Christmas before, Hannah had ridden with Amy and Scott, who was attending an Adventist college in California, to Colorado for the holidays. She had family residing in the same area as Amy and Scott's mother. Four days together on a trip that included being stranded in a storm for two days, provided Amy with a lot of time to get to know and like Hannah. Amy's dismay as to how this could have happened to a sweet, effervescent young woman deepened when the whole story was told, and I was further horrified

Hannah had been in the process of escaping from a pimp boyfriend. Tragically, he found her just feet from reaching a bus that would take her home. He ran, grabbed her, and slit her throat, there on the street. She had been estranged from her mother for months after running away and joining friends. That very morning her mother had made contact via phone, talked her into coming home, and provided a bus ticket that Hannah would never use.

For days I could not escape the questions from students. My own questions plagued me. *How did we fail Hannah? How did I fail Hannah?*

How could this happen to a girl who was an Adventist and knew God? Why was the teaching at the academy not enough to save young women from this kind of slavery and abuse? Why didn't the years of church school and the time spent at the academy protect her from "the street? Why didn't God protect her for just a few more feet and answer a mother's prayer?

Within the third year at the academy my clamped jaws resulted in damage to the nerves in my face. Electrical-like shocks into my face and stabbing pain penetrated from the jaw line. At times I became immobilized with pain and withdrew from campus while continuing to meet with students as often as possible.

With lessened duties, I had time to contemplate how to help the cases I saw on a regular basis in my office. Particularly those of incest and abuse. Further scrutiny of what I was and was not doing only left me feeling more inadequate. The pain in my face became unbearable and I sought medical evaluation that led to surgery at John Hopkins University hospital by Dr. Ben Carson, who is an Adventist, and years later would have a campaign to become President of the United States. He punctured needles through both sides of my face, and into the nerve at the back of the neck to eliminate the coating on the nerves that radiated the pain. The procedure was one Dr. Carson had developed to treat trigeminal neuralgia. The treatment did little to relieve my pain. The clamped jaws and stress had damaged the nerves to the point of no full recovery. I believe the pain was brought on by evidence of student needs which I could not meet effectively.

When I opened the door Julia was already sobbing. Her words between sobs were broken and sentences were incomplete. "It was in the church........ a room by the stairs. I know it's a man....can't see face.... no, no....but I know.....I don't know.....why?" She went on with other babblings that were hard to decipher at first, "my brother, too, my brother, I know he did, I know he did. He brought his friends." Like others before her, she came from a Christian home. One intact and one that appeared solid, religious, and full of love. I knew her parents, I knew the brother she spoke of. She continued with me session after session spewing pain and anger.

That same year another student, Melanie, sat sobbing in my office time after time spitting out descriptions of abuse from two older brothers who used her for a "sandwich" of sex. The older brother forced or threatened the younger one to do what he did. Both parents were faithful Adventist church members and appeared to be loving parents. *Why their sons?*

Then there was Marty who returned time and time again but spoke very few words, faintly nodding as I asked questions. This went on for months until she slipped under my door a note barely readable. The note revealed sexual abuse perpetrated upon her by a brother. I made the parents aware of the daughter's needs, needs they did not have a clue how to fulfill. They did eventually confront the brother, but his denial left the young woman with further pain.

As in Kathy's description given to me years before of brothers who used her sexually, these disclosures always led me to wonder: *How can this happen? Did someone molest those boys?* Most of all, I contemplated what happened to cause or allow brothers to molest sisters within the confines of Christian homes?

I begged Rachel's mother to report her husband, Rachel's father, as her daughter's perpetrator. She begged me not to report him. Much to my dismay, I relented to her begging.

After years of experience, I was still naïve enough to believe I could trust the abuse would stop in that home. I met with the Father and heard from him that it had stopped and would never continue. It did not stop. I found out from Rachel after I left the school, that he had moved on to a younger daughter. The family remained up-standing members of the Adventist Church. The mother did nothing. I did nothing.

These stories, fifteen years after I started listening to young women, remained the same. Through the years I had listened to many young women on the Christian campuses where I was employed, sob out their stories of sexual abuse and incest. After years of experience and educating myself via written word and workshops, I knew what to ask, how to give the security needed in order to reveal the pain—pain so deep that it destroyed the core of belief in self.

My experience with the sexual abuse of girls and women has always been within a conservative Church setting—the abuse of wives, daughters, granddaughters, and parishioners. I faced powerful men who denied and threatened, a Church that did not want to know, and an employer who protected the perpetrating men on the payroll.

Throughout much of this time I didn't perceive what was happening. I only knew that something was really wrong, something within my own home, my own family, my Church, and my society. *Was I naïve because there was normalcy to it? Was it fear of knowing?* I had been taught that men were "just that way," and never to question their behaviors which I perceived as abhorrent. I still feel passionate regarding the time I sat in a discipline committee meeting on the campus, and was subjected to the discourse of men's accusations that the stories of perpetration told by girls were "way overdone" and "not to be trusted." Making myself heard was difficult, but I spoke with a trembling voice, "You speak of a subject you know nothing about. None of you have a clue as to the pain a girl goes through in order to reveal this information. The abuse has damaged her very core. I have held this pain in my own heart. At this school, and at others, I have held girls in my arms in agony over this pain. What you are saying is wrong." No one spoke after my words and the subject was changed to other matters.

Though we have awareness that was not evident twenty years ago, let alone forty years ago, the abuse of girls and women continues flagrantly. We've learned how to listen and how to help toward healing, but it does not appear that we have learned how to stop this abuse.

I'm sad to say I only started addressing these issues when it was safe because I was remarried to a supportive, aware, loving male. I remain concerned for those of my mother's generation, who have not healed, for those of my generation who still do not speak of their experiences, my daughters' generation who speak more easily but refrain still with the threat of intimate revealing. I feel no relief from these concerns for my granddaughters, though they are often more informed than any other generation.

I recently found the following written on a piece of paper while searching for notes to use to write this book. It is a quote I wrote down years ago from the book WHEN GOD WAS A WOMAN by Merlin Stone 1976: "What else might we expect in a society that for centuries has taught young children, both female and male, that a MALE deity created the universe and all that is in it, produced MAN in his own divine image—and then, as an afterthought, created woman, to obediently help man in his endeavors? This image of Eve, created for her husband, from her husband, the woman who was supposed to have brought about the downfall of humankind, has in many ways become the image of all women. How did this idea ever come into being?"

The quote states my own question, *How did this notion of God being a male ever come into being?* A friend recently told me, "I don't think patriarchy or the results have anything to do with God being seen as male. It's just 'men being men.'" *Men being men?!*

20

MEN BEING MEN? And fathers being fathers? *No, I can't accept this.*

Fifteen years earlier, I sat in a modified class-room for a conference on sexual abuse. As the moderator described a perpetrator, I became aware that I was holding my breath and clamping my jaws. The moderator had just described my husband, my daughters' father. It was a chilling, heart-stopping revelation. Though I had questioned a number of counselors regarding my concerns about my daughters' relationship with their father, I see now that I was unable to allow myself to question or face what this was telling me.

Six more years went by before a frantic call from a daughter revealed that my fear had been realized. The tremor of her voice expressed to me, before her words told me, that she felt desperately afraid of something.

When I answered the phone, Lori spit out, "Mom, something is really, really wrong. I'm so scared and I don't know why," I encouraged her to go on although already my own voice trembled and my knees felt weak, "What's happened? Tell me what's happened?"

"A while ago, this afternoon, Dad came over right before I had to leave to go to the doctor's. Jon was supposed to come and stay with Lindsee, and when he didn't come in time for me to leave, Dad volunteered to stay with her. But, Mom, I was afraid to leave her with Dad and after I did I was so scared I felt sick to my stomach. Why, Mom, why? What is wrong with me?"

Roger, since our divorce, lived in the same town as Lori, and though their relationship was strained, he visited frequently.

My response was shaky and gave her no assurance that all was well. "Lori, there is something wrong, but it is not you. You are not wrong; your feelings are not wrong. For right now don't leave her with your dad, and I think that you should see a therapist about the fear." Many more words of encouragement were spoken before hanging up the phone and being thrown into tortuous memories of the past. *Is it what I think it is? Surely it is not! I would have known, wouldn't I? Is Lori overreacting? After all, she was her father's least favorite. Maybe she is only reacting to her dislike of how he has treated her. But then, how has he treated her?*

While contemplating this call, I remembered a time at the farm when Lori changed from the happy carefree, verbal eight year-old to being withdrawn and continually washing her hands. *Could it be? Could he have?*

This call was followed by another a couple of weeks later. A sobbing voice that I could not understand, yet knew was another daughter, propelled me into another fit of agony. Finally, I was able to understand the words between sobs. Brenda was desperately trying to describe feelings about her father who had left her apartment moments before.

"Mom, Dad was here. I did not want to see him. I didn't go to the door when he knocked. He kept knocking and then he started crying. I could hear him through the door, and I felt so bad, so guilty, that I went out. He hugged me and I thought I was going to faint. What's wrong with me? Why can't my father hug me without my feeling sick?"

Again, the next minutes were filled with emotion on both sides of the phone and ended with my assurance that there was nothing wrong with her, but that the feelings needed to be investigated so that she could understand her experience.

Lori sought the therapy I suggested. Brenda did not.

Brenda refused to discuss the subject any further, but I spent hours on the phone with Lori listening to her anxiety and processing the question of what to do. Roger alluded to Lori that he was contemplating marriage to a young woman a few years older than her who had three small children. We discussed our responsibility to this woman with our concern for the safety not only of Lori's children, but now the concern for this woman's children lay on our minds. We decided that we had to do something, but both felt it would not accomplish anything to approach Roger with our suspicion.

The conversations with Lori were focused on how to alleviate her anxiety—whether to allow her father to be with her daughter. We discussed the pain it would bring into his life to not be with his grandchildren. But could he be trusted with Lindsee and not do to her what he had to her mother? Everything I read and was made cognizant of, said perpetrators continue to perpetrate if not treated. We decided that even though it would be extremely painful to all concerned, we could not take the chance of letting him be with his grandchildren.

A couple of weeks after a phone call with Lori when we decided to talk with a lawyer about a court order to keep Roger from seeing her daughter and any future children, I received a phone call from my oldest daughter, Trudy. Roger's complaints of chest pain had led to a hospital stay and she had flown out to be with him. Her voice was strained, but in control when she said, "Mom, Dad had a heart attack a few minutes ago and died."

She went on to say, I called the girls, but I don't want to call other family. Could you please call them?"

I hung up the phone and cried. He was the father of my daughters, and though I was discovering the damage his relationship with them had engendered, I still felt compassion for him. *Why God? Because the pain we were going to give him if we went to court would be too painful? For him? For us? Why couldn't there have been healing? I'm sure he loved you. I don't think he wanted to hurt his daughters. He loved them. Why, why the damage? The pain? For him? For them?*

There were feelings of relief. Especially for Lori and I.

We would no longer have to pursue the court ordered protection for grandchildren. Nor would we need to approach the woman he was dating.

The relief of not having to confront Roger was eventually overshadowed by the difficulty of healing. Their memories of him would remain conflicted with love and disgust. Healing would be a process that they had to go through individually and differently, considering the level of molestation and their individual willingness for forgiveness.

21

ANOTHER LEAVING. ANOTHER beginning. Loren resigned as principal the fourth school year at the academy, to pursue his dream. Contacts in California convinced him that funding was available to bring the group homes to fruition. I continued at the academy while he pursued the possibilities. Nothing had materialized by the end of the school year. My resignation from academy and Church employment to join Loren in his renewed determination to open group homes in California, also meant another move. Away from the academy and away from Adventist education. We had tried to make a difference. Loren felt stifled by conference administration. He needed the freedom to do for kids what he had determined they needed. Neither of us believed that religion was what they needed. The love of God, yes. Unconditional love. The love that assures each person's value.

A small apartment above an assisted living home for seniors, where I could exchange work for rent, became our home. It was a difficult move. We were living the unknown again. *What's next? Where now? Why doesn't it work out, this dream of ours? And the doubts begin. Are we being punished? Should we have stayed in Christian education?*

Loren's epiphany at seventeen to care for troubled kids had not been satisfied. The call would not go away. He was driven by a desire to work with those considered by most to be throw-aways—those adjudicated by the courts and those not acceptable in the foster care system. All of his other endeavors to make this dream come true had failed. He couldn't stop trying. I supported this "trying." Tired of moving, tired of no income, I still believed we should move ahead with the plans that absorbed Loren's every waking hour. He spent few hours in bed. Often leaving it in the wee hours of the morning to the closest Denny's because they were open all night, where he could study and write undisturbed except by those filling his coffee cup. While we were at the academy the closest all-night restaurant was forty-five minutes away. Still he went, and it was there that he sat and designed the program for the group homes he was determined to open.

Six months after the move from the academy, his determination was rewarded when contact was made with a physician who financially supported two group homes in Napa Valley in California. They were failing in treatment and financially. He needed someone to take them over. Though I had supported his dream and wanted to be a part of it, when I left the Church educational employment I thought I was done with counseling teen girls through the horror of abuse and dysfunction. When the door opened to assume this business of group homes for adjudicated teenage girls instead of boys, Loren asked me if I would join him in this venture by becoming an administrator on a daily basis. He did not feel adequately prepared to manage homes for girls. I said, "Yes." We moved into a large three story house—one of two used as a group home. The large master suite on the second floor became our home.

I thought the emotionally disturbed girls I had counseled regarding abuse and family dysfunction had prepared me. *Surely six girls in a house can't be harder than eighty teens in a dormitory. I can do this.*

The anger, distrust, and apathy of these girls was different. Tentative glances, accompanied by whispers, angled to someone else's ears, let us know we were not welcome. They did not trust nor did they like adults.

The adults in their lives had neglected, abused, and exploited them. They didn't treat me any different than those who had betrayed them. *Were they going to give me a chance? How do I show them I am different?*

I learned a hard lesson within the first six weeks. Thirteen-year old Angel was a very small child in a young woman's body. She was a black teen from the foster care system. Meaning she was a dependent of the state. Her disruptions in the foster home and attempts to run away had brought her to this group home before we arrived. She was skittish, agitated, and at times seemed to leave reality.

I started "tucking her in" at night at bed time. Sometimes going over with her the day's events, explaining anything she didn't understand, and always ending the conversation with "I love you." I assured her over and over again that I would "always be there." Loren and I had discussed at length how to introduce spirituality to the kids in our group homes. We came to the decision and determination to do it by showing them love—introducing them to the idea that God loved them. I wanted each one to see themselves as loveable. It was a very difficult task and I failed over and over but never as I did with Angel.

Months of her misbehavior, and then apologizing remorsefully only to escalate to destructive behavior again, she spewed hate and threats. This behavior led to a psychological evaluation that affirmed she had the same disorder as her institutionalized mother. Her social worker came for a visit and informed staff that she was removing Angel to a psych unit. When I received the report, my heart hurt and my mind rebelled, "This can't be. We haven't had enough time with her. Maybe we can change it." We were told that there was nothing we could do for Angel.

I cried when they came to take her. There was no relief from the pain when I told her, "Angel, I will always care about you, but I cannot keep you here. It is out of my hands. I am sorry." She responded defiantly. Her pain was greater than mine. Pain exacerbated by her removal from a home where she had felt love. I had unknowingly set her up to be hurt at a level far deeper than before I came.

The pain of that experience stays with me till this day. *Could I have somehow prepared her for what was coming? If I had known, what would I have done that could have helped?* This played often in my mind for months after. What I did learn was to not say, "I love you." To say it brought hope I had no right to give. This sounds hard but the truth is, I did not have control over their lives. They could be removed from my presence at any moment and I would not be able to be in contact with them. I decided that I needed to express my love, but in another way. I started saying, "I care for you." In my stumbling with Angel's departure I had tried to reassure her that I didn't want her to go, "It's not what I want, Angel. I can't change it. I would if I could." It didn't matter what I thought or wanted.

Within the first few weeks I also experienced something else I had never before felt. The fear of another human being. Amanda stood facing me with clenched fists and raised voice, "I'll smash in your fucking face." Postured in front of her, I did my best to appear confident, sure, and in control. Inside I was trembling, near panic, as my mind raced with a prayer for protection. I said shakily, "Amanda, go to your room. I will not talk to you now."

With these words I spun around, stepped into my office, locked the door behind me, and picked up the phone. As Amanda pounded threateningly on the door demanding, "Open this fucking door or I will break it down," I dialed the office two miles away at another group home we managed, to speak to Loren.

"Loren come now, Amanda is going off and I'm afraid," I sputtered.

I sat at my desk in tears. *What was I doing? How can I do this? I thought I could. I thought it would be easy after all the girls I had in the dorms. These girls are so different. I feel so incapable, so vulnerable.*

Amanda had the ability to hurt me though only fifteen years old and three inches shorter than me. She was two-hundred pounds of angry, and a street-toughened survivor. She eventually told me about the drive-by shootings she had been a part of as though it was an innocent teenage drive down a town strip on Friday night.

Loren came into the house before Amanda broke down the door and talked her into returning to her room. She knew that without a weapon he had the upper hand and relented to his power and control of the situation.

My desire when we moved in was to make this house into a home for the girls. I placed my dishes, pots and pans, utensils, and anything else I took out of boxes into the cupboards as if the cupboards were mine. First mistake. The girls filed in and out of the kitchen as I worked. The sneers and comments were aimed to let me know further that this was not my house. I planned nutritious meals and included desserts that would satisfy appetites that ranged from near starvation to indulgence. The girls were assigned tasks that put them in the kitchen with me. Working together slowly broke down barriers leading to conversations so I could get to know each one individually.

Barbara gave me my first introduction to the name calling I would get used to. "Why you think you gotta do that?" was her sneer. Turning to face her I asked, "What do you mean?"

"Why you gotta come in here like you own the place, bitch. This ain't you place." I had never been called bitch! At least not to my face. A response stuck in my throat. "Well, well, I guess I am doing this stuff in this kitchen because this is where I live too, and I want to cook good meals for you." Instead of responding, she spun on her heels to leave the room sputtering, "Don't know why the bitch thinks she belongs here. She gonna learn." And learn I did.

I was used to girls coming to me with their problems. At the academies and the college, my schedule was always full of girls wanting to see me, to talk to me, to ask for advice, and to thank me for the help they perceived I could give them. The girls in this house not only did not come to my office, they didn't want to see me, period. They did not even know they had problems, and their pain was buried so deep it was non-existent to them. Their only question was, "What do I have to do to get out of here?"

They were not locked in and could walk out the door anytime. We could discourage them from leaving but we could not hold them. State licensing demanded an open door policy. The only thing that held these girls was fear of the unknown country surrounding the house. In the city they would have run. Many did run when they got points enough in the system to go on outings off the mountain and into more suburban communities where they could catch rides. Dangerous as it was for them to depend on these rides, most wanted to return to the familiar. They felt safer on the city streets than in the country.

One Saturday afternoon, I decided to take them to a park for a picnic. I thought getting out of the house and into nature would be good for all. I drove the van with six girls anxiously taking in the scenery as I drove. I parked in the parking lot, started to get out of the van and one of the girls said, "I'm not getting out here. There are trees."

I responded, "Trees won't hurt you."

Two more voices added, "Yes, they can. They can fall on you." Then the stories followed, "My aunt........and a tree fell and killed her." Not one of the girls would leave the van. We went back to the house to eat our picnic.

After months of therapy and behavior modification, Amanda improved her behavior and attitude to the highest level of the program. My relationship with her grew into mutual respect. She came to my office one day, knocked on the side of the open door and meekly said, "We gotta talk." I knew what she wanted to talk about but did not make it easy for her.

Three days before, Amanda had lost control in an argument with her roommate two years younger and eighty pounds lighter. Though very fond of her, she had thrown her to the floor with pounding fists. Iris was a very irritating fourteen-year-old that never shut her mouth, and argued about everything. Personally, I had become so annoyed with her when she would not return to her room when told to, that I marched her up the stairs forcefully with my hand on the back of her neck. This I reported to the licensing agent and received verbal reprimand—we were not to touch the girls with any correction.

I understood Amanda's loss of control. However, because I perceived what Amanda's response with a different protocol would be, I decided not to administer the normal consequences for a fight by returning her to juvenile hall. This was very disconcerting to the staff, but my demands that they give it a chance to succeed played out in my favor.

Immediately after the encounter, I confronted her demanding an apology, "Amanda, this is unacceptable behavior. You have hurt someone you care about, and we expect an apology to Iris in person and in writing."

Tears came to her eyes, "What cha gonna do to me?"

"I'm not going to do anything to you," I said as I left the room.

"What, what? You gotta do something," were the last words I heard.

Amanda displayed distress the next three days and now had come to my office to implore me to punish her, "You have to do something. I feel really bad about what I did to Iris." The tears were brushed away angrily as she repeated again, "You gotta do something."

I smiled and said, "Amanda, you are punishing yourself and that is enough because it shows me that you are truly sorry. That is all I need to see."

A few months later, we unknowingly brought into the house a fellow gang member from Amanda's past. Within a few days, she was convinced to run away. I was greatly saddened by Amanda's departure. I checked with her probation officer now and then but for months heard nothing from or about Amanda. Then late one night I received a call from Amanda, "I wanna come back," were her first words.

Recognizing her voice, I asked, my voice raised with emotion, "Amanda, where are you?"

"I'm at a pay phone and I gotta come back," she replied.

Amanda was still on probation. I could not pick her up so I said, "Tell me where you are and I will have an officer pick you up. It's the only way you can come back." She did not argue but gave me the address and promised to wait there until an officer came. Officers did go to the location. Amanda was not there. She was never heard from again. Her probation officer never found her or heard anything about her. He did not know what had happened to her. He should have heard something if she was alive. *Was she in danger the night she called? Is that why she wanted to come back? Was she murdered? By a gang member? Her own or a rival one? I will never know.*

I don't understand why the girls ran away not only from a warm bed, good food, and safety, but the caring that we displayed. It especially hurt when it was someone like Amanda who knew we cared for her, and she had shown she cared for us. I understand more about someone like Sara, a twelve-year-old prostitute who was with us just days and who convinced two other girls to run with her back to the Tenderloin District of San Francisco.

Lizzy, who came in large bibbed overalls, had been in twenty foster homes. She was wary and surly. She ran with another girl within the first couple of days she was with us. When one of the staff followed, she found Lizzy huddled in the ditch alongside the road a short distance from the house. Lizzy was more frightened by the country road than the unknowns of the program, and willing to return. She eventually revealed to us the incidents of abuse she experienced in twenty foster homes. Most of the abuse was sexual in nature. Lizzy remained in the program for eighteen months and was released without graduating because she did not want to leave and kept misbehaving so she could stay. Our fondness for her grew as she became a poised young woman determined to improve her life by education. When she was released from our program and social services, the volunteer sponsor she met through our program paid for her to attend a Adventist boarding academy. She even went to college for a semester.

However, the emotional damage from all the sexual and physical abuse was not healed, and Lizzy eventually went back to the streets. She found me through Facebook years later and called leaving a message with a phone number. When I called, the phone had been disconnected.

One of the saddest stories I heard was told by Selena, a thirteen-year old Latino girl from the Mission District of San Francisco. She was pretty with long, dark hair framing her face with curls. She was even-tempered and mild in manner compared to most of our residents. She lived with her father, but spent most of her time on the street with her gang. Late one night when she could not sleep, I asked her to come down to my office and talk with me. She had been with us long enough to know I was non-threatening, and that I cared about her. I encouraged her, "Tell me about your gang. Why do you belong to one?"

"For protection," was her reply.

She did not go into detail about the exploitation of the girls and how they had to prove their loyalty to the gang through numerous sexual liaisons, but she did tell me a horrible story. "We were holed up in a room one night in this old building that didn't have a bathroom and I had to go. I told em I had to go. Luis said he'd go with me. We went out and around the corner to the alley. I moved to the back to pee and Luis stayed at the entrance to keep watch. While I was peeing, I saw Luis turn and get under a car that was parked at the front of the alley. These guys from another gang had seen him. They came up to the car and shot him. I was so scared, but they didn't know I was back there so they just left."

This story came out of her mouth with no show of emotion. I was aghast and could hardly talk. "I'm so sorry, Selena, that you have had that kind of experience." She shrugged her shoulders and changed the subject to talk about her anger with her father. The topic of the shooting was dropped and never talked about again.

I have thought of her often. She returned to the Mission District because she had a parent that was supposedly taking care of her. And she went back to her gang because they would take care of her on the street. I ask myself *how do these young women survive?* Yet, I know how. They survive by getting tough, by becoming as mean as the boys, to protect themselves from abuse.

Progress made with the girls was often cursory, at best. The probation officers and social workers were only concerned with correcting behavior. As soon as a girl was able to show improvement by gaining points and levels in the system demonstrating cooperation, she was removed to be replaced by another. They were released from the program to return to homes with absent parents which meant going back on the street, or to foster homes. So frustrating! We spent months caring for a girl, getting her to trust us, teaching her better behavior, and attempting to create healing. Then often she was forced to go back to where she came—where the damage had been done in the first place.

Samantha came to us off the streets of Sacramento where she had numerous other relatives in the gang she participated in. She plopped down in the chair next to my desk one afternoon when I called her down to investigate why she had lost numerous points due to a blow up. She was on track to be released in three weeks, and this display of anger was out of character. When I said, "Samantha, I see that you lost a lot of points yesterday," she shrugged her shoulders while looking down at her lap.

"You are due to be released. If you are going home, you know you have to maintain the fourth level. What are you doing?"

She looked up as tears sprang into her eyes. With the voice of defiance I had not seen in months, she said, "Yah, you want me to be this nice sweet girl but you're sending me back to the street where I have to live. I'll get killed out there. I gotta be tough. I can't be nice or I'll die."

I can still feel the horror I felt when this statement was spewed at me. Despairingly I admitted, silently, *she is right. We are expecting her to be nice. Nice is going to get her killed!*

This experience convinced me, more than any other, that correcting behavior did not avail these girls of what they needed in their lives. I had continually voiced to whomever would hear, "These girls need healing, not correction." They needed love and acceptance. They needed self-worth and personal power in their lives.

Years of listening to pain that I could not heal and employees who couldn't see beyond correction, came to a head the day Loren supported the decision made by the Mental Health Director to dismiss Lisa after I said she needed to stay. I had talked with the house manager and the girl creating an agreement in writing of behavioral expectations. I told Lisa if the agreement was broken she would be dismissed from the program. A couple hours after leaving the meeting and returning home, I received a call from Lisa. Crying and loud she said, "You told me I could stay. Why did you lie to me?"

My first question was, "Where are you?" I knew she could not be in the house because she could not have used the phone there.

Her response brought blood quickly to my head and ache to my heart. She said, "I ran. I'm using a pay phone. They told me they were taking me back to the hall."

"Lisa, please go back to the house and I will fix this," was my plea.

"I'm not going back. I'm not going to the hall. You lied," were her last words and she hung up. I had no way of contacting her.

I called Loren, "Did you tell Marie that she could take Lisa back to the hall?" I was spitting nails mad! I was the Program Director, the boss, the staff should never go around me to Loren and he should not have let them. We had dealt with this before and I thought we had the understanding it would not happen again.

I said, "I quit. I'm done. Don't talk to me about it. Don't ask me any questions. You want to run the show, then run it," and hung up. I made the choice right then, to be Loren's wife and not his business partner. I never stepped back into any of the houses after that day. I never again guided staff, or argued with administration about treatment. Not even

Loren. I thought this decision was forever. It was for a long time, and then it was not.

I was angry. Hurt. Most of all dismayed. *Too much pain. So little healing. I can't do this anymore. I don't have to do this. I have to discover the whys. I need answers. Why is there so much pain in the lives of girls and women in the Church, as well as, in the homes of America? My spiritual journey depends on my answering these questions. Not for anyone else, just for me.*

22

BEFORE I RESIGNED from the partnership with Loren, and while I still served as the program director responsible for the management of the homes, I took a walk one morning in the beautiful Napa Valley near the condo where Loren and I lived. When I walked in upon my return, the telephone message light was blinking. I did not hesitate but hit the play button, concerned that I might be needed at one of the homes.

My heart beats fast even now years later, as I remember the voice that spoke. "Paula, Paula, please be there. Oh, please pick up. I need you. I need to talk to you. Oh please, please."

It was Loren's voice. It was "not" his voice. There was terror in that voice. It was something I had never heard before. The call ended with a sob.

Trembling and stuffing sobs, I dialed numbers, one after the other. *I have to find him. Where is he? Something is very wrong. God help me.*

In between jabbing numbers to his cell phone that kept going to voicemail, the phone rang. As soon as I heard Scott's voice I knew that he knew the same thing as his father. His first broken and hesitant words were, "Have you heard from Dad?"

"Scott, I got a terrible message from Dad, but I can't find him. He doesn't answer his phone. What's wrong?"

"You really need to find Dad," was Scott's next breathless statement. "You need to find him. I just gave him some terrible news."

"Scott, tell me, what is wrong? What has happened, please tell me. I have to know."

His voice was filled with a horror he was hesitant to impart. He kept saying, "Oh, I can't. I can't. I can't do it again. I can't say it again."

In between these heart-rending words, I tried to ask, "Scott, is it Juliette?" speaking of his wife of two years. "What is it Scott, please tell me." He kept saying over again and again with what seemed like long minutes, "I can't, oh, I can't."

By now I too was crying, shaking, nauseous, and near hysterics. Finally, after what seemed a lifetime, Scott said, "It's Amy. She was in an accident. She was killed."

An involuntary scream escaped my lips. The very thing he feared. He had already heard horrific responses from his mother and his father.

There was no comfort to give. My body and mind went into shock, and the only thing I thought after hanging up was that I had to find Loren. Minutes later a call from the office informed me that he had called to have an employee come pick him up from where he was eating breakfast as he could no longer drive.

The next steps were as agonizing as hearing the news from Scott. I now felt the same reluctance as Scott to express these terrible words. I had to let the family know. I called each of my four daughter's husbands. I could not bear to tell the girls myself, and I did not want them to be told while they were alone without the comfort their husbands would provide.

I had married Amy's father ten years earlier when she was twelve. In those ten years she had become my fifth and youngest daughter. Trudy, Kim, Lori, and Brenda had embraced Amy as their little sis. The fact that my blood did not run through her veins did not lessen the love I felt for her. And now, did not lessen the pain.

It was decided to have a closed casket. Each family member and friend could decide to view her body if they chose. I chose to see her. As I stood with my hand in her father's, looking down at the broken body, I said, "She is not there." Those that heard me looked at me as if I had said something strange. I had. For no one in that room believed Amy was anywhere else but asleep in Jesus to be raised "in a moment, in the twinkling of an eye, at the last trump." (ICor. 15:52) This was the Adventist view of death. I had recently questioned it and discovered for me a different belief.

As I stood before Amy's casket, the pain was severe, but peace was present with me that she, out of this body, was okay. In fact, Amy's body had been thrown out the passenger window while it flipped five times down a flat highway. As I peered at it, I said, "I'm glad she did not stay in this body. It is too damaged, and she would not have wanted to live as a cripple."

I knew Amy was okay. I had risked the judgment of family and friends and reached out to discover answers to questions that plagued me. One of the questions I pondered because the Church's answers did not satisfy my inquisitive mind was "what happens at the time of death." I stood before this casket so thankful that I no longer believed the broken body before me was Amy. I knew she was no longer present here, but in Spirit—back with God.

Amy walked spiritually with God. Not religiously, but spiritually. Just months before the accident Amy had gifted me for my birthday with Depak Chopra's book, "*The Seven Spiritual Laws of Success: A Practical Guide to the Fulfillment of Your Dreams.*" This was the first indicator I had of her new search to understand God. She wrote inside, "I hope you enjoy the book. I know it's packed full of principles you'll love."

Later I would be even more assured when I read the last entry to God in her journal: "I will keep moving forward even if they are baby steps. You have given me or blessed me with a good spirit, a kind heart, a warm personality. I have a wonderful outlook on life knowing this is just the beginning of a life beyond words. Thank you Lord that this is only temporary......" This was Amy, a kind trusting heart, and a warm personality.

The change in my beliefs about death had come slowly. The continued face pain I had developed at the academy drove me to search for relief. I had slipped into the office of an Ayurvedic doctor in the middle of Napa Valley, and moved to a chair far in the corner of the waiting room, away from the windows. I had come with trepidation. Against my own conscience. Not because of *why* I had come but *because* I had come, come to a place where a Christian should not be. The Church I was still a member of declared that all Eastern religions, and what they taught, were of the devil. I had to find out why.

The comfort I experienced with the doctor led to further appointments. I began to read books I saw in the doctor's office. I read in private, when no one was around, including Loren. I was hesitant to be questioned about why I was reading *The Tibetan Book of Living and Dying.*

This book offered an entirely different way of thinking about death. For fifty years I had accepted the view of death that my grandmother and the Adventist Church had given me. Death is sleep. All those who die before Jesus comes and have accepted him as their Savior will be raised again to life everlasting in the bodies they had lived in on earth.

I didn't question this belief before reading the book, but I prayed earnestly and sincerely to *know* Truth. The only way I knew to *know* Truth at this point in my life was to listen to my inner voice. That inner voice was comforted with what I read. It *felt* right. Death was not permanent. Death was the soul leaving the body. This meant I was something more than the body. I was not satisfied with the explanation of "going to heaven" as read from Church doctrines.

I was so thankful I knew Amy still existed. She was not sleeping. She was not in her body. I did not know at the time what this meant, but the belief that she was okay sustained me through the months to come. Loren struggled with anger and the disturbances this caused in his life affected mine. He could not accept Amy's death as God's plan or that "the devil" was to blame. For six months I did not know if Loren would come back to living and sometimes wondered if he would find a way to experience death that he might find her. He was not ready to accept or even listen to what I believed. He had to find out for himself where his daughter was. This strained communication between us but we loved each other and were committed to allowing each other to search with acceptance.

The experience of Amy's death and the change in beliefs about death evoked the springboard for more discoveries. I continued to stretch beliefs. One daughter encouraged, three daughters questioned, my husband withdrew from discussion. Friends and family did not know I questioned or what I discovered, for I did not discuss my path with them.

Kim who encouraged my search also encouraged me to meet with a woman she called a Spiritual Intuitive. I did not know what a spiritual intuitive was, but since I was on this path of discovery and could not stop, why not find out? I had no expectations.

Shari, the intuitive, lived in a subdivision outside of Prescott, Arizona. Her small, one-story house was well kept. The door I knocked on was opened by Shari who looked like a homemaker stepping from her kitchen chores. Nothing indicated there was anything special about this woman. What small fear I had was dissipated by her warmth.

We entered a small room that for others would have served as a bedroom. Shari sat on a couch next to a stand with a tape recorder on it and invited me to sit in a chair opposite her. She explained that she would turn on the tape recorder, close her eyes, move into meditation, and begin to speak anything that the Universe revealed. She would share with me what she heard and what she saw. I was to answer any questions the Universe might have and could ask any questions that came to mind.

Shari began, "Paula is here this day to receive from the Universe anything that can help and guide her on the journey of life." She paused as though waiting for an answer on a telephone line. She expressed messages about my health and then ask ed what I could do to improve it. Repeating what she said the Universe was telling her she told me I needed to concentrate on becoming healthy or I would experience physical and emotional disorders in the near future. She testified to my need to change the lifestyle of relentlessly pushing myself to achieve or complete work. This brought a smile to my face, but I remained silent.

Half way into the hour-long session and recording, Shari started stuttering with distress. She said, "Someone has entered the room. It is of female energy, young female energy. Oh, oh wait, wait."

She was speaking as though out of breath and asked, "Please back off, it's too much." She said the entity had not been removed from earth very long and was still weak so was draining her of energy. She explained that it was difficult for the young woman to come into this vibration but that she, "had to come and take this opportunity to be with you."

I felt a change, my skin vibrated, and I felt the warmth of love. I knew it had to be Amy. Amy was a great hugger. She hugged with the warmth and energy of no one else I had ever experienced. As the tears rolled down my cheeks I absorbed the love I felt from her and smiled.

"She cannot stay long, it is too difficult," Shari said. "She wants you to know how much she loves you. She also wants to ask the family to stop calling her back. It makes it difficult to move on when she is being pulled back to this vibration. The vibration is too heavy for her."

Within minutes Shari said, "She must go now but she says 'You are in her heart. You are in her heart.'"

The vibration stopped, my tears fell a few more minutes and the experience of Amy faded into more sharing of what the Universe had to say to me.

What an experience! *The dead are not asleep. Thank God I risked walking into the doctor's office the day when I was introduced to the book that changed my view of death. And that I stretched into coming this day to meet with Shari. I wouldn't have had these moments with Amy.*

Shari also said, "A male energy has entered. He wants to be here to tell you he is sorry. He says he was troubled in this lifetime. That he is healing. That he is stronger." I believe her description was of Roger. This experience brought me the gift of closure that I sought but did not have with him.

The encounters facilitated by Shari stretched me far beyond the ability to return to the beliefs of the past. I was on a journey that led me further and further away from the doctrine of the Seventh-day Adventist Church and beyond established beliefs of Christianity. I would discover Truth for myself. I did not need to convince others of my experience and shared it with few.

Passionately motivated, I continued to read, and to discover the Divine. I was more convinced than ever that it was not as I had been taught and accepted for so many, many years.

23

My departure from managing the group homes allowed me time and desire to put more energy into being a homemaker. This included being a wife instead of business partner with Loren. His life remained taken up with the twenty-four hour responsibilities of caring for troubled youth. This caused some division in our interests, but did not distract from our rekindled love and appreciation after the tension of my leaving administration of the homes. I still supported what he was committed to, in any way I could, without involvement with staff or residents.

I also could focus more on our growing family. Many hours spent on the phone with my daughters as mothers kept me in touch with the happenings regarding the grandchildren. A trip east at least once a year and catching up on the phone, allowed a soft bonding with Erik and Brendan, Trudy's sons. Lori birthed a daughter, Katelyn, while we were at the academy, and a son, Jeremy, the fall before we moved to California to the group homes. I managed to be present within hours of Katelyn's birth and in the hospital with Lori when Jeremy was born. Brenda's daughter, Taylor, joined our family a month before Jeremy. I was able to attend her birth as well. Now I was a grandmother of six and soon to be seven when Kim gave birth to Laurel in the same hospital near by where Taylor was born. Once again I was able to hold a new grandchild.

While my family was growing and I was becoming more and more a grandma, I was also growing. Growing in the knowing of my own individuality of thought. Though Loren did not agree with what I was learning, he supported my right to discovery.

A recent move from one duplex to another in the same neighborhood, introduced me to Charlotte, a therapeutic massage therapist. She introduced me to a new way of thinking about body and soul. A few days after our move-in, she invited me next door to have a massage. This in itself was a stretch into the unknown. I hesitantly removed clothing, leaving on underwear, and climbed upon her massage table. Surprised at how good the pain she produced felt, the tenseness in my neck and back dissipated. At the next appointment a week later, I happily climbed on the table without the underwear and relaxed while Charlotte worked her hands into my stiff, sore muscles.

Her introduction in regard to metaphysical thought stretched me even further. Our conversations led to discussion of life experiences and shared beliefs that revealed how different our lives had been. And how different our beliefs were. Weeks after my acceptance that massage was not only okay but therapeutic and not New Age, she approached me with, "Come with me to a friend's house and have your hands read."

I hesitated in my response, "I'll think about it and let you know." *What am I going to tell her? I can't go. Isn't that the devil's ground? Hand reading? Palmistry? Maybe she will forget she asked me.*

But a few days later she approached me again with the same request, adding, "Come on, it'll be lots of fun."

I tried to place within my mind the thought that there can't be anything wrong with fun. But what if family and friends found out I went to this type of party? My thoughts were dominated with *would God think it was okay?*

I hesitantly said "Okay, I'll go with you." Because, again, I had asked to be directed by God and had prayed for courage to walk through any door that opened. I'd prayed she wouldn't ask me again unless it was okay with God.

Though fearful and tentative, I did believe that I was led by God. I was trusting God when I said, "I'll walk through any door you open for me." I did not believe He would allow me to be deceived. Others would say, "It's the devil talking." Though I heard this through my years of discovery, I never gave into it because of my trust in a loving God who could protect and care for me, not allowing for deception. Otherwise, why pray in faith if the devil could deceive me?

The house clung to the hillside of Sausalito, California. Three small stories housed the International Institute of Hand Analysis and a home for Richard and Alana. A view of the San Pablo Bay met my gaze as I entered this small living room simply decorated with Native American paraphernalia. The resounding drip of splashing water on rock drew my eyes to the corner where a small fountain sat on a wooden table. A sweet smell permeated the room. A smell that was unfamiliar. The room was crowded with a three-person couch against one wall and folding chairs lining the other. In the corner opposite the fountain, a tape recorder and microphone next to an overstuffed chair indicated space for the teacher of this class of Hand Analysis.

My foraging into unknown beliefs brought me to this place in the fall of 1995. The drive that morning from Napa Valley and along the southern edge of Sonoma Valley was through the vine filled hills of wine country. It was fall, the green of summer fading, and the aroma of harvested grapes intruding the senses. The drive on winding highway 116 across to 101 and south on this cool early morning should have included fun filled chatter between Charlotte and me. It did not. I was very nervous about this new experience, and was more silent than usual.

As I waited for this first class to begin, I tried unobtrusively to observe the other women in the room. Their attire of loose-fitting, free-flowing dresses decorated with beads and sequins and their chatter about goddesses and witches led me to ponder, *how am I going to fit into this mix? It looks like New Age stuff. I don't think there is another Christian here. Witch, goddess, meditation, incense? What are they talking about? I think I am in the wrong place. I can't leave, I brought Charlotte. I'll just have to wait it out and keep praying.*

I was at a crossroads and felt this crossroads strongly. When I drove away from the academy five years before, the Christian radio station I listened to was repeating words from Jeremiah 29:11: "For I know the plans I have for you, declares the Lord, plans to prosper you and not to harm you, plans to give you hope and a future." We went to a couple different Sunday worshipping churches. We felt fulfilled for a short period of time and then moved on. Nothing religious stuck with either Loren or me. It was the doctrine of each church that I could not accept. The rules from the past, that if broken could cause me embarrassment and shame, no longer dominated my life. I walked free, toward whatever doors opened for me.

When I left the class that Friday evening with my friend, Charlotte, and before we had traveled very far, I asked, "Have you heard of goddesses?"

With a chuckle and twinkle in her eyes, she said, "Yes."

My first introduction to the Goddess came from her library. She implored me to read Jean M. Auel's series starting with THE CLAN OF THE CAVE BEAR. I did not read novels but relented to her suggestion because I was so curious about the things I had heard in the class. Reading the series opened up my thinking to possibilities I had never been exposed to, and produced within me more questions about why I had only thought of and believed in a male God.

Through the ensuing months thoughts regarding a goddess kept invading my mind. *Why was God a word okay to use but not Goddess? Why not Goddess? After all the female body is the body of creation and birth. We call God the Creator—the most compelling of characteristics. The female creates life. Why hadn't I thought of this before?!*

Unable to still the questions, I started searching. I searched first for where the title Goddess came from, and then why this title created such anxiety for me. My search led me into many avenues of discovery, from biblical to metaphysical with archaeological in between.

I realize now that I needed a softer, gentler God—a nurturing God. I was missing something in my relationship with God. I had continually tried to vision climbing on to God's lap for comfort, but I never felt comfortable.

I started studying in earnest to find out about this Goddess or Goddesses I was hearing about. Other events would distract me from this endeavor, but it was constantly on my mind. *Who is God really? Why can't I be satisfied with what the Church says He is?*

24

THE DOOR KEPT opening to new Thought, and I kept walking through with trepidation. I took a year-long class, consisting of a weekend a month, at the hand analysis institute. At the end of the year I became a certified hand analyst. Reading hands taught me a lot about family members, and opened my understanding of some of the disturbing actions of others. Loren's divergent behavior of sometimes being present and sociable and then other times being withdrawn, was explained by the reading of his heartline. The heart line shows our emotional relating. On one of his hands it is long across his hand heading toward the pointer finger. He is wired on one hand to be focused on the needs and desires of others. On the other the line is short showing his need to spend time alone and focus on self. It had disturbed me for years that he insisted on going to a coffee shop in the morning by himself. Once I understood this need, I no longer feared he was trying to get away from me.

Reading my daughters' hands gave me insight into their way of being. Three of them have what my teacher described as a Gina Lolabrigada heart line. This line helped me accept their need to be in the center of attention, self centered, but not selfish. They were wired to be sociable and passionate relationally. The fourth daughter has a line showing that she focuses on what others want and need. To a fault sometimes when her sisters do not want to receive what she has to give.

I read grandchildrens' hands. They found the act of having their hands printed a delightful experience. Sometimes asking to do it over and over again. I discovered with their hands who had a computer brain and thought and thought, creating it difficult for them to make decisions and those who jumped to conclusions and decisions easily. This knowledge helped their mothers to know when to give more time and when to encourage more time before decisions were made.

Most of all I had fun with what I had learned. I continued to walk this path of new thought for a number of years. Metaphysical became a word that replaced New Age. I attended and read hands at numerous fairs and became acquainted with many in the industry, reading their hands in exchange for their psychic readings and massages. I enjoyed it but always felt there was something missing. I began to search for what was missing.

During this time Brenda lived nearby while her sisters and step-brother lived across the United States. The girls orchestrated a reunion each summer that brought us together to create new bondings. Brenda's son, Colton, and then Kim's daughter, Kara, joined the family while we lived next to Charlotte. I was present at each birth. Loren had and continued to welcome each grandchild as his. He was the only grandfather they knew. We were both thankful to be able to build strong relationships with each of them. Telephone calls and note writing kept us in touch. There were no cell phones, no FaceTime that we would experience in later years with great-grandchildren.

My bonding was especially close with Brenda's children as she came apart. She was partying more than I liked, but I kept my thoughts to myself. I took care of the kids anytime I could, regardless of the idea that I might be enabling. First, there was a divorce with Taylor's father and divided custody. Then, a new marriage, Colton's birth, a year later a divorce, and divided custody. I didn't like divorce. The havoc and pain it caused for the children became mine. I tried to make up for it by responding to any call Brenda made for help. And I stuck my head in the sand about what was truly happening. While Loren managed the group home business, I did my best to manage family. It was my identity. My goal in life. More than anything else, family was my purpose.

Then a move changed my focus and my ability to be there with Brenda and her children. Loren and the team he now worked with wanted to have a horse program for the kids they served. It was too expensive to do this in California so plans were made to extend the program to Colorado. We were the ones to move and make this happen.

Though I wanted to move to Colorado to expand our group home business, the act of leaving Taylor and Colton was heart-rending. Brenda and the kids came to help with the last loading in our car and to say goodbye. To this day, I tear up and my heart lurches when I think of that day. I left California with my sobs mingling with the sobs of five-year-old Taylor who called me on her mother's cell phone just moments after our departure. For years after Taylor would ask me, "Grandma why did you leave me?" *Had I not left could I have prevented the pain coming? Should I have interfered somehow? Was it all to be the way it played out? Is that why I left? It was their path to walk? All three walking a painful walk?*

I visited as often as I could over the years of separation and was made aware of the chaos in their lives. Brenda was a single Mom working long hours as an emergency room nurse in the Bay Area. One of the times I visited their home, I found a syringe with a needle attached in the trash. I did nothing. Well, I did something, I rationalized. *It must be from work. She probably had it in a pocket. Surely she would not be injecting herself. It would not do any good to confront her. She would lie. I'll pretend I didn't see it. It could make things worse if I confront her. Maybe she won't let me see the kids.*

Like always I just tried to "fix" things. I cleaned and cooked and babysat to make things easier for Brenda so that she would not be stressed—so that she could be more peaceful—happier. I was in denial. The co-dependent, enabler, denied what I saw and knew, just like I had most of my daughters' lives.

She became more and more distant. When we were together, we pretended all was well. When apart we spoke briefly and about the kids. It came to a head one day when I called her after our move from California. She was in an especially defensive mood.

Tears flowed down my cheeks. I pressed the phone hard against my ear and stifled the sobs threatening to escape from my chest. I wanted to hang up, but couldn't. As Brenda spewed her contempt into my ears, I tried to break into the barrage of words. "Bren, I, I," is as far as I got before she spit out again, "Mom you don't understand so don't try to. You're white and you're religious. You don't really care about anything but looking good. I don't even want to hear what you have to say."

I mumbled out, "Okay, okay, I need to go now," hung up the phone and let the sob I released turn into a scream of anguish.

Brenda was involved with someone in a hispanic gang. I know now that the words she flung at me about being "white" and "religious" were to drive me away. She did not want me to know what was happening in her life—to her.

Hours later I wrote the following letter, but never sent it. It still sits in a file marked "Brenda."

April 2, 2002

Oh, Bren, how I long to hold you to myself that you might feel the love I and all the Universe has for you. How hard it is to hear and see the pain you continue to embrace.

You don't know me, Bren, it is the only way you can say I am judging and that I am "white," unknowing and selfish. For some reason you are unwilling to "see" me. Is it because you are so afraid of loving yourself that you can't accept my love? To see others as loving maybe you first have to see yourself as loveable. Remember a few years ago when you spoke so well of the fact that it was better to tell a child she/he was "loveable" instead of loved – because to say "I love you" puts the emphasis on me and my goodness for loving you. To say, "You are loveable," puts the emphasis on the other. Well, Bren, "you are loveable." I mean that sincerely and would give my life for you to accept that message – twofold: 1) that you are loveable and 2) that I see you that way.

The old patterns of my life pull at me and I have to fight to not let what has happened this past year in your life to place me in the place of a victim. It is such a family trait to become and stay a victim and I refuse. I refuse to stay where I have been. The only way I can continually choose to move forward with my life of healing and growing is because of my inner wisdom that tells me I truly am here in this place and at this time for a purpose.

No one can heal me, no one can heal you. Our help and/or salvation is not outside of us, it is inside us. The only thing that really matters is our own contact with God, Higher Power, Spirit, or whatever name you want to use.

I surrender you, Bren, I've surrendered you to <u>you</u>. For you see I have and would like to heal (fix, if you want to call it that) you but realize that is selfish to think I can and dysfunctional to think I should. I would take your pain if I could and that too is dysfunctional for it is yours alone – no one can take it and taking it would rob you of the opportunities of growth.

You are a very passionate person and have the capacity for strong compassion. Having compassion must start with ourselves. Be compassionate with you. Do the things for yourself that you'd do for others if you were being compassionate with them.

Compassion is part of unconditional love and the secret to unconditional loving is that we are all the same, holy beyond our imagination. We are all one.

I appreciate more than you can imagine your willingness to be honest about feelings. I'd rather hear hurtful, honest feelings than have no communication or hear dishonest feelings.

I've thought often about nurturing and my lack of it – receiving and giving. I thought of your dreams of my missing or being killed, etc. Learning to nurture – how to give and receive is a journey. I encourage you to look into the possibility that your nightmares represent your need to love and nurture yourself.

You haven't walked/aren't walking a difficult path for naught. If you will grasp hold of the belief in who you really are – divine – your pain will subside with the addictions and you will help transform the world with your wisdom.

This is my belief ---- Love unconditionally,
Mom

Three weeks later I returned home from a trip to California where I had not seen her because she was in a psych unit on a seventy-two-hour hold. I talked with her on the phone and she begged me to come get her out. It was heartbreaking to deny this request. The children were with their fathers. The fathers were considering, along with her sister, Kim, to get custody. Those seventy-two-hours, placed within Brenda the knowing that she needed help. Upon her release, she made an agreement with each of the fathers to give them temporary custody of the kids, got in her car and headed east. She ended up in Michigan at my sister's home, who helped facilitate her entrance into a treatment facility near-by. Years later she told me that her intention when she left California was to commit suicide, but instead was pushed internally to go to Aunt Sue's.

During this time, Brenda refused to speak to, or acknowledge me with anything but angry emails describing my failure as her mother. At the time I wrote the letter, Brenda was at an impasse. Would she self-destruct or heal?

I could not remove the troubling, agonizing thoughts of failure as her mother. *How did I fail so miserably? I helped many other girls, why not my own? How could I fail my own daughter so blatantly? Should I have reported what I suspected but did not address? Would it have made a difference? Would she have accepted my help? Why was I so afraid of her reactions?*

I sat in my office begging for forgiveness, understanding, and peace. I walked around the house peering out windows that gave no answers. I took long walks in the fields around our home while sobs erupted from some incomprehensible truth I had ignored. Fear twisted my insides and left me speechless as I sat in the middle of the field asking for forgiveness and strength to go on, "Please release me and fill me with light and love."

I stood at a window peering out into the field behind our home, "Please, please, God protect Brenda. Surround her with light and love."

An inaudible voice said to me, "She is more mine than yours. She does not belong to you. I will care for her because she is mine."

I hung on to this message for relief from the agony of failure. *She'll be taken care of. I don't have to. I can trust God to care for her. He won't fail. I surrender.*

I had insisted upon raising my children in the country away from negative influences. I had raised them in a conservative, religious, environment. I had stayed married to their father though I was extremely unhappy because I believed it was best for them. I had worked long, hard hours to provide what I thought was a better life for them. I thought our devotion to the Church and Church beliefs would save them from the world. I thought I was preparing them for a better life out of devotion to God.

I taught them to obey—to keep the rules. I allowed no swearing, not even gee, gosh, or darn. There was no rock music or movies in our home—we had no TV. *Where did I go wrong?* My struggle to protect, guard, and survive distanced me from them emotionally. I was so concerned about raising them *right* that I did not know it took more than rules and obedience. I did not show enough love and support. I did for them what my grandmother did for me—I taught them about God's rules and not about God's love.

I thought I was giving them a new "dad" when I married Loren. He had definitely become grandpa but only Lori called him Dad. There was fondness but still distrust and a lack of respect not only for him but for men in general. I myself still struggled with lack of appreciation for the male while I held my grandsons as precious, loved my husband and stepson and sons-n-laws.

What I perceived as my failure as a mother pushed me further to question *why.* I had been so taken up with the Church, so conservative, so literal, trusting that God would guide me at all times and protect my children as I asked. I had been faithful in following the Christian life. I had been faithful in Church rules (except for the affair), and yet here I was with the pain of Amy's death, the pain of all four daughters in the throes of what appeared to be the results of incestuous behavior from the man I chose as their father.

I hung on to my belief in a loving God by the skin of my teeth. Always I came back to this belief when I could not adhere to others. I was dissatisfied with the answers any church I visited gave me. I searched outside the Christian Church and still was left with unanswered questions.

I contemplated: *What if I had believed in a female God? What if a Mother-Father God? Would I have had a better self-image? Would I then not have accepted the abuse from father and husband? What if I had pictured myself sitting on the lap of a Mother instead of believing I should accept God as a Father? Further, would there not be the abuse in our culture for me to accept or deny if our culture was not inundated with the belief that God is male?*

At the same time that I spent hours contemplating my failings and the why's, I, also, started to study more deeply to discover answers to the whys. The time would come to reestablish a relationship with Brenda and her with the family, but in the meantime I needed to find healing for myself, and do that through understanding.

I questioned not only my role as a mother, but how did my being a Mother relate to God's being a Father?

25

"OH, MY GOSH," escaped from my lips as I reached for the light orange paperback book I'd just spotted. On the spine in bold black letters were the words *The Woman's Bible*!

I love book stores. All book stores, but especially used book stores. For many years I only searched the Christian stacks because I did not read novels and believed only Christian writers were trustworthy of sharing acceptable thought.

The day I discovered *The Woman's Bible* I had allowed myself to venture to shelves of metaphysics. I had completed my course in hand reading, read about goddesses, and read other Eastern teachings. That day I was looking for old books on hand reading.

Finding the book I held in my hands was serendipitous. I had no idea such a book existed, or I would have been seeking it. I caressed the book gently. It was old.

As I turned the first pages I noted the published date of 1898. Over a hundred years ago! The year Grandma Courser was born. Wow! I was amazed, and questioned. *Why didn't I know about this book?*

Elizabeth Cady Stanton, who, with a Revising Committee, published *The Woman's Bible*, wrote on the second page: "Genesis Chapter 1 says

Man and Woman were a simultaneous creation. Chapter II says Woman was an afterthought. Which is true?"

I was captured by this question. I couldn't wait to get home and devour the book!

The Preface describes the first Woman's Rights Convention held in Seneca Falls, New York in 1848. Fifty years before the publication of *The Woman's Bible*, Mrs. Stanton, a housewife and mother of three sons, sat down with a small group of Quaker and abolitionist women and decided that the wrongs done to women should be made into rights.

At that time, in the eyes of the law, the main-stream churches, and the government, women were not allowed the freedoms assigned to men. Women could not vote, hold an elective office, attend college, or pursue a career. If married, it was very difficult for them to make legal contracts, divorce an abusive husband, or gain custody of their children.

This small group of women presented a Declaration of Sentiments based on the language and content of the Declaration of Independence. This declaration stated that "all men and women are created equal……The history of mankind is a history of repeated injuries and usurpations on the part of man toward woman, having its direct object the establishment of an absolute tyranny over her."

Among the eighteen grievances listed in the Declaration, the second in particular rings true to my experience:

> "He (man) allows her in Church as well as State, but a subordinate position, claiming
> Apostolic authority for her exclusion from the ministry, and with some exceptions, from
> any public participation in the affairs of the Church," and, "He has usurped the
> prerogative of Jehovah himself, claiming it as his right to assign her a sphere of action,
> when that belongs to her conscience and to her God."

Elaborated in the preface is the fact that the Church of England, after much expressed dissatisfaction with the Authorized Version of the Bible published in 1611, appointed two groups of scholars in 1870 to prepare a revision. Similar groups were formed in America, but no woman was invited to participate in any group. Some American women believed that at least Julia Smith would be included since she had made five of the most literal translations to date. Though this fact was also recognized by other male scholars, she was not invited!

What were the men afraid of? Why wouldn't they want female in-put if God's Word is for the female too? This was only one hundred and fifty years ago. This happened during Great Grandma Millie's lifetime!

I wonder if my great-grandmother knew that there were women contemplating and planning objections to this treatment, this belief system. Surely, as the oldest great granddaughter and granddaughter, if she or my grandmother had questioned, I would have at least heard bits and pieces of discontent in this regard. I did not.

In 1982, during a visit home, I mentioned to my mother that a female friend was pursuing the idea of ministerial ordination within the Adventist church. I was amazed at how adamant she was when she said, "God never meant for women to be ministers. The Bible says that women are not to be in the pulpit."

When I asked, "Where have you ever read such a thing in the Bible?" she said, "I don't know, but I'm sure it must be in there."

My mother spoke with emotion and assurance. I dropped the subject immediately, and never brought it up to her again.

In *The Woman's Bible* Eleanor testifies to the fact that, "We have found ourselves to be in a position of conforming to the cultures, attitudes, and systems of male dominance rather than seeking to transform them….we have supported male dominance within the church itself….we tend to read and interpret the Bible selectively, emphasizing what supports our biases." This influence was surely apparent in my mother's responses.

It is easy for me to understand why the males in our culture would conform to the belief of God being male. After all, it gives them supremacy and dominance. It is harder to understand why women not only conform, but support and perpetuate it. Maybe because many genuinely believe that God is male and that this *fact* testifies to men's rights to dominate. They may also think that this naturally entitles men to prerogatives given by the authority of God.

This assumption has significantly affected my personhood and the personhood of my great grandmother, my grandmother, and my mother. Not only has it affected the personhood of my ancestors, but it continues to affect me, my daughters, and my granddaughters in the same manner. Although the imprint is less, given the women's rights now provided in our culture, the effect of the assumption remains.

Mrs. Stanton concluded that, "self-development is a higher duty than self-sacrifice and should be woman's motto henceforward." Though written one hundred and fifty years ago, I resonate with this statement. It is what motivates my questions: *Who am I in relation to this male God? Who are we as a woman, part of the human race, in relation to a male God? Where does this belief in the "male" God come from?*

Some, who appear to be rational individuals, assume that male dominance is a direct order of God. Stanton's statement in the Introduction to *The Woman's Bible* that, "The Bible teaches that woman brought sin and death into the world; that she precipitated the fall of the race; that she was arraigned before the judgment seat of Heaven, tried, condemned and sentenced," speaks to why some ministers I've heard preach, say this is so.

Placing responsibility on the women who are unwilling to oppose their position of a subordinate, Stanton states: "We have many women abundantly endowed with capabilities to understand and revise what men have thus far written. But they are all suffering from inherited ideas of their inferiority; they do not perceive it, yet such is the true explanation of their solicitude, lest they should seem to be too self-asserting."

This inheritance that she speaks of is mine, and that of my daughters and granddaughters. It is the inheritance of every female born into the *family of God* as defined by the Bible and the Koran. Both speak of the same God. Abraham was the father of both Isaac and Ishmael. Both claim God to be male.

I question the belief that God created woman subject to man, created him first and her from him. What kind of God would create a woman who is the creator of life within her belly, and also support the religious beliefs that degrade her? As long as women accept the position that religions assign her, her emancipation is impossible.

"So God created man in his own image, in the image of God created he him; male and female created he them." (Genesis 1:27) This scripture declares the equality of the genders. The feminine traits of vision and nurture and the masculine traits of manifestation and aggression balance each other—are essential to all of life.

It is not my intent to discredit the Bible, but to question the interpretations and translations that have perpetuated the belief within the culture I live that women are less capable or less important. This domination does not come from God. In fact, does not come from the Bible, but from the translations of men.

One of the greatest blocks to advancing civilization has been the degradation of woman. The birth of a son is often considered more significant than the birth of a daughter. I gave birth to four daughters and heard the sadness in many voices when they were told I did not produce a son. To this day in the United States of America, there are families of my acquaintance that make statements declaring joy when a son is born to carry on the name of the Father and disappointment when daughters are born, "Oh, I'm sorry you had another girl."

Stanton wrote:

> "We scarce take up a paper that does not herald some
> outrage committed on a matron on

her way to church, or the little girl gathering wild flowers on her way to school; yet you
cannot go so low down in the scale of being as to find men who will enter our churches to
desecrate the altars or toss about the emblems of the sacrament; because they have been
educated with some respect for churches, altars and sacraments. But where are any
lessons of respect taught for the mothers of the human family? ....They who would protect
their innocent daughters from the outrages so common today, must lay anew the
foundation stones of law and gospel in justice and equality, in a profound respect of the
sexes for each other."

These statements are as pertinent today as when written. Domestic abuse of women far outweighs that of men and is still considered a dirty secret. Often the women themselves dismiss abuse with statements of, "He didn't mean it," or "I made him angry, it isn't his fault." Whose fault is it? I declare that it is the fault of a society that accepts the dogma of God being male, and therefore males have more importance and value. It comes from mothers and fathers who teach their children that there is a difference—that there is not equality. It permeates our society with subtle clues that we are not aware of or not willing to investigate.

I volunteered for Victim's Advocates from the year of 2005 to 2010. During the required training I was told: three U.S. women are killed every day by a current or former partner; approximately 300,000 adult American women are raped each year; domestic violence is a major cause of death among pregnant women, and domestic abuse makes up twenty percent of violent crimes against women. During the year 2010 more than one third of American women reported being abused by a partner at some point in their lives.

I found this statement from Stanton correlates with experience I had in 1963:

> "Males are the race, females only the creatures that carry it on…Men never fail to dwell on maternity as a disqualification for the possession of many civil and political rights…men will declaim at once on the disabilities of maternity in a sneering contemptuous way as if the office of motherhood was undignified and did not comport with the highest public offices in church and state…Why should representative American women be incapable of discharging similar public and private duties at the same time in an equally commendable manner?"

I worked as a Teacher's Aid in the public school I had attended for thirteen years and from which I graduated. I was married and had a young daughter. When it became apparent that I was pregnant with my second child, the principal called me into his office to announce that I needed to take another position if I was to remain employed by the school—that of serving the student body "behind" the counter in the administration office.

"It is not appropriate that you mingle with the students in your condition."

Today I am still not amazed at his demand, but amazed at my effortless capitulation to the demand.

In DREAMS FROM MY FATHER. [2005] Barack Obama, now President, describes his heritage by listing his ancestors: "First there was Miwiru. It's not known who came before. Miwriru sired Sigoma, Sigoma sired Owiny, Owiny sired Kisodhi, etc. My thoughts while reading this manifested a retort in my mind: "*sired, sired? What about birthed? Who birthed, who sustained this life with the milk from her breast? What about the one whose body gave the life?*

He wrote: "The women who bore them, their names are forgotten, for that was the way of our people."

And I thought: *The way of our people? It is the way of all the people I know. It for sure is the way of all people who believe in a male God.*

For I remembered I Chronicles, chapter one: *Adam, Seth, Enosh, Kenan, Mahalalel, Jared, Enoch, Methuselah, Lamech, Noah. The sons of Noah: Shem, Ham and Japheth.* And I remembered chapter two of I Chronicles: *These were the sons of Israel: Reuben, Simeon, Levi, Judah,* and so forth, and so forth, and so forth.

Recently I proposed a question to a new acquaintance after a few minutes of discussion about religion: "Don't you wonder how we have accepted all these years that God is male?"

She looked at me as though I had slipped into a foreign language. She took a breath, looked the other way for a second and responded: "You need to read the Bible and trust what it has to say."

While I took my own deep breath, I concluded in that suspended second that she was saying that she did believe God is male. I started with a retort on my lips and got out something like, "Well, you know the Bible has been written and interpreted by men."

She reiterated with, "Whenever I have doubts about what to believe I go back to the Bible and am always reassured."

I changed the subject.

Lunch with Susan, an ordained, retired Methodist Minister, was refreshing and revealing. Of course we talked about religion. Susan made the confession that she is spiritual and not religious—one of my favorite confessions.

She had recently resigned from the position of chaplain at a treatment center where she counseled women with addictions. She spoke of how she implored the women to recognize their own personal power. She further shared how difficult it was for the women to accept and believe in their own personhood. She said, "When I told them they did not need a man, that they were able to care for themselves, they did not understand how I could be saying those things."

I leaned forward over the table; looking directly into Susan's eyes, wondering if I was going too far, and said, "Susan, maybe it is the cultural indoctrination that God is male that keeps women from believing they are anything more than second class citizens."

Her response, "Yes, I know that has something to do with it," led to further conversation regarding mutual belief and understanding of what this religious belief has done to our culture in the United States. We agreed that the United States was founded upon Christian beliefs and though there have been many changes, the belief that God is male and the male has supremacy, still lingers in a powerful way.

Susan also supported my thoughts with the idea that "religions have made God in the image of man." Further that, "Changing this belief within a church setting is very difficult."

Her statement, "I rarely attend church anymore," echoed my sentiments exactly, as she went on to say, "I'm so fed up with the same ole doctrines of who God is."

"So am I," I said.

26

TEARS SPRANG TO my eyes as I looked down into the face of a sari-wrapped Bangladeshi woman. She was silent, looking at me through her own tears, as I said a heart-felt, "Bless you." The feeling was intense.

We did not speak the same language. She lived in a small hut with dirt floor and dung slapped on the sides for burning fuel. I lived in a three-thousand square-foot brick home with carpet and tiled floors. In an effort to respect her culture, I stood there sweating in a long cotton skirt to cover my legs, a long sleeved blouse to cover my arms, and sandals on my feet, dirty from the sand we stood upon. Peering down at her I wondered: *What is she feeling? Why did tears come to her eyes at the same time as mine? How could two strangers living not only miles, but centuries apart, feel this bond of emotion?*

I traveled twenty-three air hours and an additional six ground hours to be in this Bangladeshi village. It was foreign territory, yet I felt touched with emotion by everything I saw and experienced. I was definitely touched by this woman—as though we were long-lost friends. *Was it about our human connection? The Oneness? Or simply our feminine hearts reaching out to each other without words, but with understanding?*

We were no longer members of an Adventist church, but we kept contact with many acquaintances and friends who were. Hence, the invitation from a wealthy Adventist gentleman to visit a couple of orphanages he supported in Bangladesh. He had received information about Loren's past principalship within the Church and his present licensed school for the group homes. He needed some help with the schools within the orphanages, and asked Loren for a ongrounds consultation. Scott, Juliette, and I were invited to go along.

Our arrival in Dhaka was late in the evening. By then the streets had been emptied due to political unrest. We traveled to the only hotel safe for Americans on dark and dreary streets with numerous burned out vehicles lining them. It looked like a war zone. It was my first trip to an underdeveloped country. I thought I had prepared for the poverty. I had not. My senses screamed.

The next morning we ate breakfast in the hotel, loaded the back of the small two-seater truck with our luggage, and climbed inside. The driver was a young Bangladeshi employed by the gentleman who sponsored our visit. As we drove out of the locked and guarded hotel gates, my apprehension mounted and then overwhelmed me as we left the side street onto a main thoroughfare. The morning light disclosed unmitigated poverty that astounded me though I knew that Bangladesh was one of the poorest countries in the world.

Traffic, diverse with rickshaws, bicycles, smoke-spewing trucks and buses, and numerous weaving motorcycles, clogged the road. The smell of kerosene burning in the smaller vehicles filtered into the truck. We slowed to a crawl and then stopped for long minutes at a traffic light. Beggars clamored for our attention. On the left side of the truck stood a young girl surrounded by boys and men, like a flower amongst a field of weeds. The blue dress and a drooping blue bow in her hair gave prominence to her presence. She held both hands outward with unseeing eyes. On the right of the truck posed an old woman between two teenage boys. Her mouth moved as she spoke, but the cacophony surrounding us drowned out her voice. Her right hand extended and her eyes met mine.

A sob broke loose from my chest making an animal-like sound. I covered my face with my hands and cried with all the empathy present in my body. Able, after a minute, to gain some control, I looked into the eyes our young twenty-three year old driver reflected in the rearview mirror and between sobs stammered, "I'm not afraid….I want…..I want….to help. I can't help it. I'm sorry….it hurts…..to see this."

He spoke English and said to me very firmly, but with compassion, "You must not give. Do not look like you will give. We will be overtaken and unable to move the vehicle. Do not look." I turned my eyes straight ahead and tried to keep them there. How could I ignore, or be complacent? Nothing had prepared me for this.

He went on to explain that the old woman and the young girl were being used by the boys and the men surrounding them. That in fact the girl's eyes had been blinded for the purpose of begging. He further stated that the government was trying to stop beggary. With his compassionate yet concerned voice, he said, "I will tell you when to give. Sometimes it is okay." Later on our trip he gave me coins of his own to give to someone when he indicated.

Bangladesh is the seventh most-populated country in the world. Men are seen everywhere you look, which magnifies the absence of women. The two females, little girl and old woman, were the only ones I saw on our trip to the airport where Loren and Scott were to board a helicopter to visit an isolated orphanage further north. Juliette and I stayed in the truck that would take us to a closer orphanage six hours away where the men would meet us later in the evening.

At the airport men and young boys were rushing hither and yon, imploring with their desire to be of service—all the activity to collect any coins made available by carrying luggage, opening doors, selling trivia.

After dropping Scott and Loren off, a couple who were to help at the orphanage for a few weeks, entered the truck for the six-hour journey of trepidation to the southernmost orphanage. The road was a lane and half wide compared to two-lane paved roads in the United States. Rickshaws, motorized and pedaled, were engulfed by large buses with people hanging on the sides and squatting on the top. The large trucks took up most of the road allowing only a few feet for vehicles they met. Holding my breath soon became commonplace as trucks and buses we met on the right passed by my window within two or three inches—maybe closer, as sometimes I closed my eyes expecting the crunch of metal. I was glad we were in a very small truck as we also sped around families in fragile rickshaws on our left. The driver told us, "If we have an accident I will disappear."

"What?" spewed out of my mouth before thought could stop it.

"They stone drivers who have accidents," he responded without emotion. The fear of his possible departure leaving us to deal with angry men with whom we could not talk, added to my fear already in abundance!

We did arrive safely at the orphanage and enjoyed four days of visitation that included the village where I experienced the toe to toe emotional intimacy. I also had the delight of visiting other villages where men and boys were conspicuous while women and girls were elusive, appearing slowly and demurely from open doors. Juliette and I toured a small hospital, more comparable to small animal hospitals in the United States. The gentle caring physician touched each of the patients as he introduced us to them.

I spent as much time as possible in the austere, cement building—not a toy, book, or stuffed animal in sight—that housed one-hundred under-school-age children. At my first visit I knelt down to be at the children's level and accidentally fell backwards, engendering bedlam as the children laughed uproariously. I repeated my first-appearance act daily just to hear their laughter, added to mine as we enjoyed the camaraderie.

As the helicopter lifted, taking us back to the airport for our return flight home, hundreds of orphans and orphanage personnel waved from the ground. Once again I apologized. This time to the pilot. I could not contain the sobs. I felt sad and torn—part of my heart was staying there with the women and girls I had met and hugged.

The trip into a third-world country affected me greatly. I set up a foundation to facilitate sending money to help feed those I met in a small factory that employed single mothers. But the experience that affected me most profoundly was the few seconds I stood before the woman in the small village whose eyes had sprung tears the second I looked into them. I thought of her often in the days, weeks, and months after the trip. I wished I had been able to talk with her. I had so many questions. *Why did her eyes tear? What was she feeling? Was she sad? Was she looking at me for encouragement? Was she ashamed? Did she know I was not looking down on her? Did she know what my heart felt?*

Our visit was in April of 2002, just seven months after 9/11. I had not reacted to the devastation of that day as most around me did. I felt a deep sadness for both the families of those killed and for the Muslim people who felt the wrath of the American people. I did not feel anger.

Not knowing much about the Muslim religion, I still did not believe it was "of the devil," as I heard some around me express. The trip to Bangladesh bolstered the beliefs I did have about Americans unfairly maligning all diversity. I came home wanting to understand more.

As I read, I discovered that the similarities in the lives of the Muslim women and my life were greater than the differences. The woman I stood toe to toe with in silence, my eyes filled with tears, was a woman caring for her family the best she knew how. I remembered the absence of women, and surmised that she believed she was less important than the husband who had control over her life. Her experience was graphic, mine was subtle.

Reading her book, *My Hope for Peace*, I found a comrade in Jehan Sadat, wife of Anwar Sadat, slain King of Egypt. She wrote: "As a consequence of 9/11.....I have found myself trying to evaluate my own life. I have been both praised and excoriated for being a 'feminist,' hailed as a pioneer for women's rights in the Arab world and deplored as a destroyer...."

About Muslim women she says, "...there is no single truth, for Muslim women contain multitudes. Like women of every faith, we share the same goals for ourselves and for our families: happiness, health, peace, and prosperity. We want to matter in our societies."

I also found similar, even familiar, expressions in the writings of Ayaan Hirsi Ali, Azar Nafisi, and Nonie Darwish. They all denounce the Muslim faith. The questions and doubts that Ayaan spouts in her book *Infidel,* continually reminded me of those I struggled with regarding my faith. She writes, "By declaring our Prophet infallible and not permitting ourselves to question him, we Muslims set up a static tyranny. The Prophet Muhammad attempted to legislate every aspect of life." As a conservative Seventh-day Adventist every aspect of my life was dictated by the Prophet Ellen White's writings. Supported by the Church and advocated from the pulpit, they guided my life. I not only read the Bible judicially, but her writings too—adhering to the dictums faithfully. For me, Ellen White's admonitions were woven into salvation beliefs that caused me to question whether I was good enough—whether I measured up to God's expectations. For some within the Church, her words had more dictum than the Bible and some used her writings to translate Bible texts.

In the article, *Subjection and Escape: An American Woman's Muslim Journey,* written for the magazine, FREE INQUIRY, Lisa Bauer speaks of her experiences from being raised a Catholic, to becoming a Muslim. She writes "....my mother disliked much about the Church. She'd been sent to a Catholic school as a child and had had some extremely negative experiences there, with the nuns verbally abusing her and treating her like garbage. She loathed the sexism inherent in the patriarchal structure and the rules of the Church." And yet this mother raised her children in the Church! Lisa says: "......the entire time that I was supposedly a model Catholic girl, I was tormented by doubts about the whole enterprise."

Lisa explains that, like me, she thought it "was important to try to follow the dictates of the Church......I didn't feel that any such practice was forcibly imposed on me. In fact, *I* tended to be the one who scrupulously tried to follow the rules." I too never felt *forced* to obey the dictates of the Prophet and Church. I obeyed to be saved and not punished by God.

Lisa tells that her search, also like mine, to understand the background of the religion with the rules, "paved the way for my interest in Islam, however, in that many of the concepts and ideas found in (Orthodox and historical) Judaism, such as the emphasis on sacred law and the importance of orthopraxy (correct behavior), are also found in Islam. Over the years, I've come to realize just how strikingly similar the two religions are, which makes it all the more perplexing why there would be so much hatred between them." I, too, found similarities, and I was amazed to find that the verbiage I used from the Bible resonated with that used by the Muslim women regarding what they read and understood from the Qur'an.

I have heard and read much criticism for the wearing of the burqa, and how terrible husbands are for "making" their wives wear them. Justine Hardy in her book *In the Valley of Mist* tells us that in the area where she lived: "Full black burqas are also a part of the Valley's tradition, and one that was not just confined to Islam. For centuries it was also the measure of man's success. If he could afford to put his wife under the burqa when she was moving around outside the house, it was a sign that the woman did not have to work. That there were enough servants in the house to fetch and carry, clean and cook, freeing the woman of the house to be fully covered, and therefore unable to carry loads on her head."

She also quotes a Doctor from Srinagar as saying: "You see, so many of you foreigners just assume that the women wear the burqa because their husbands will beat them if they do not...... This is there, both these things. But it is the women as much. They cover themselves, they teach their daughters to do the same, and so it goes. Some of them do it because they just know that all these men are just not able to control themselves. They are too scared to take off the burqa, both for the shame that they believe it will bring on their families, and because they do not have any faith that men will be able to keep control of themselves if they all take off their burqas."

These comments rang true to me, for I remember the times I felt responsible for a man's arousal. I have felt angst walking past a construction site where the men yelled unseemly comments making me wish I could cover myself and not be seen. I, also, remembered the times I heard girls complain that their father refused to let them leave the house because of a short skirt or being braless. These men undoubtedly were concerned about how other men would look at their daughter, and endeavored to protect her—cover her up.

Jehan Sadat reports troubled thoughts that, "The burka-clad woman became a mute archetype for the Oppressed Muslim Woman, and thereafter, it was not too difficult to imagine that this entire benighted population was in need of rescuing—and not just from a corrupt and inhumane political regime that took hold as a result of the spectacular misery of recent Afghan history, but also from Islam itself. Western concern about the 'plight of Muslim women,' well-meaning as it may be, has often played into stereotypical ideas that we are oppressed and intimidated, voiceless and victimized."

She admits that while "many Muslim women wish to shake off the oppressive practices and ideologies that presuppose they are less worthy than men, Muslim women do not require, nor do they desire, liberation from Islam."

She also makes a declaration that I believe the women of the United States need to hear: "People, not Islam, infringe on the rights of women. Time, tradition, customary law, and the collusion of men unwilling to have their authority challenged have combined to undermine the status of women." *Interesting! She's saying what I want to say and have been afraid to say it so pointedly. I think this is true. I am saying it now.*

Another astounding observation she makes is: "In marked contrast to traditional Christian doctrine, Muslims do not hold Eve responsible for

Adam's sin and the subsequent Fall. Islam has never entertained the idea of woman as 'cursed' or morally inferior to men. ….in Islam, Eve was not created as an afterthought or appendage from Adam's rib; rather, men and women were created from a 'single soul' to complement and give comfort to one another: 'It is He Who created you from a single soul. From that being He created his spouse, so that he may find comfort in her' (Qur'an, 7:189). 'I will deny no man or woman among you the reward of their labors. You are the offspring of one another.' (Qur'an, 3: 195)."

A Gallup Poll she speaks of states that "a majority of Muslim women said that the thing they liked least about the West is a 'culture of moral decay, promiscuity and pornography' that they see as degrading to women." American Soap Operas exported to Muslim countries do not show the true picture of women within the United States, any more than the sensational stories that abound regarding honor killings and female abuse that abound in the USA about the Muslim world.

It is interesting to me that both "Islam" and "the West" find each other's acceptance of treatment of women objectionable. Jehan says that, "women the world over—whether they are Oriental or Occidental, inhabitants of the developing world or the industrialized—have yet to achieve the full measure of political, economic, or social equality that we deserve." This is a worldwide issue.

She concedes that the Muslim family is patriarchal, but says that "men are not given license to abuse their status as heads of household. Husbands are instructed, 'Live with their wives on footing of kindness and equity. If you dislike them it may be that you dislike something in which Allah has placed a great deal of good' (Qur'an, 4:19)." This is a stronger language than I find in the Bible for support of the woman.

Jehan also addresses another major concern of mine when she says: "Here in Egypt, I hear men, and some women, too, proclaiming that women should be content to stay at home, removed from public life. Though I realize that some women are weary of and worn down by the fight for equality and feminist movements, Arab and Western, which have not ushered in a golden age, I find this archaic attitude alarming. Right now, millions of women and their children are falling deeper and deeper into the chasm that separates the haves and the have-nots. As a result, the middle class, men and women alike, is losing footing."

Like me, she voices the concern that because "younger women have never known a world in which women were barred from civic and economic participation," they may take for granted gains made by feminist pioneers. She says, "Women—in Egypt *and in the United States*—have not yet arrived at a point where those who wish to raise families and have successful careers can comfortably 'have it all,' so, faced with the struggle and sacrifice of the daily lives, some women may even long for what they believe were simpler times." (Emphasis on the United States is mine.)

I believe more women within the United States should do as Raya Idliby, Suzanne Oliver, and Priscilla Warner did. Each being of a different faith, they came together to learn from each other about their religious beliefs. They described the experience and results in the book: *The Faith Club: Three Women Search for Understanding.*

After 9/11, Ranya Idiby, an American Muslim of Palestinian descent, reached out to two other mothers, Priscilla Warner a Jew, and Suzanne Oliver a Christian, to try to understand and answer the questions her children were asking. These women were willing to confront the age-old differences of their religions. They instead were stunned as to how much their faiths united them.

Suzanne testifies that she "can't justify the fact that most Muslim countries deny women equal rights,.... But that says more about the condition of these societies and their legal systems than about Islam. I don't think that is what Muhammad intended. If we look at his actions in the context of time he lived in, he was revolutionary. He championed women's rights. He gave women marital rights and inheritance rights. A woman could divorce her husband if he did not satisfy her sexually! He put an end to the desert practice of killing female babies. I don't see him as a discriminator but as a liberator." Though the description is different, we Christian women have often pointed out that Jesus made a point to support women regardless of the culture at the time.

Suzanne also says that after reading the Qur'an: "……I began reading about Islam's view of creation, I found things that appealed to me more than the Catholic doctrine I had learned in school. In the Quran, Eve does not trick Adam into eating the apple. Adam and Eve act together. More importantly, the transgression of Adam does not mark humanity with "original sin" as taught by Catholics when I was in school." *I wonder. Has the Qur'an had translations and interpretations as the Bible has had? As a woman, if I read the Bible from the very first original script, would I interpret it differently? Could it say to me that the woman wasn't at fault?*

Ranya says that, "As a Muslim, I am called upon to believe that the diversity in human faith traditions is intended by God's design and not a random occurrence. The universality of God and his accessibility to all is emphasized in the Muslim understanding that all religions have sprung from the same divine source and that God's message was sent to all people and cultures of all nations (35:25). Different communities are united in their devotion to God, yet what sets them apart is their good work, not the merit of one faith tradition over another."

Near the end of the book Suzanne makes the statement: "I had become a universalist. So why was I so scared? Because I suddenly didn't know where to find truth. If all religions were equal, how did I know what to believe when they disagreed? There was one big area of agreement: that we should love God with all our heart, soul, mind, and strength and love our neighbor as ourselves. I was fine with that. But what about the other stuff? Religion was easier to think about when I thought I had the right answer." What Suzzane says here, mirrors my thoughts and my beliefs.

Priscilla's input at the end of the book is simple, yet profound: "I now realize, as Ranya has pointed out to me, that on September 11, the whole world was praying to the same God, the God I feared had disappeared.

Whatever you call prayer, wherever you do it, we're all doing it for the same reasons, toward the same end—to feel connected, to fill a void, to feel whole and strong and somehow in control, even if we are surrendering that control to a higher authority in order to feel in control."

During the time I was reading books written by Muslim women, Rulon T. Jeffs, leader and prophet of the Fundamentalist Church of Jesus Christ of Latter Day Saints was being spouted in the news as a fugitive. Uncle Rulon, as he is known to his followers, traces his ordination as the leader back to Joseph Smith. While the leadership of the Latter Day Saints Church has worked to persuade the modern church membership, and the American public, that it no longer supports the doctrine of polygamy, the Fundamentalists contend that by abandoning support of that doctrine, the LDS leadership has abandoned one of the religion's most crucial theological tenets.

I was as vaguely acquainted with the Mormon faith as I was of the Muslim faith. I have been acquainted with a few followers of the Mormon faith. I knew the church's record of non-support for female leadership. More than once it was reported to me that women of the Mormon faith were dependent upon the husband they married to achieve salvation—dependent to the point that they would not be in heaven after death unless married to a Mormon man of good faith. This report I never verified. However, reading the stories of women who have left the faith of the LDS Church and the Fundamentalist Church has convinced me that here in the United States of America, women are being treated as property.

In his book *Under the Banner of Heaven* Jon Krakauer makes the statement: "As the TV prohibition suggests, life in Colorado City under Rulon Jeffs bears more than a passing resemblance to life in Kabul under the Taliban."

And another: "According to (Mormon) dogma, wives do not belong to their husbands, nor do children belong to their parents; all are property of the priesthood and may be claimed at any time."

In *Refuge* Terry Tempest Williams, born, raised, and living as Mormon, questions her faith due to the treatment of women. She says, "What I do know, however, is that as a Mormon woman of the fifth generation of Latter-day Saints, I must question everything, even if it means losing my faith, even if it means becoming a member of a border tribe among my own people. Tolerating blind obedience in the name of patriotism or religion ultimately takes our lives."

She asks the question I am asking: "Where is the Motherbody?" And she goes on to say, "We are far too conciliatory. If we as Mormon women believe in God the Father and his son Jesus Christ, it is only logical that a Mother-in-Heaven balances the sacred triangle. I believe the Holy Ghost is female, although she has remained hidden, invisible, deprived of a body, she is the spirit that seeps into our hearts and directs us to the well. The 'still, small voice' I was taught to listen to as a child was 'the gift of the Holy Ghost.' Today I choose to recognize this presence as holy intuition, the gift of the Mother."

She goes on to say that her prayers no longer bear the 'proper' masculine salutation. She, like I, now includes both "Father and Mother in Heaven." *How different would my life be and the life of my daughters, if I had always prayed to a Father and Mother God?*

She writes further, "My physical mother is gone. My spiritual mother remains. I am a woman rewriting my genealogy."

Yes, my physical mother is gone, too. And I search for my spiritual mother. I wish I knew as strongly the Mother that Terry describes.

We—Terry, Jehan, Ayaan, Azar, Nonie, Lisa, Justine, Ranya, Suzanne, Priscilla, Quanta, Davar, and others—are rewriting our genealogy, and including The Mother.

27

THE TRIP TO Bangladesh and the experience of the subjection of the women by evidence of their absence, led me into further study to discover the wheres and whys of misogyny. Though this practice is much more apparent in Bangladesh, I had experienced it at home. Growing up I accepted the preference my mother and aunts gave to the men in their lives and to sons. As an adult I was angered by it in the Church. I experienced it in my first marriage and fought against it in my present marriage. I also learned for the first time the word patriarchy.

On the first page of the first volume of three books titled: *The History of Women I,* I read, "These volumes, edited and written by historians recognized for their work on the history of women, demonstrate what the study of gender can include, how fascinating it can be, and where it can lead."

Lead me, God. I am not sure what I am doing, but I have to. I can't stop searching. Why have men been more important in history?

I delved in. Well, I *tried* to delve in. Reading was laborious. The language was scholarly and at an academic level new to me. I often reached for a dictionary while taking copious notes.

Chapter one begins: "At one time a history of women would have seemed an inconceivable or futile undertaking. The roles for which women were destined were silent ones: motherhood and homemaking, tasks relegated to the obscurity of a domesticity that did not count and was not considered worth recounting. Did women so much as have a history?" *Good question. Do we have a written history? Seems as though history textbooks only speak of men.*

As I read my way through, I felt anger rise with statements like the quote of Ado of Cluny who died in 942. He quoted John Chrysostom, a Greek Arch Bishop of Constantinople, an important church father (347-407AD). Cluny writes, "Physical beauty is only skin deep. If men could see beneath the skin, the sight of women would make them nauseous...... Since we are loath to touch spittle or dung even with our fingertips, how can we desire to embrace such a sac of dung?" *The contempt in that statement! Bishops taught Christianity! No wonder women were so discredited and maligned if this is what* ***important*** *church fathers preached!*

Reading on revealed to me that it was not just the church fathers who spoke of the degradation of women. From a Greek philosopher Lucuis Mestrius Plutarch (467-120AD) in his brief essay *The Virtues of Women,* written in the early part of the 2nd century AD: "I do not hold the same opinion as Thucydides (a Greek historian 460 BC – 395 BC). For he declares that the best woman......ought to be shut up indoors and never go out."

And another quote from the year 1105 from Geoffroy, who himself fathered a number of children through shameless affairs, warned Bishop Hildebert of Lavardin: "Take heed, venerable prelate, lest the women take advantage of your guileless nature and compel you to act against your mother, The Roman Church. The female sex is in the habit of deception......the female sex deceived the first man and misled the apostle Peter. It drove the first to sin and the second to renunciation. The sex thus discharges its office in the manner of a guardian of the gate: those whom it seduces, it either excludes from life, like Christ's Peter, or admits unto death, like Adam of Eden."

And a quote from Mansellis from around the turn of the 12th century: "The female sex poisoned our first ancestor, who was also husband and father to the first women, it strangled John the Baptist and delivered brave Samson to his death. In a manner of speaking it also killed our Savior: for had woman's sin not required it, Our Savior would not have to die. Woe onto this sex, which knows nothing of awe, goodness, or friendship, and which is more to be feared when loved than when hated."

Is this why women are blamed and maligned? We are responsible not only for Adam's departure from the garden, but the death of John the Baptist, Samson, and Jesus?

As late as the 14th century in a paper by Florentine states, "A horse, whether good or bad, needs a spur; a woman, whether good or bad, needs a lord and master, and sometimes a stick." *Ouch! Chattel?*

When I read and searched into Aristotle (384-322 BC), Greek philosopher, student of Plato and Socrates, and teacher of Alexander the Great, I experienced vindication for my suppositions. The Christian Church had perpetuated patriarchy and misogyny under the banner of God being a male and men being created first.

Such quotes as one attributed to Jean-Jacques Rousseau in book five of *Emile,* "To please (men), to be useful to them, to raise them when they are young, to take care of them when they are grown, to advise them, to console them, to make life pleasant and agreeable—these are the duties of women in all ages, duties which they should be taught from childhood," rang true to my experience. I'm sure my grandmother, mother, nor my aunts, read anything like this, but they lived it. This is what I believe my mother tried to teach me—as I also tried to teach my daughters until my overwhelming experience of unhappiness caused me to search for different beliefs.

Rosseau's views were much like that of Aristotle's. Rousseau had an excellent classical education in a Catholic school that included the study of Aristotle. Duby and Perrot go on to report that, "Aristotle, for his part, held that women are systematically inferior to men in every respect—anatomically, physiologically, and ethically—and that this inferiority is a consequence of the metaphysical passivity……this unanimous belief in the inferiority and inadequacy of women, in their shortcomings, deformities, and incompleteness, makes the thinking of the Greeks distinctly unpalatable."

Aristotle? Wasn't what he said considered really important?

Paul Strathern says in his book *Aristotle in 90 Minutes* "In Roman times Aristotle was acknowledged as the great logician but his other philosophy was largely eclipsed by (or absorbed into) the evolving Neoplatonism. *And over the centuries this was in turn largely absorbed into Christianity.*" Further he states, "Christian thinkers quickly recognized the usefulness of Aristotle's logic: thus Aristotle now came unto his own as **the supreme authority** for the philosophical method." And, *"Aristotle's theologically unobjectionable logic thus became an integral part of the Christian canon."* (Italics and bold are mine.)

Along with statements regarding Aristotle's "supreme authority" affecting the Christian church, Strathern also states: *"almost all Islamic philosophy was derived from interpretations of his thought."* (Italics mine.)

Further quotes in *Aristotle in 90 minutes* informed me how effective Aristotle has been with his beliefs and writings regarding women. Such as: "Thomas Aquinas was deeply attracted to Aristotle and quickly recognized his supreme worth. He devoted much of his life to reconciling Aristotle's philosophy with that of the church. In the end he "succeeded in establishing Aristotelianism as the philosophical basis for Christian theology. ….The Catholic church pronounced that the teachings of Aristotle—as interpreted by Aquinas—were The Truth and could be denied only on pain of heresy (a situation which remains in force to this day)."

The philosophy expounded by Aristotle influenced Roman law. Roman law has affected European and, therefore, American law. I found in the reading and studying, mostly from the *A History of Women* series, that Aristotelian and Greek philosophy not only has had a significant effect on the status of women within Christian churches and Muslim mosques, but that it influenced the laws that kept women from owning property, and maintained that their own children were owned by the father.

Yan Thomas in *The Division of the Sexes in Roman Law says,* "Under Roman Law women did not form a distinct judicial species" and "under Roman law a woman by herself could not establish the legitimacy of her offspring." That, "For Romans sexual division was not simply a fact but a norm."

Yan Thomas in *The Division of the Sexes in Roman Law* says "marriage was indispensable only to men, and it was exclusively for them that the (Roman) city instituted it." Exclusively for men? Marriage was instituted for men?! *So that they could own wives and daughters?*

My pulse quickened when I read that a question was proposed to Aristotle as to whether or not gender determines if one has an aptitude for specific tasks, and Aristotle answered with, "No. All men and women possess various talents. But there is an important proviso; the gifted male always outstrips the gifted female in any particular type of performance."

He then goes on to aggravate me further by adding, "Let's not waste our time talking about weaving and making pancakes or boiling stews, things at which women appear to have some talent and about which people would laugh if a woman were bested by a man." Can you imagine, "waste our time?" I would guess it was not wasting time for women to fix his meals, or make, mend, and wash his clothes!

I read on while reminding myself that there was a lack of medical knowledge at the time. Aristotle pursues the idea that males are the ideal, and the "intended" being by declaring that "woman, born female because of some impotence in her male parent, owing to youth, old age, or some similar cause." He also says, "menstrual blood is analogous to sperm, but it is imperfect sperm because it is uncooked….the male is capable of transforming blood into sperm." He goes so far as to say that the female does have something to do with the creation of life through gestation and birth but says, "the menstrual blood contains the parts of the embryo's body," yet "it is mere matter." However, he repeatedly expounds about the male being the precursor of children, allowing only that the female provides the body! *The body? The creator? Giving life?*

The quote from Aristotle that "The progeny that does not resemble its parents is already, in certain respects, a monster, because nature has to some extent departed from the generic type. The very first deviation from type is the birth of a female instead of a male," distresses me but at the same time allows me to understand further the origin of the perpetuated belief that the birth of a male child is often preferable.

Carla Casagrande in the chapter titled "The Protected Woman" from *A History of Women* tells us, "Women were exclusively wives, mothers, or daughters; their function was exclusively to produce and rear children; their work exclusively domestic. Preachers found confirmation of what they were saying in the clear unequivocal language of Aristotelian politics, which also provided the foundation of their moral vision; in order to be a part of society, women had to be a part of a family—forever."

Duby and Perrot also support my perspective that men have incorrectly written women's history: "How did images and fantasies of women evolve? …When the virtuous woman is portrayed as a spinner of yarn in a society indifferent to the value of labor, or when feminine beauty is associated more with adornment than with the body itself, all but shapeless and hidden from view, then we can begin to glimpse the way in which the feminine has been perceived. From such manifestations we can determine not how the sexes actually stood in relation to each other but how men *construed* their relation to, and thus their representation of, the opposite sex." (Italics mine)

They also point out: "Often the men who spoke were those - clergymen for instance - whose status, function, and predilections ensured that they would have least to do with women and who imagined them from a distance and with a certain dread, at once drawn to and frightened by this indispensable yet unruly Other. 'What exactly is a woman?' they asked."

It was impossible, disintegrating, Casagrande said, "to support a liturgy that exalted a masculine God image and encouraged women to lead limited, subordinated, clerically-defined lives."

Study of the 13th, 14th and 15th centuries reveals how the new ethics of marriage slowly emerged from the incessant need for the obedience, temperance, chastity, and silence of women. But still, society as a whole accepted that women by themselves were deemed incapable of controlling their desires or regulating their relations with others. They still needed fathers or husbands to control them.

Around the 14th century in her book, *The City of Ladies,* Christine de Pison writes: "I despaired that God caused me to be born in a female body." She blamed God for this misfortune that she believed encompassed all her sex, "as if nature had given birth to monsters." When she went on to dissect the roots of her misery, she came to blame her misfortune on a "series of authorities." Who were these "authorities" I ask? As Belknap says in *A History of Women,* "The written word was controlled by the clergy, men of the cloth and of the church, who controlled the flow of knowledge and determined how people conceived of women, or rather woman. Much of our evidence about medieval women derives from the fantasies, certaintics and doubts of the clergy."

It appears to me that Aristotle, Socrates, and Plato before him, were some of these authorities who passed belief on to the Jewish, Muslim, and Christian Church. It was men—men of the church—who were educated and often the ones who published as well as spoke on such things from the pulpit. Men were "the authorities." They were who stood in the pulpits, sat as judges, educated others, and recorded history. Men from the same bolt of cloth, who describe women pitifully inadequate, put the Bible together. Men wrote, interpreted, and translated the Bible.

Clergy write with the authority of God, do they not? God said it, it must be true. For the first fifty years of my life, though I had female teachers, what I was taught and what I accepted as truth came from men—my religious beliefs, my beliefs about history, and my beliefs of who I am.

My beliefs came primarily from the Seventh-day Adventist Church, and though the church purported a female prophet, men interpreted "the word of God," and interpreted her words for the Church.

Belknap also wrote, "......occasionally they (women) rejected those images (by men) that men held up for them to see. Occasionally they rejected those images, but inevitably the imposed images inscribed themselves in women's very flesh and shaped their lives." *Yes, pervasively and subliminally it has happened to me and every woman I know.*

I found it very difficult to let go of what I had been taught within the Church. Searching and accepting new theology was a heart-wrenching experience. Moving beyond theology, was even more so. The fact that I was disgruntled with the power of men within the Church did not make it easier.

Years ago, a husband of a friend, employed by the Seventh-day Adventist Church, was called into his supervisor's office and told he must get his wife "under control." She was wearing jewelry, and this was unacceptable to the standards and doctrines of the Church. I know of other incidents when Church issues with women were discussed and processed with husbands, instead of the women involved. Sadly, frustratingly, this tells me that the influence of history still reigns.

I do not remember any female in my life even occasionally questioning the images given by the Church regarding the status of men and who God is. Yet, I've questioned—haven't been able to stop questioning. I've tried to shake female relatives and friends into questioning and looking at this belief system that perpetuates the notion the female is second class. I have had little success. No relative or Church acquaintance has joined me in this search.

Has the status of women changed from the ancient times I've described? Yes, women have fought for rights and won them. But as Belknap has said, "these messages are inscribed upon the female psyche." It was there for my generation, it was there for my daughters, and it is there for my granddaughters. Not as evident, not as intrusive, but still subversive. It permeates our culture at a level that continues to affect the self-worth of many young women today. I have found it rare in the dormitories and treatment centers in which I have served, to find a young woman in her teens with a self-worth that defies these messages.

I don't want the young women of today to forget how far we, as women, have come nor what it has taken for us to get where we are today. But more than this, I want women to be willing and take the risk of looking at the male God many of us have accepted, and ask: "Where is Mother?"

Isabel Allende in *The Sum of our Days*, says: "Many women of my generation have had to invent a spirituality that fits us, and if you had lived longer, maybe you would have done the same, for the patriarchal gods are definitely not suitable for us: they make us pay for the temptations and sins of men. Why are they so afraid of us? I like the idea of an inclusive and maternal divinity connected with nature, synonymous with life, and eternal process of renovation and evolution."

I like this description of God as Goddess, but it does not fully answer for me who God is. I still search for understanding as to why most of the Christian Churches, and readers of the Bible just simply accept God as male. Maybe if I understand this, I will be satisfied enough to stop searching.

I believe prejudicial statements permeate the fabric of who we are as women, at an indistinguishable level. I believe a form of misogyny still permeates the churches—shown by many denominations' reluctance to ordain women. And further reiterated from the pulpit of many churches by the expression that man is the head of the home. It is reflected in the rap music of the ghetto and the subjection of the board room. It is prevalent in the records of spousal abuse and rape in the court systems of this nation.

I believe most of all we must look deeply into "where is our Mother God?" *How can the Mother aspect of God be brought to the Christian Church today?*

28

THE MOVE FROM California to Colorado in 1999 had its ups and its downs. To start with, we left one family and moved closer to another. As described earlier, it was difficult to leave Brenda, Taylor, and Colton. I had been involved with their lives as a caretaker. A role difficult for me to walk away from. We now lived close to Scott and family. Back to the days of sunshine that I had missed. Our family was spread across the country, with Trudy and family in Indiana, Kim and family in Arizona, Lori and family in Washington, Brenda and family in California, and Scott and Juliette with us in Colorado. Within two years, Trudy, having divorced, moved to Colorado with Brendan, leaving her oldest son, Erik in Indiana. Kim and Philip also joined us in Colorado with Laurel and Kara. Having family around us was delightful. We were able to get together for holidays and birthdays, and welcome together Blake, Ashton, and Sienna as they were born to Scott and Juliette. The cousins loved getting together. My greatest joy was when all my family was together. I never dreamed this gathering would ever cease— that joy could be taken out of my life. That, too, caused by the men in our lives.

Our family grew in numbers and in years. We traveled back and forth across the United States for graduations, birthdays, presentations, school plays, and just to be together. Our family was knit, supportive, and loving.

We bought a thirty-five acre plot of land in the foothills of the Rocky Mountains with a beautiful brick house and another brick building Loren was able to use for his Colorado office. We added a loafing shed and fencing to accommodate three horses. A dream-come-true for me, the horse lover. The group home business flourished. I focused on home and family. We traveled, like the trip to Bangladesh, and then a month in Europe visiting France, Italy, Greece, Greek Isles, Slovenia, Slovakia, Germany, Austria, Turkey, and a wedding in Croatia. Friends invited us on this trip and paid for much of it. When the plan was made, business was doing well. By the time of the trip we were stressed, financially and emotionally.

California was having a difficult time paying their bills and started giving IOUs instead of checks. One of the managers had made a huge mistake by not reporting abuse in one of the houses and caused a hold on all intakes. Thus a sixty thousand dollars a month loss. Colorado was taking a closer look at the financing of group homes and cutting their budget that put residential treatment facilities, like ours, out of business.

We had a contract on the sale of ten acres of our thirty-five and a contract on land up in the mountains to build a dream house. We had thought we could pay for the European trip from the money of the ten acre sale. The sale was postponed. Friends encouraged us to go on the trip regardless. Since the closing date was set after our return, we went. We came back from the month long vacation to discover the sale was dead and contract broken. We couldn't afford a lawyer.

Then the proverbial shoe dropped when it was discovered that the Chief Financial Officer had embezzled funds and hid the fact that he was not paying the payroll taxes. Devastation! There was no mercy for unpaid payroll taxes. Within days the business financial situation was dire. Money was borrowed against our property for the business. Money was borrowed from friends. All to salvage our company to which we had given our lives. We struggled, we fought - with the IRS and with each other. I went back into the office to work with Scott who was at this point president of the company and trying his best to hold it together.

Sitting in the office one afternoon I received a phone call from the owner of one of the houses the company rented in California. He was furious, having just discovered that the house was empty and filthy. He had not received a notice and had not been paid rent. I, too, was infuriated. I had had enough. Nothing was working. I could not keep up with the falling cards as they were batted around back and forth from and to California. I picked up a piece of paper, wrote a note addressed to Scott and Loren, "I am done. I am not coming back into this office again. Do not talk to me about business."

My world fell apart and I could not stop it. I was devastated. I was angry. Infact, more furious, more heart broken, more confused, more everything than the last time six years before when I had stepped away from partnership with Loren in business.

I didn't feel like a partner. He talked like I was his partner. He expressed his appreciation and endearment of me, but I never felt listened to. Others, all men, had more influence on his decisions, our decisions, than I did. This time Scott was included in that feeling experienced as fact. I did not feel that I had any influence with his decisions either. I felt disrespected and disallowed by both of them. By all men. My value was second to the men in their lives regardless of titles. All those making the decisions were men. Men deciding what was best for everyone - including me. I truly had had enough.

At home when Loren approached me with the note I had left in the office, I would not talk about business. I said, "I am moving to the mountains. I will find an apartment up there."

He asked, "What does that say about me?"

I said, "It says whatever you want it to. You can come with me or not. It's up to you. Right now, I really don't care." And I didn't. I only knew I had to protect myself somehow from the brokenness around me. I felt broken. It wouldn't be the last time.

We had no income. Again! The bank took the house and the cars. My horses were given away or sold. Even the loafing shed had been torn down and sold to another. This beautiful place, with all the beauty I had brought around and into it, was no longer mine. We had to move.

The Saturday after my declaration of moving to the mountains, Loren and I sat on lawn chairs, on an island in the middle of a creek in the mountains and talked it out. I was honest about all my feelings and he accepted them, and encouraged me to not give up on us. We found a condo to rent, sold everything we could sell and moved up to the mountains. Not up in stature, not up in prosperity. Just up the mountain. It would be years before we walked up the mountain of debt.

Loren continued his pursuit of reestabiling treatment centers. This time with the emphasis on sexually abused teen girls. We found in the group home business that over ninety percent of the adjudicated or foster care girls coming into the program had been sexually abused. We believed the emphasis in the program needed to be on healing and not on correction of behavior as it had been previously.

His first pursuit to reestablish was in Michigan. We made the trip together. He to do business, and I to visit family. After a few days visiting, I returned home and he stayed to try and bring fruition to his pursuits. I arrived home late at night and went straight to bed. While unpacking late the next morning the telephone rang.

I was surprised and immediately anxious as it was Scott. "What's up Scott?"

"Well, Dad isn't feeling good so we are going to take him to a hospital."

My response, "What do you mean, 'not feeling good?'" led into his attempted sharing of the circumstances without scaring me. Well, it's probably his diabetes, but maybe a heart attack." He went on to say that he would call me back when they knew for sure.

I said, "Scott, don't beat around the bush with me. You tell me the truth of what is happening."

He called back within minutes to tell me that Loren had been taken to a local hospital, and that it was determined it was a heart attack. "I will keep you in touch," were more words.

I walked the floor in tears, distress and fear, phone in hand. The next call from Scott told me that Loren was being rushed by ambulance instead of helicopter, due to bad weather, to Fort Wayne, Indiana. All I could think of was that I had to get to him.

My anxiety was too high to focus on what it would take to make arrangements, so I called Trudy who lived near the airport, "Loren's had a heart attack. I need to get to Fort Wayne as soon as possible. Can you get me a ticket and take me to the airport when I get down there?"

Of course, she said, "Yes, I will take care of it."

I flew into Indianapolis, Indiana, and Trudy's ex-husband, Bob, picked me up and transported me to Fort Wayne. What a blessing that was.

I arrived in Loren's hospital room at two-thirty in the morning—less than forty-eight hours since leaving Michigan. When Loren opened up his eyes, moments after my entrance into his room restraining tears, being brave, I asked, "You are staying, aren't you?"

He knew what I meant, and replied, "I am planning to." While I was traveling toward him, the doctors had determined that he needed open heart surgery to insert six by-passes for his arteries. All were plugged.

The next morning I walked into the financial office of the hospital, asked to speak to someone who was responsible for billing. I wanted so much to be brave - to know that all was well. But just weeks before we had lost our business, our house, our cars, and any security. When I opened my mouth to tell this to the women sitting behind the desk, I broke down in tears. My words included, "We have nothing, no income, no insurance, no way to pay this bill." Seeing my distress, she asked no further questions than what was necessary, and assured me that the surgery would be done. She told me there were other ways the bill would be paid. I was relieved with this assurance, though later we would be sued for the $140,000 bill and have to file for bankruptcy. Since we lived in Colorado, Indiana's medicaid would not pay the bill. Since the surgery was done in Indiana, Colorado medicaid would not pay the bill.

The fear of how we would move forward after the surgery was tucked away. His life, his health was most important. I knew we would survive this too. We'd survived so many other losses, changes, and moves. *We'll survive this too.*

We needed income. I went to work. First, as a hotel maid and later as head of the janitorial services for a senior living complex. I did not want managerial responsibilities so did not search for employment that would require administration. Though the work was hard physically, I enjoyed the independence it allowed. I have always been hands on. As a dean, I often cleaned the dormitories myself, and though I was administrator in our group homes, I cleaned the house whenever taking a shift of duty.

Loren recovered quickly. Within a couple of weeks, he was back again planning how to move forward with plans of treatment centers and group homes.

The condo we returned to after Loren's surgery, had a small closet-like room that I claimed as mine, and had carried in my desk, my collection of angels, my bookcase and books. Besides working at the motel, I ignored the rest of the world and continued my search for the Mother. I knew there had to be a Mother in the Godhead. I knew I was not a second class citizen. I just felt like one at the time. I didn't know why I could not stop reading and settle into what I knew at that moment. I had to search for more. I needed to understand.

29

A FEW YEARS IN my twenties, when I voted for President of the United States, I voted straight Republican ticket. This act was passed down to me from my mother, and to her from her father. Unlike my sister, Susan, who served as Township clerk for over thirty years, I did not become involved in politics at any level. I was involved in the Church, and Church politics only. But in 2008 the first woman was running for president and I took notice.

The first time I heard Sara Palin speak, I said out loud, "Oh my gosh, she sounds just like one of my cousins." *The truth of the matter is that she actually sounds like me, thirty years ago. If she had run for office then, I would have voted for her.* A Mother of four, I too, focused on the religious right. I voted Republican. I was a strong, Bible-thumping Christian with the "truth" on my side. I could shoot a gun, target shot rifles many times with Dad and uncles. I climbed within the arena I served (the Church) by my good looks and out-going personality. Without a college degree, I too, moved upward in administration, and climbed the ladder of success. I advocated for women leadership and spoke up to the men in charge when I disagreed. I also thought I had to be tough. *Don't show weakness or anything that could be portrayed as weakness—like tears. Show the men you are capable.*

I gave up voting, early on, for a political system I could not consciously support. Neither party had leaders I could ethically support. I know - heard it many times - I should vote for the best of two so I don't give a vote by not voting. I was focused on other things. Could not bring myself to focus on politics, and could no longer just vote down party lines. I accept the accusations of failure to support those women who fought for women's right to vote. But there you go again: "fought."

Less than one hundred years ago, not until 1920, women were granted the right to go to the polls and vote. The women who picketed the White House, carrying signs asking for the vote, were jailed. Thirty-three, wrongly convicted of "obstructing sidewalk traffic," were beaten by forty prison guards wielding clubs and their warden's blessing. Lucy Burns was chained by her hands to cell bars above her head and left hanging for the night, bleeding and gasping for air. Dora Lewis was hurled into a dark cell, smashing her head against an iron bed and knocking her out cold. All because they wanted to vote! So, we women owe it to these women to strive to keep women's rights alive. But do we have to fight to do it?

In 1984, new ground was broken for women in the United States when Mondale chose Geraldine Ferraro as a running mate—the first woman in history to be on a major-party ticket. I didn't even know this at the time, showing how little I was aware politically. It was new ground, but not what I'd call a major break-through. It was twenty-four years later before we experienced another. *Why did it take so long?*

In 2008, women friends of mine rejoiced in the female good fortune, while I could not. I felt that neither candidate, Hillary Clinton running for president, nor Sarah Palin, running for vice-president, represented me or what I believe femaleness represents. One a beauty queen who handles a gun as well as a man, and one who has allowed herself to be used and abused by a husband and a political party. Each demonstrates her savvy with evasiveness and deceit.

My sense is that both women demonstrate they have the male qualities believed necessary to fill the role of president. But I also perceived the lack of the female qualities necessary to fill the role of president as a balanced individual to bring both masculine and feminine qualities to the office.

A NewsBank article of June 21, 2010, states that Palin is seen by some as, "a modern-day prophet, preaching God, flag, and family—while remaking the religious right in her own image." The article says that the Christian right is a women's movement, and Sarah its Jerry Falwell. The writer of the article, Lisa Miller, says "a certain kind of conservative Christian woman worships her." And she says that, "These Christians seek a power that's pragmatic, which means formally acquiescing to male authority and conservative theology, even as they assume increasingly visible roles in their families, their churches, their communities and the world."

Also in 2010, Lisa Miller wrote another article describing women and politics. Following Palin's description of herself being a "mama bear," Lisa describes in her article *The Bear Truth*, three other female politicians as "Mama Grizzlies." This new crop of religious, conservative women is out to protect their children. This is good, right? Or not?

While these Mama Bears declare that they are out to protect their young and that government needs to get out of the way, their records show that they do not always support issues that others say are good for children. Like voting "no" on a domestic-violence bill designed to improve restraining orders; voting "no" on a measure that would create a program for at-risk kindergarten kids; voting "no" on a bill that would give parents paid parental leave.

The statements I am most concerned about from some of these women are those that support war, or describe placing someone or some group in "cross-hairs." And the Twitter message of "Don't Retreat, Instead—RELOAD!" as Palin did. Or like Bachmann, the pro-life, pro-Creationist, who not only voted for the war in Iraq, but stated that if made president she would reinstate water-boarding used in questioning terrorists. In my estimation, these are masculine views, and part of a patriarchal belief system that perpetuates the lack of value in the feminine.

I believe that the female energy of nurture and intuition balances the male energy of dominance and cognition. The feminine energy – whether in man or woman – has qualities of passivity with strength, enhanced by the gift of intuition. Women contribute creativity, sensitivity and perspective to the male personality. All persons have male energy and female energy. When these energies are in balance they create the healthiest functioning being possible.

Nancy Pelosi, first female Speaker of the House, writes in her book *Know Your Power,* that while studying about America's Founding Fathers, she learned about the qualities of leadership and that "A President's vision and judgment enable him or her to act intuitively to make the right decision." She goes on to say, "When we were studying these aspects of leadership, I couldn't help think about how women were especially blessed with heightened intuition to decide or to advise." This will be true if the woman blessed with intuition uses it for the good of all, and not for power of party or self. It's questionable how Polosi, herself, has used such a gift.

I perceive that when a woman recognizes the strengths in her gentle nurturing aspects she becomes what every child (and country) needs. These qualities, versus the qualities described by Mama Bears, are qualities that will enhance the service of presidency whether in a male or a female. *The meek shall inherit the earth! Strength in gentleness versus brashness.*

I was reminded of the strength that comes with feminine qualities when I read the book *Gabby.* Gabrielle Gifford and her husband, Mark Kelly, wrote the book as Gabrielle (Gabby) was recovering from gunshot wounds to her head from an assassin's bullets.

A statement Mark makes in the book about Gabby delighted me, "She looked forward to redoubling her commitment to serving her constituents in southeastern Arizona, including those who didn't like her or her positions. 'I represent them, too,' she said." A female politician talking about "liking" instead of "fighting"!

He also quoted her as saying: "we cannot succumb to partisan bickering. The challenges—and the cost of failure—are too great." Speaking of Gabby, her sister says, "Most human beings care about a relatively small group of people. They care about their family, their friends, their neighbors, some of the people they work with. Maybe that adds up to fifty people. Gabby's number is way past 50. Her number is in the hundreds of thousands—or the millions. I started realizing it when we were kids. That makes her different from the rest of us." *How refreshingly different! My kind of politician.*

In philosophical discussion about the meaning of life, Gabby is quoted as saying, "We are here to care for each other." Not to protect as a grizzly with claws that ravage, but to care. I'm impressed that Gabby has found balance in the masculine and feminine qualities. *This balance in a person could bring it to the political system? What will it take to bring balance to the divisive, masculine system of our government?*

According to Elizabeth Sandford's 1842 epistle titled, *Woman, In Her Social and Domestic Character,* society received its "balance and its tone" from women. "She may be here a corrective of what is wrong, a moderator of what is unruly, a restraint on what is indecorous," Sandford asserted. "Her presence will be a pledge against impropriety and excess, a check on vice, and a protection to virtue." Nineteenth century statements, and yet so true, and yet unheard in a society that puts the word "fight" before every cause! These statements have been made for many years and by many others. When will we see the results?

The window I looked through as a child brought me to the belief that men were built to be in charge and women were not. My mother's response to women in charge or running for office was judgmental, "who does she think she is?"

I would like to support a woman for president. But more than a woman for president, I support the balanced qualities of male and female in whoever is president. I look forward to the day when a woman runs for President without fighting but caring. *Is this possible? Am I being foolish to believe it is possible? Am I guilty for not voting because I don't see these qualities and can't or won't support the lack of them*

30

A COUPLE YEARS INTO my janitorial employment, my brother, Lewis, asked me to become the president of his geological consulting company located in California. Though living in Colorado, being President of the company in California was possible due to the technology that kept me connected with the office. I visited the office as often as possible to meet with staff, and inspect operations.

On one of my monthly trips to California, the following experience spread my belief of love needing to be inclusive. I was only in the office ten minutes when Donna said to me, "Ginger is really anxious and needs to see you right away. See her now, and we'll go over things later."

I knocked on the side of Ginger's office door and entered with a smile of reassurance. "You wanted to see me?" I asked.

She swirled her chair away from her desk to face me as tears sprang to her eyes with a nod of her head. "I really need to talk to you but…..but I'm not sure how to start."

"Ginger, I am willing to hear anything you have to say. You are an employee I value, and want to help in any way I can. Please, I can tell you are hurting, trust me with what you have to share," was my attempt to put her at ease and encourage her to open up.

She began, "I've been having some real issues like, well, like puberty.

I'm thirty-one years old, and shouldn't be having any of these symptoms. So I went to the doctor and my doctor couldn't find what was wrong so he sent me to an endocrinologist."

Stumbling through phrases, she tried to explain in language I could understand, what the doctor had told her. "He said my testosterone was off the charts, and he didn't understand this. So he ordered more tests to find out why."

Ginger spent the next half hour telling me her story between bouts of emotion. After the many tests that included x-rays and a MRI, the doctor told her in medical terms that she was more male than female—that she had no vagina, and they found testicles within her body.

She continued to express her dismay, "I've always *felt* like a boy. I did all the things boys do, I liked all the things boys do like tractors, trucks, dirt." She had emulated her father and resented her mother's insistence she dress and act like a girl. "When my breasts started developing, I took a knife and tried to scrape them off. I hated them," she said.

"Ginger, I am so sorry you are hurting. What did the doctor say caused these feelings and the mix-up in your body?" I encouraged, with compassion.

"Well he didn't know what had caused it, but said I needed to ask my parents about my birth." Her parents had been unaware of her recent struggles and did not know she had appointments with a doctor. She approached them at their next visit. After explaining the results of her recent medical exams she asked, "Do you know what happened to me?"

Her parents, with mom doing most of the talking, told an amazing story that Ginger had never heard. She had been a twin. When one twin aborted, her mother was given a drug to keep the remaining fetus.

"The drug I was given is not used anymore because it disrupts the sex development of a baby, and that is what happened to me," she said. Going on, she described what her parents told her. When she was born, the doctors came to her parents to report the sexual mix-up in their child and asked, "Did you want a girl or boy?"

"My parents told the doctor that they wanted a girl, and since the doctors didn't know for sure what I was, they made me a girl. I don't feel like a girl. I am stuck in a girl's body," came out slow and with rancor.

I could feel her agony. The same agony I had heard through the years from those discovering and afraid that they were gay. She made the statement, "It's not like feeling gay. I feel masculine. I *feel,*" said very strongly, "like a man."

Through the lump in my throat I asked, "Ginger, what are you planning to do with this information?"

She lifted her eyes to mine and said, "I don't want to lose my job. I love it here."

"But why do you think you will lose your job?" I questioned.

She stated, "Because of what I might do." More tears, more sighs, and then, "I know your brother is very conservative, and I'm afraid he won't let me stay if I do what I feel like doing."

Her fears were real and justified. Lewis had picked me up at the airport and during the thirty-minute drive to the office, he had expounded on his disappointment in Ginger. He stated with disgust in his voice, "She is starting to look like a guy. She's dressing more like it all the time." He ended his diatribe with, "I'm afraid she might be gay."

I responded only with, "Really?" Going through my head were thoughts of how differently my brother and I relate to situations such as this. His conservatism concerned me, and I wanted to point out the judgment in his voice. But our discussions regarding his beliefs usually led to arguments and caused distance between us. I didn't want that during this trip when I was staying at his house. I just listened and contemplated: *This must be why Donna said I needed to see Ginger when I got to the office. I will deal with what Ginger has to say, and then communicate with Lewis.*

Now I knew what I was to deal with—it was big and painful. I did not mention to Ginger what Lewis had said, or that we had a conversation about her just moments ago. Intentionally looking into her eyes I asked, "What do you mean when you say you could lose your job over what you might do?"

"I can go through some surgeries like removing my breasts and some hormone shots and I can be male. I just don't know. I don't know if I should." Her family was not supportive of her making the change. She was a practicing Christian and so was her family. While they couldn't say she was going against God because of the parental choice that made her female, they felt it was "wrong." Ginger herself struggled with the right and wrong of it—the choice made and the choice to be made.

Returning to the issue of Lewis' conservatism, I said, "First of all, Ginger, I do the hiring and firing around here and I will not fire you. Secondly, if we fired you for the reason of a sex change, you could sue us."

Then I said, "Yes, Lewis is very conservative and definitely opposed to anything that looks like homosexuality, but he has a big heart. I believe you and I should share your story with him. I think his heart will win out."

Trying to remain professional with an employee, yet compassionate, I rose from my chair and facing Ginger asked, "Can I give you a hug?" Her "yes" mixed with more emotion allowed me to reassure with touch what words couldn't portray. "So if I talk with him first and prepare him for your story, will you go with me and tell him what you are going through?"

Hopeful with the statements I made, she said, "Yes, I'll try, but it'll be hard."

"I know, I know. But we can do it. We have to do it. I am here for you and we can get through this," I said as I left her office.

Forty-five minutes later after a short conversation with Lewis explaining to him that Ginger had something serious to talk with him about, and asking that he please listen to her with his heart, I opened his office door to Ginger's knock. I reassured her with a smile and told her, "It is safe for you to tell Lewis your story."

She started the story the same she had with me, explaining the medical issues she had been having. Halfway through her story, as tears slipped down her cheeks, I looked at Lewis and saw tears standing in his eyes.

When she completed the story and looked directly at Lewis indicating she was through, he wiped tears that had flowed down his cheeks and said, "Whatever you decide to do, I support you. We need never talk of this again unless you want to and I will be here for you." And then, "If anyone in this office ever gives you any problems, come to me, and I will deal with it. You have my support."

At that moment I was more proud of my brother than any other time in our lives—even more pride than when he received his doctorate degree. His heart had won over his head. He "heard" someone's pain and could not judge the actions.

Had Ginger not shared her story but moved ahead with her desires to live the male life, Lewis would certainly have condemned her and probably tried to get me to fire her. She did make the sex change, and in the office paper-work we terminated Ginger and hired Levi. He is very happy and much, much more peaceful, as well as healthy. He and Lewis work together as two men.

My brother's conservatism, as with many others I know and relate with, comes with a lot of judgment. A couple of years before this incident he had called me to complain about an experience he had just had. He and his wife accepted a three-year-old boy and his sister of eight months, into their home as foster children with consideration for adoption. They had adopted two brothers a few years before, now aged seven and six, and they had a younger biological daughter, three years old. Their communication had been that these two children would round out their family.

Lewis' call was to tell me that they had decided to return the children. "They are too difficult and won't work out. We took the kids back to the social worker's office to leave them with their new adoptive parents," he told me. And then explained, disgustedly, how when he and Tami got to the office, there were two men in the office with the social worker.

"I naturally thought one of them must be the father and the other another social worker. So when they were introduced, I asked which one was the father, and was informed that *they* were the parents."

He went on to tell me how Tami broke down crying because she had told the children they would have a new mommy who would love them even more than her. The explanation from one of the men that his mother was going to be very involved in the children's lives relieved Tami, but did not absolve Lewis' anger, and he walked out of the office.

My response to his diatribe was to tell him that I did not disapprove of gay men adopting children - even girls - if they were going to be loving parents. I said, "Your fear of those men abusing this girl or her brother, is unfounded. There are far more cases of heterosexual males sexually abusing children than there are of homosexual males." "Furthermore," I told him, "You did not love those kids, and if these men love and adore them they are going to have a better life than being with parents who can't love them unconditionally." I believed that Lewis and Tami were abusive with the kids—to the point of his calling the boy "a son-of-a-bitch," and Tami leaving the girl in her crib for hours. I had been distressed about their possible adoption.

Years of hearing agonizing stories from students who were afraid they were gay had convinced me that homosexuality is not a choice. How could it be a sin? I know the Bible verses I am often pointed to when I make these statements. But believing homosexuality is a sin now conflicted with my stronger belief that God is love, and that a loving God would not create a human being in an unchangeable sinful state. I was made aware of those who seriously, genuinely tried to change and could not.

Like my friend's son, Dorian, who upon returning from a year of college in England, had announced he was gay. My friend told me, "He was brain-washed over there and fell in with friends who are homosexuals."

She explained to me that they sent him to a camp in the south that would rid him of these beliefs. She said he was now home from the camp and dating girls so they were sure God had "cured" him.

While I listened to my friend's relief, I thought: *You will make sure that he marries a woman and has children and then some day he will hurt them all by "coming out."* I was remembering the young woman who came go my office at college hurt and distressed regarding her father who had been an evangelist for the Church, and recently announced he was gay. I didn't express what I was thinking, but said, "Betty, your son is a very loving and caring young man. Why would he choose this way of being and hurt his family?" She did not answer and changed the subject. A couple years later a mutual friend distastefully informed me that Betty's son was now living "in sin" with another man. I only nodded and said, "I'm not surprised." I thought: *Thankfully, he did not take his parents' and Churches' beliefs to heart, and inflict pain upon a family that he did not truly want.*

Another friend in his fifties spent thirty years faithfully serving the Christian church with his wife as music ministers. They met in college and became close friends. Craig, committed to God, shared his fear of being homosexual with Mindy. They sought counseling from a minister before their engagement to marry. The minister assured them that God would change Craig. They married, birthed two children, and were successful in the ministry they had committed to. But Craig, after years of praying, begging, and believing in change, became suicidal.

He was surrendered to change, begged for change, and yet it did not happen. He loved Mindy, she was his best friend, but he came to the conclusion that he could not be who he really was and stay married to her. Craig was relieved and encouraged with our words of understanding and support, but words did not give him the courage to continue to live his life "a lie," as he described it. More than anyone else I had listened to, I was convinced that Craig was a committed Christian surrendered to God's will in his life. My heart ached for him as it does for others who face this condition as Christians, and receive only condemnation. Craig and Mindy divorced. Now a family is torn apart and all question God's unwillingness or inability to make the change they needed in their lives.

Another friend, Barbie, is a delightful, loving care-taker who served a church for years as a Christian counselor, knowing that she was gay. Married and divorced, she lived the straight life until she fell in love with a female parishioner, and for the sake of sanity and the relationship, "came out" to the pastor of the church she served. She was asked to leave her position as counselor with the church, and left the church as a member. She did not leave God. Her commitment to Christianity remains, but so does the pain of the rejection.

In *Christianity, Social Tolerance, and Homosexuality*, John Boswell states that the historical breadth and revolutionary study of the history of attitudes toward homosexuality challenges preconceptions the Christian church has proposed. He reports that the people of Sodom were destroyed because they forsook the covenant which was about relationship—hospitality issue, faith issue, not a sexual orientation issue. Further he reiterates, as others with degrees in biblical studies like my friend Barbara have, that here is no biblical instruction for or against the marriage of same-sex individuals. *Why do Christians make such an issue of other's sex lives? Why is what we don't understand, so maligned?*

My brother and sister also oppose abortion. This is another issue I was forced to wrestle with as I counseled students. However, another experience of my brother's brought it closer for introspection. Unable to get pregnant, he and Tami decided to participate in vitro fertilization. Tami's eggs were impregnated by Lewis' sperm in a test tube and implanted within the womb. Three impregnated eggs became triplets. Joy was supplanted with sorrow when at five months all three babies were born dead due to infection within the womb. Months later another group of fertilized eggs were implanted. One egg survived producing a baby girl. Stepanie, the baby girl born healthy and darling, was three years old when they talked of having another child. Did they want to have more children? What were they to do with the eggs that were left?

They did not have another child, and I don't know what they did with the eggs left over. I didn't ask.

If a baby is produced by a sperm impregnating an egg, aren't babies being killed when a number are implanted only expecting one, two, or maybe three to survive? What about destroying the eggs that aren't used? Is that murder—as abortion is called—by anti-abortion groups?

Or, what if the sperm, impregnating the egg, is only producing a vehicle for a Being to inhabit while on earth? What if destroying the body is not destroying a baby, or a Being? What if we are eternal spirits that cannot be destroyed?

31

I LEFT THE INDIANA border under steel grey skies and drove north through the middle of the mitten of Michigan. Tomorrow would be Thanksgiving. I had traveled from Colorado under continual dreary skies to spend the holiday with family. Eighteen months had passed since I visited my mother who resided in an assisted living home in the town where she had lived in or near, all of her life.

She did not recognize me the last time I visited. Communication other than cards I sent her had been non-existent, she was not communicating. I hoped for recognition this time. She sometimes recognized her sister and even chatted. Maybe, just maybe, she would know me.

It was late afternoon when I walked up to the door of Mom's residence. Through the window, I saw the only person visible, slumped in a chair, asleep. Was this her? Yes, it must be her. But so diminutive? She had always carried more weight than needed and at the height of five foot three, was considered plump. Now she appeared tiny.

I paused at the door to take a breath of resignation. I was okay with Mom not recognizing me. Or was I?

No knock was required to come into the common room, so I entered, walked across the room and knelt before her. I touched her knee and spoke quietly, "Mom. Mom." No response. No movement. Only her breath indicated life.

I remained there, kneeling and looking at the face I barely recognized as my mother's. She no longer wore glasses. She no longer read. Nor did she care about what was across the room or out the window. Life was over for her. Or was it? Would she awake with recognition? I hesitated to awaken her. Now I could wish. In minutes I would know.

I longed to have her know me, to be able to speak with recognition one more time. I still had questions to ask and things to tell her. I wanted to heal the past for her and for me. *Was this to be?*

The room was suddenly filled with the yapping of a Chihuahua. I had been discovered and soon two caretakers entered the room. The yapping had not awakened Mom so one of the caretakers more aggressively touched her saying, "Look, Mildred, Paula's here. Wake up Mildred, see Paula is here." Mom opened her eyes. She saw me. She burst forth with a high pitched sound like the whine of a motor stuck on start.

Still on knees, I backed away as Shelley, the owner of this home, said, "It's her way of crying." No tears appeared. Only a blank stare accompanied the whine. There was no light of recognition, I wanted to believe she cried because she recognized me and that tears of joy would soon form. They did not.

The caretakers left us as I remained kneeling before her. The whine soon stopped but she continued to stare into my face with no movement or hint of recognition. The stare remained blank like an empty page awaiting the pen. I tried to write upon the blankness with comments of, "I love you, Mom. I miss you." With a smile on my face but pain in my heart, I tried to awaken her to who I was, "It's your daughter, Mom. I am Paula."

I talked about family, "You have seven grandchildren. And now you have fourteen great grandchildren."

Nothing I said brought any response until the dog returned, yapping. Her brow knitted in a frown and then relaxed when the dog left. There was someone in there. She responded to something she did not like. I said, "You don't like the dog, do you?" She frowned again, brow deeply knit.

She could be awakened by what she did not like and respond to it, if only with a frown. This brought evidence to her thought processes. Why couldn't she respond to the pleasure of seeing me? Was it not pleasurable? At least it was tolerable, for she gave no sign of displeasure as she looked upon my face.

Mom had always responded more to displeasure than pleasure. She spoke often and easily about anything that she did not like. This had been her focus in life. She never said, "I love you," until I was thirty-five years old and pointed out this fact to her. She had stumbled through the first time, and with my urging, said, "Of course, I love you." From then on, she repeated, "I love you," when we hung up from calls I made to her, always with a catch in her voice.

The recognition of displeasure on her face drove home more now than ever before, her inability to see the joy in life. Any pain of living, and especially the pain of Dad's death, was unexpressed. Her refusal to talk of pain or acknowledge other than displeasure or anger left her a hollow person unable to recognize a reason for joy. I tried through the years to get her to talk about Dad but she would tear up and refuse to talk. Always saying, "I don't want to talk about it."

Sadness seeped into me. Sadness for her. Sadness because the things that could prick the bubble of pain in her life, she no longer recognized.

Twenty-four hours later after Thanksgiving dinner, I crouched down before her again and put my arms around her to say goodbye. As I held her in my arms, tears slid down my cheeks and I stifled a sob. Very slowly, she raised her right arm and put it around me. It was a response I did not expect. I remember no other time that my mother gave me comfort within her arms.

The last time I saw Mom, she lay in bed in the same assisted living home. I received a call the day before that she was dying. Loren and I drove through the night from Colorado to Michigan to be with her. Shelley awaited our arrival with lights on in the early morning hours. She left the room for needed sleep and I climbed in to lay next to Mom. She was unrecognizable. Barely breathing. I spoke softly and as lovingly as my voice could be, "Mom, I am here." I continued with, "It's okay, Mom. It's okay to leave. You're safe." It felt like she was hanging on. *Hanging on to what?*

Then I remembered how she had told me, "Your dad hung on and would not let go. He was waiting for you to come." I knew she was waiting for Lewis. Of course! He was her favorite. He had always protected her. And she, him. He never complained about or to Mom. Susan and I did. Often. She was waiting for her protector.

I next said, "Mom don't wait for Lewis. He's always late. You know that. Don't wait for him. It's okay to go." Lewis had always been late to family events. Sometimes he was days late. On one of the last Christmases we had together, his nieces hid his gifts because he was two days later than expected. Mom was very upset that they would do that to their Uncle, even if done in fun.

Susan had relayed the message to me earlier that Lewis was on his way, but I knew it could be days before he arrived. I believed he did not want to be there at Mom's passing. He was afraid of his own emotions. I kept encouraging, "Mom, it's okay to leave." After a few hours of sleep, Shelley returned to Mom's room and bid me to go get some sleep. Three hours later, she called to say that Mom had "let go."

Mom's death had nowhere near the emotion for me as Dad's had. Probably because Dad died while much younger and I had already said goodbye to Mom many times while she lingered in the assisted living home with no true living. I was ready for her passing. I had not been ready for Dad's until the very end when I asked God to take him from the pain. Mom had no pain. Her birth certificate states: failure to thrive. She did not want to live. She had shut herself off from living. It was by our efforts and prodding that she lived as long as she did after Dad's passing. He was her life.

Three days later I met with family and friends in the afternoon for a service that we, my siblings and I, arranged in order to honor the life of our mother. After the service our cousins were invited to my sister's home to visit with my brother and I who lived in other states.

During the two days after Mom's passing, and before the funeral, I spent time with cousins to talk to them about their mothers. Mom's younger sisters lived in a care facility eighteen miles from where my mom had been living. Aunt Jane, eighty-six, and Aunt Martha, eighty-two, were not doing well. They would not be able to attend Mom's funeral.

I loved seeing my cousins and catching up with their lives. As the oldest granddaughter of my mother's family, I babysat many of the nineteen cousins, and felt closer to some than most people do with their siblings.

During the conversations with my cousins about their mothers, it became apparent that both families were in turmoil. The siblings struggled to make decisions regarding their mothers. The older brothers of both families wanted to be in charge, and the younger sisters didn't trust them. The mothers favored the sons and yet depended upon the daughters for caretaking. I was aware of the disparity with which my aunts treated their sons versus their daughters, for I had experienced it within our family too. Though my mother definitely favored my brother, it wasn't portrayed as strongly in our family due to the fact that I was the oldest.

Conflict, anger, and even hate had developed between the siblings of my mom's younger sisters, just as it had amongst the oldest sister's family before she died. And now that their mothers were becoming dependent, they were being forced to work together, lend support, and make decisions together for their mothers' best interest. They were managing, but the tension in both families was taking a toll on each member. Especially upon my aunts.

I met and talked with the male and female cousins separately, stretching myself to understand both sides. I encouraged them to work together for their mothers' sakes, and also I did my best to explain the dynamics within the families that had produced the pain and distrust we were now all experiencing.

As for Jean, I had listened to her brother and her in conversation concerning their mother and sensed their distrust of each other. In the last moments of saying goodbye, and after her brother had left, Jean made the statement, "I hate him because of what he did to me." This was when I pulled her away from others standing in the hallway and into my sister's bedroom to talk further.

I asked, "Are you speaking of sexual abuse?"

Hesitantly, yet adamantly, she said, "Yes."

Then she added, "And Uncle Bill, and your brother, too." She went on to state, but not describe how it had begun with her Uncle Bill, a step-brother of her father's. Then she said that her brother and my brother, who were the same age, "used to corner me and other cousins and……." Not able or willing to go on, she closed down. Tears spilled as she ended the tirade with, "I hate him, I hate him, and when Mom's dead I won't have anything to do with him."

I pushed a little further by asking, "Have you ever said anything to him?" Anger flaring again, she responded, "Yes, and he said I couldn't blame him. That after all he was a teenager and couldn't help himself." Disgust and pain filled her eyes. I asked, "Have you ever said anything to your mom about this?" She answered, again with anger, "It would not do a bit of good."

Her accusation resonated. It never did any good to complain to my mother about anything my brother did, either. Others were waiting for Jean, in order to leave, so our conversation was cut short. With my condolences and assurance of understanding she left.

Seven years before Mom's passing, at eighty-one, she visited me during a time when I was spending hours examining my memories and beliefs.

Our conversations were stifled due to my own aggrieved feelings regarding my father's abuse of me and her defense of my brother.

During the above mentioned visit, Mom became more distant and appeared pained after a call from my brother. She would not discuss the call nor why she appeared upset. The day after his call to her, as Mom and I sat at the dining room table sharing tea and cookies, he called to speak with me. He said, "Tami says I have to tell you something I did. I already told Mom, but I'm sure she hasn't told you, right?"

I responded, "No she has not told me anything, but I know that she is upset."

He went on. "Well, um I, I have to tell you that I had an affair with Deanne." Deanne was an adopted daughter of his and Tami's—one they had given their last name to. Though she was only seven years younger than Tami, she was definitely young enough to be his daughter, and much younger than my daughters.

"What do you mean you had an affair with Deanne?" I asked.

"I had sex with her," he replied.

"Oh, no, Lewis, you didn't!" was all I could say. I did not say much during this telephone call. I felt anger. When angry I turn to silence.

A few days later when I had cooled, and he called again, I expressed my feelings strongly. I said, "You may call it an affair, I call it incest."

When I hung up from that first short phone call, I turned to my mother and said, "So you know what your son did." She said, "Yes," but then started to defend him, "Tami was not treating him ……."

Before she could get through the first sentence of defense, I jumped. "Mom, don't you dare go there. Don't you go to defending him. This is no one's fault but his. Do you realize what this means? She is a daughter—he made her his daughter!"

Mom broke into sobs, "I know, I know, but….."

Still wanting to make it sound as though it wasn't his fault, she then started in on Deanne. "The way she acts, it's no wonder….."

I adamantly put my hand up in the stop position and said, "Mom, we are not going to discuss this until you are willing to look at what your son has done, and not at Tami or Deanne."

She stood up to leave, then turned back to me with slumped shoulders and chin down, "…your father, he's like your dad." These words stumbled out and I was not clear what she was saying. Nor prepared.

"What do you mean, he's like my dad?"

She sat back down at the table, defeated. Between sobs and nose blowing she told me what I had never suspected about my father. I was not surprised about the sex he partook during the war while stationed on the front lines of Germany—didn't even feel as though it was an issue. She went on to say there were other times. She wasn't sure how often, but that just recently her sister, Martha, had told her about a time, one that had happened thirty years ago. The issue for me was not what my father had done, but that my mother at eighty years old was carrying the pain as though it had just happened. She had never talked about it and admitted that she had never allowed my father to talk about it.

She told me that as he lay dying he tried to tell her something, "But I wouldn't let him cause I think he wanted to tell me what he had done." Even though on his deathbed, and she believed he wanted to say he was sorry, she would not let him. Not from any vengeance. It appeared as though she did not want to feel the pain.

The flow of words in the cracks of her years of silence went on, and what she confessed next was the most disconcerting to me. She stumbled through a story. "My brothers had sex with me. I had to sleep with them and John……well, he did it."

I asked, "How old were you?"

She answered, "Eleven or twelve." And went on to explain that her three sisters slept in one room with one bed, and she slept in an attic bedroom with her two brothers in another bed. She was the middle child—often lamenting this along with her articulation regarding neglect. Her verbal expression of anger was toward her mother, "How could she do that to me? Why did she make me sleep with them?" I asked her if she thought that Grandma knew what was happening and she said, "How could she not know what was going on?" She looked at me with pleading eyes and once more asked, "How could she do that to me?"

I felt compassion for my mom for the first time. I wanted healing for her, but after this conversation she would not speak of it again. Nor would she answer any more questions. My suggestion of therapy fell on closed ears.

My unverified suspicion of sexual abuse within the family was now substantiated! *Did my Grandma who was a very religious person really perpetuate this? Was she naïve? Was she in denial? Did what happen there in that home precipitate the abuse in my family, and in my home? Or is it a cultural trait? Is this abuse of girls and women precipitated by the belief of a male God? Would the belief of a Father-Mother God help alleviate the abuse that is so prevalent in our culture and even in Christian homes?*

32

VISITING MY FRIEND in California had always been a pleasure. Especially, to sit at her table with good food beautifully presented in a comfortable setting. But sitting at her table now, I was uncomfortable. We had been discussing grandchildren with statements of how much smarter they are today compared to our childhoods and even that of our children. Then Karen told the story of her four-year-old granddaughter asking her, "Gramma, where is God's Mother?"

What a great question. One I had been studying for years—ever since Charlotte, my next-door neighbor in California, introduced me to the thought of a Goddess.

I had never said anything to Karen about my inquiries or the answers I found. She was a conservative Adventist in thought—as were the ones now sitting at the table with me. Adventists did not talk about God as being anything but male—a Father. I couldn't bring myself to face the horrified looks if I brought up the topic of God's mother or a Mother God, or worse yet, a Goddess.

I asked instead, "What did you tell her?"

Karen answered, "I told her to ask her mom or dad. I wasn't going to get on that topic with her. It is so difficult to explain."

Yes, it is difficult to explain where Gods' mother is and difficult to understand why you, my friend, aren't also questioning what your four-year old granddaughter is. Why aren't you asking that question?

I had found out I was not alone, nor searching in vain for God's mother. It was a lonely search, however, since it seemed I was the only one I knew who was searching. Volumes of material by some of the foremost men and women surprised and delighted me. They are educated, degreed, and research-savvy individuals, who spent years studying the subject of what happened to the Goddess.

William Dever, in a book by the same title, asks, "Did God Have a Wife?" It was important to read the research presented by men, because for many years men were the only ones presenting material regarding the archaeological finds related to the Goddess and Great Mother. These findings were often slanted or distorted due to the influence of the patriarchal view of God. Findings were further misinterpreted by men who looked at the woman's body as sexual and not spiritual. William goes into depth sharing his research, and ends his book with the statement: "With the full recognition of women - the other half of humanity – in religion and society, the spirit of the Great Mother will at last be freed. Here I have tried simply to anticipate her emancipation by showing that in the world of ancient Israel, among other places and times, she was once alive and well, at least until she was driven underground by men who wrote the Bible. Archaeology brings her back to life."

I especially appreciate the encouragement Dever presented with the statement: "….we are beginning to speak less of the 'Fatherhood of God,' and 'the brotherhood of man;' and more of 'God the Father and Mother' and 'the whole family of humankind'." I was also surprised because I had not heard any of these statements from anyone before reading this book.

Many of the women I read asked the very questions that were circling in my head. Karen Armstrong, a free-thinking and highly respected expert on religious history and a prolific writer about the Goddess, made a profound statement that both delighted and pushed me into further reading of the material that she had researched and shared through many books. "As I grew up I realized there was more to religion than fear." This statement I related to. After all, it was my willingness to set aside fear that allowed me to even read her material.

In *A History of God,* she said, "The more I learned about the history of religion, the more my earlier misgivings appeared justified. The doctrines that I had accepted without question as a child were indeed man-made, constructed over a long period…."

I felt so relieved to know that others, more educated than I, had the same misgivings, and that my questions and discoveries aligned with theirs.

In her book, *Heart Song*, Ceanne De Rohan wrote, "Trying to make sense of things has told me this; there's a gap in here someplace where I need pieces filled in, something about love lost and Original Sin. What happened to Mother has to be told." My sentiments exactly! A very provocative question from her pen is: "If Mary was the doorway through which love could come, then why isn't the Mother a loving part of One?" She goes on to say that because of leaving the Mother or feminine out so many times in history, "women are a mere shadow of themselves." This is testimony I myself have experienced personally, and over and over again with young and older women I have related to and counseled. However, I had not thought of what she wrote: "until men figure out, in a real way, not just in their minds, that they have no real power to live unless they empower their women, who in return, then empower them, they are also mere shadows of themselves." Indeed, a powerful statement from Ceanne to contemplate!

In *The Feminine Face of God* Sherry Ruth Anderson says: "I've been identified with patriarchal values for so long now that whenever something deep within me begins to ask questions, I feel guilty and disloyal. Then I scramble around trying to make my feelings and beliefs all fit together somehow. It's very hard to put into words, but something uniquely feminine in me is asking to be expressed, and I don't know how to let it come out."

Oh how familiar this sounded to me. Something in me had been expressing the desire to get out, and I was reading this material because of that very sense. I was struggling to understand why I was questioning. At first I did not know what I was missing in my continued search for God. When I discovered that it was the lack of the feminine, I lamented over the dissatisfaction I felt with the Christian Church and the people within it who have determined that God is male.

Sherry Anderson writes that she came to the place where "religion didn't 'feel' right to me and yet who was I to question the learned—the men who taught, who wrote the Bible, who went to seminary." Many times as Dean of Women at the Adventist College, I grappled with this very issue: *How can I question what the learned men within the Church, college, and seminary say about God? They have the degrees, I do not. If they say it is thus and so, why can't I just accept that?* Now I realize that there were few women in positions of influence within the Church or college. The ones who were there may have questioned, but undoubtedly were shut up by men in authority, as I was when I asked questions that threatened the status quo.

Merlin Stone, as a pioneer of the Women's Movement, has influenced greatly the reclaiming of the Great Goddess tradition of the Western world. Her book, *When God was a Woman,* further aroused within me a greater desire to know what happened to Goddess worship. She came in contact with ancient Goddess images first through her artistic work as a sculptor, and then she pursued her interest in archaeology and ancient religion. Her work helped to reclaim the Goddess and women's role in prehistory and also laid the groundwork for those who continue to research pre-patriarchal history. Stone spent a decade on extensive research regarding the Goddess. Her work describes her theory of how the Hebrews suppressed goddess worshipping religions practiced in Canaan, and how their reaction to what she asserts as being the existing matriarchal and matrilineal societal structures shaped Judaism and, thus, Christianity.

Stone's hypotheses were reported as radical. They challenged the accepted views of male scholars, but she pressed on with the question of what effect the worship of the female deity actually had upon the status of women. In *When God Was A Woman*, archeologically documented, is information regarding the religion of the Goddesses who are known by many names - Ishtar, Astarte, Isis.

Stone found that women's roles, under the worship of a Goddess or the Great Mother, differed greatly from those in patriarchal Judeo-Christian cultures. She affirms that women not only bought and sold property, but that the inheritance of title and property was passed from mother to daughter. Stone asked and answered, in part, the question that continued to plague me: How and when did the change in our perception of God come about? She answered this question by documenting the wholesale rewriting of myth and religious dogmas, and the revelation of an ancient conspiracy of the patriarchal *re-imaging of the Goddess* as a wanton, depraved figure. The Biblical texts revealing this "wanton woman," are what I had experienced, until now. (Italics mine)

Like Stone, Marija Gimbutas' work was quite controversial. She was tenacious in asserting her hypotheses, and as a result, she had both strong proponents and strong opponents. She gained fame and notoriety with her books: *The Goddesses and Gods of Old Europe; The Language of the Goddess.* Her book, published in 1991 before her death, *The Civilization of the Goddess*, presented her speculations on the housing patterns, social structure, art, religion, and the nature of literacy in Neolithic cultures across Europe. Her prolific writing and attention to detail in hundreds of scholarly articles and twenty books translated into many foreign languages, attest to her diligence in searching, understanding and communicating the presence of goddess worship in Old Europe.

Gumbutas, as a professor of archaeology at UCLA from 1963 to 1989, directed major excavations of Neolithic sites in Southeastern Europe between 1967 and 1980. She unearthed a great number of artifacts from daily life and of religious cults, which she researched and documented throughout her career. In her final book, *The Living Goddesses,* published after her death, she asserts: "We can see that the Baltic pantheon remarkably preserves an almost complete Old European family of goddesses and gods. Neither the presence of the Indo-Europeans, nor the five centuries of intensive war between paganism and Christianity exterminated the oldest layer of Baltic beliefs. Best preserved are the goddesses, who were life and birth givers, healers, protectresses of households and communities, bringers of earth fertility, death messengers, and life regenerators. Until recently, people kissed Mother Earth as if she were a human mother, in the morning and in the evening, before Christian prayers were said." *Aren't we women today the same? Aren't we still the life and birth givers, healers, protectresses of households and communities, bringers of earth fertility, death messengers, and life regenerators?*

Gimbutas related social respect for the female to religious respect for the female - the worshiping of goddesses - and states that Old European matrilineal societies therefore honored both mortal females and female deities. Consequently, in her opinion, these cultures were egalitarian in social structure, honoring both women and men. *Isn't this how it should be today – equal representation of male and female input in all aspects of our lives?*

While Gimbutas' material convinced me further of the presence of goddess worship and matriarchal societies, Stone in her writing asked questions so relevant to mine that while reading her material, I became excited and agitated, often putting the book down and walking back and forth trying to absorb what I was reading. She asks, "Why is it continually inferred that the age of the 'pagan' religions, the time of the worship of female deities was dark and chaotic, mysterious and evil, without the light of order and reason that supposedly accompanied the later male religions, when it has been archaeologically confirmed that the earliest law, government, medicine, agriculture, architecture, metallurgy, wheeled vehicles, ceramics, textiles and written language were *initially developed in societies that worshiped the Goddess*?" (Italics mine)

In taking this question further I ask myself, *why, as a woman, did I so readily accept the teachings of the Bible in this regard?* It was declarations from Stone, like this one, that brought clarification to my mind: "It was the ideological inventions of the advocates of the later male deities, imposed upon that ancient worship with the intention of destroying it and its customs, that are still, through their subsequent absorption into education, law, literature, economics, philosophy, psychology, media and general social attitudes, imposed upon even the most non-religious people of today." In other words, having been raised in the Christian culture of my youth, as well as today, I did not have a chance to see it any other way. As she too says: "The lessons learned in the Garden of Eden were impressed upon us over and over again. Man was created first. Woman was made for man. Only man was made in God's image…and the male god favored men and had indeed designed them as naturally superior."

It was so enlightening to read her research and that of others. I danced my way through book after book. I had to take breaks. I did not always understand the deeper meanings and explorations. But my most profound questions and doubts were finally being addressed.

Freke and Gandy in their book *Jesus and the Lost Goddess*, write "When this impoverished form of Christianity was adopted as *the official religion of the brutal Roman Empire*, the original Christians were violently suppressed, their scriptures burned and their memory all but erased. The Roman Catholic Church fabricated its own account of the origins of Christianity, still believed today, which dismisses the first Christians as a minor cult of obscure heretics." (Italics mine.)

Once more it shows up—the Roman Catholic beliefs determining what history shall be. The rewriting of History.

Often when I have tried to share with other Christian women my questions and my doubts about a true identification of God, and the lack of the Divine feminine, they remind me about Mary and her being the Mother of God.

In *A Woman's Journey to God* – Joan Borysenko says: "There is a wealth of myth and story, as well as archeological evidence, about ancient Goddess Worship. At the time of Jesus, Judaism was still waging a battle against worship of the Babylonian goddess Asherah. Mary, who was not originally venerated in early Christianity, gradually drew a following because she was a natural extension of the Goddess. Since the "pagan" fascination with goddesses could not be wiped out, the church fathers allowed it to be transferred to Mary and wisely co-opted the earlier forms of worship and veneration. Although Mary is not technically a goddess but the Mother of God come to earth in human form, she is nonetheless worshipped as divine by many people around the world."

If Mary is truly the Mother of God, why didn't my friend Karen easily answer her granddaughter's question of, "Who is God's mother?" with the announcement, "Why darling, it is Mary?"

It is time to bring the facts about the early female religions to light. They have been hidden away for too long. The facts in Stone's book (and others) helped me to understand the earliest development of Judaism, Christianity, and Islam and their reactions to the female religions and customs that preceded them. With these facts, I am more able to understand how the political attitudes and historical events that occurred as these male-oriented religions were forming—attitudes and events that played a major part in formulating the image of women during and since those times -- continues to play out in the lives of the women today.

Reading the research, studies, and conclusions of others has changed the way I look at history, and the way I perceive organized religion. How different would my walk with God have been if I had believed there was a Mother God? Or better yet, what if I had been taught that God was masculine *and* feminine—male and female? What if I had been able to be hugged and encouraged by a God with the masculine traits of strength, protection, courage, perception, <u>and</u> the feminine attributes of nurturance, vision, and gentleness? How differently would I have raised my daughters?

Of course, I don't know for sure *how* differently, but I do believe their lives would have been improved. Certainly, the counseling I gave young women would have been enhanced greatly if my personal value as a woman had come from the position of believing in a Mother and Father God.

Immediately after completing my research, I understood and believed there was a time of Goddess worship, but it still did not affect my life. What was I to do with a Mother God? What was the practicality? How would it change me? I was still focused on church and how the Church had deceived me into believing so many things that the further I studied the more distant I became from God. I could no longer read the Bible with commitment of heart. The Bible had deceived me. Or was it the teachings of others about what the Bible said, that deceived me? As Karen Speerstra states so beautifully in her book *Sophia,* "I had to figure out how to find Sophia (Mother God)—or to make the space for her to find me."

How? Through prayer? More study? Surrender? Meditation? How?

33

WE RARELY ATTENDED church services. Only if there was a purpose like the one a few years ago when our program for the treatment of trafficked teens was being presented to Scott's church congregation with Loren's desire to get the church to back the program financially. I sat next to Loren on a hard wooden pew in a beautiful church that covers half a city block. The sanctuary, added to the north side of an old brick church, seats two-thousand people in a semicircle facing the pulpit where a minister I have known since he was twelve years old, stands, giving a sermon.

I listened intently to Ray as he talked about his and his wife's experiences while adopting a daughter from Ukraine. He told of all the miracles and of God's interventions on their behalf. He spoke of God's love for this young woman, and how He has provided so they could become her family.

I could tell that Ray was finishing the sermons by the statements he made, and by a look at my watch. I started to relax and thought *this has been nice*, when he said, "Our Father gave us the family."

I started to rise, tempted to walk out. But I sat. I whispered to Loren, "How can he say that? God can't just be a Father." My feelings were overpowering. I felt like crying or screaming. I didn't allow the tears to come. I processed in my head instead. *Why does this upset me so much? I can't do this anymore. I'm not going to church anymore. It doesn't make sense that the Christian Church, as a rule, puts so much emphasis on the family—on marriage between a male and female. How can they leave a Mother out when they talk about God being a Father, and giving us the family?*

I'd spent so many years searching for answers to the questions I hadn't been able to stop. My studies propelled me beyond the patriarchal belief and teachings about God as male. The knowledge and understanding I now had left me devoid of tolerance for religious beliefs that do not include a feminine aspect to God. In one of Ray's earlier sermons he spoke of the Holy Spirit as He, and further emphasized "him" being as real as Jesus. I had the same emotional reaction then, as now.

It seems so obvious to me that God cannot be a male with no female in the Godhead. There is extensive material from dedicated spiritual researchers and teachers that propound this truth. *Why doesn't the Christian church get it?*

During one of my foraging of used bookstores, I was drawn to a very thin black and white covered book: THE ESSENE GOSPEL OF PEACE. As I fingered through the book, my eyes lit upon three capitalized lines. The author was quoting Jesus:

> FOR YOUR HEAVENLY FATHER IS LOVE.
> FOR YOUR EARTHLY MOTHER IS LOVE.
> FOR THE SON OF MAN IS LOVE.

Excited, I hurried to the checkout counter, bought the book, and went home to read. *What possibilities this book holds! Jesus really did talk about a Mother God.*

The paragraph under the above three lines in the middle of a page of quotes says: "It is by love that the Heavenly Father and the Earthly Mother and the Son of Man become one. For the spirit of the Son of Man was created from the spirit of the Heavenly Father, and his body from the body of the Earthly Mother."

Edmund Bordeaux Szedely, the translator, was born in Hungary in

1905, and died in 1979. He was a well-known philologist in Sanskrit, Aramaic, Greek and Latin, and spoke ten modern languages. He is the author of more than 80 books, published in many countries, on philosophy and ancient cultures. The book is from material he translated from the original Aramaic while studying at the Vatican. From the language Jesus spoke!

The book represents about a third of the complete manuscript dating from the third century which exists in Aramaic, in the Secret Archives of the Vatican. *I wonder how much more is in those secret archives that could help dispel the beliefs of Christian Patriarchy?*

Throughout this ancient text the writer quotes Jesus' use of Mother and Father when speaking of God. One quote, "As the hen protects her chickens, as the lioness her cubs, as the mother her newborn babe, so does the Earthly Mother protect the Son of Man from all danger and from all evils," reminded me of the times I was away from my children and I thought of and repeated Matthew 23:37: "...how often I have longed to gather your children together, as a hen gathers her chicks under her wings."(NIV) I always pictured one of the Rhode Island Red hens we raised on the farm, all fluffed up, with her wings sheltering her chicks. Roosters don't do that! Hens do! The author quotes Jesus as saying, "And then your Heavenly Father shall give you his holy spirit, and your Earthly Mother shall give you her holy body." *Is Jesus saying that the Mother is the creative aspect of God?*

Szedely translates another section, ".... he (Jesus) sat down among them, saying: 'It was said to them of old time, Honor thy Heavenly Father and thy Earthly Mother, and do their commandments, that thy days may be long upon the earth.'" *This sounds like the Lord's Prayer! Isn't it probable that Jesus prayed to Father and Mother? The Mother was shut out, crossed out, diminished at the time the Bible was put together by Roman Catholic priests?*

The purpose for Szedely's work of translation was to prove that the Essenes were vegetarians. But the numerous quotes taken from material written two thousand years ago told me that Jesus recognized and emphasized a Mother in the godhead. I felt encouraged. Another someone, educated and well written, has produced answers to my questions.

The clearest vision I received of Mother's love versus Father's love and the need for both, I found In THE ART OF LOVING by Erich Fromm. He says: "Mother's love is unconditional, it is all-protective, all-enveloping; because it is unconditional it can also not be controlled or acquired... Mother's love is based on equality...All men are equal, because they all are children of the mother, because they all are children of Mother Earth."

He also backs up my discovery that: "There can be little doubt that there was a matriarchal phase of religion preceding the patriarchal one—at least in many cultures." In the matriarchal phase, the Mother represents the highest being.

Frohm goes on to say, "The next stage of human evolution, ...is the patriarchal phase. In this phase the mother is dethroned from her supreme position, and the father becomes the Supreme Being, in religion as well as society. The nature of fatherly love is that he makes demands, establishes principles and laws, and that his love for the son depends on the obedience of the latter to these demands."

In the Jewish religion, the Mother aspects of God are introduced by the various currents of mysticism. In the Catholic religion, the Mother is symbolized by Mary as the Mother of God. I never have found the mother in Protestantism.

Why has it remained hidden in Protestantism? Isn't it time to find the Mother?

While visiting my friend Charlotte, the one who introduced me to hand reading, I told her the title of the book I was beginning to write. She said, "I have a book I think you should read." Directing me toward a bookshelf, she began to search and handed me THE RETURN OF THE

MOTHER by Andrew Harvey. Harvey is an internationally renowned mystical scholar. He has studied a variety of religions extensively, including Hinduism, Buddhism and Christianity. At the tender age of 21, he became the youngest person ever to be awarded a fellowship to All Soul's College, England's highest academic honor. I wanted to hear what he had to say, so I read.

THE RETURN TO THE MOTHER was published in 1995, fourteen years before Charlotte shared it with me. When I read the passage on the first page of the Foreword: "Everything, I believe, **now** depends on how the human race imagines and relates to the sacred feminine and the Mother," I turned back to see when he wrote it to understand the **now**.

One of his first statements, "It is time that Westerners realize that mystics are scientists of their domain," caused me to consider my relationship to mystics and mystical writings. I am so literal and concrete in my thinking, that anything figurative or metaphorical can disturb me. I want to understand—to make what I hear or read factual. I have difficulty with poetry and art. I want to understand what it means, why that figure, why that word, why that color?

I think this is why I have been driven to understand God. The discrepancies in Church teachings disturb me. Having a Father God and no Mother disturbs me. Attempts to understand have led me to read the mystical. I still try to *make literal* what I read, but I am learning to *be* with what I read. Andrew Harvey's writings have helped with this dilemma.

He writes: "The tragic imbalance of the masculine has brought human kind to the point of disaster, and unless we recover the feminine powers of the psyche, the posers of intuition, patience, reverence for nature, and knowledge of the holy unity of things, and marry in our depths these powers with the masculine energies of rule, reason, passion for order and control, life on the planet will end. This sacred marriage of the masculine with the feminine has to take place in all our hearts and minds, whether we are male or female."

Reading Harvey has continued to point out to me how mental I remain in my spirituality. Religion has kept me in my head. Spiritually I use my heart and feel God. It is this *feeling* that lets me know when I hear Truth.

Harvey says in his latest book, RADICAL PASSION: "The human race will not really be honoring the Mother until every starving person is fed; until every homeless person is housed; until every sick and poor old person has free access to medicine; until every woman everywhere is free from all kinds of oppression; until every human being everywhere, whatever his or her sexuality, feels free to love openly; until in fact, *all* the man-made distinctions between white and black, male and female, poor and rich, straight and gay, are radically transformed so as to express in both individual and social, spiritual and political ways, the equal love of the Mother."

This is the world I want to live in. It is the world I want for my grandchildren, great- grandchildren, great-great-grandchildren.

I believe that if the women of the world embrace this desire, it is the world we will have in the future. It is not only the love and acceptance of the Mother aspect of God that will cause it to happen, but the love expressed by the Mothers of the world now living on this planet with me.

Harvey writes further: "This is a stage beyond both matriarchy and patriarchy. It involves the restoration to human respect of all the rejected powers of the feminine. Not only should we invoke the sacred feminine, restore the sacred feminine, but this union between the matriarchal and the patriarchal, the sacred marriage, must be accomplished in the *spirit* of the sacred feminine for it to be real, effective, rich and fecund. It must occur in her spirit of unconditional love, in her spirit of tolerance, forgiveness, all-embracing and all-harmonizing balance, and not, in any sense, involve a swing in the other direction."

Crucial is the fact that we cannot afford to reject everything masculine, scientific, or patriarchal. A real marriage between the masculine and feminine is a union based in profound mutual respect. A purely matriarchal or patriarchal solution, on their own, will simply not work. I advocate for acceptance, as described in this poem included in Andrew's writing:

> I honor the God and Goddess,
> The eternal parents of the universe.
> The lover out of boundless love
> takes the form of the beloved,
> what beauty!
>
> Both are made of the same nectar
> and share the same food.
> Out of Supreme love,
> they swallow each other up,
> But separate again
> for the joy of being two.
>
> They sit together
> in the same place,
> Both wearing a garment of light.
> From the beginning of time
> they have been together,
> Reveling in their own Supreme love.
>
> The difference they created
> To enjoy this world,
> Had one glimpse of their intimacy
> And could not help
> But merge back
> Into the bliss.

Found in their union.
Without the God
There is no Goddess,
And without the Goddess
There is no God.

How sweet their love!
The entire universe
Is too small to contain them,
Yet they live happily
In the tiniest particle.

I ask, as Harvey does, that you "keep the subtlety and message of this poem in your minds."

34

THIS IS THE end of my story for now. We have made many more moves, Loren and I, physically and spiritually. Loren continues to focus on his dream of establishing treatment centers. I continue to focus on family and home. My search has not stopped. While I am confident that there is a Mother God as well as Father God, I am not sure what that means - what it looks like. I am tired of searching to understand, but cannot stop. The thought of *where is the Mother?* drives me, pulls at me. I think this poem describes what I am trying to say:

It is a hard fight and a weary one,
This fight of the truth-seeker:
for the vow of the truth-seeker is more
hard than that of the warrior,
or of the widowed wife who
would follow her husband;
For the warrior fights for a few
hours, and the widow's struggle
with death is soon ended:
But the truth seeker's battle goes
On day and night, as long as life
Lasts it never ceases. Kabir

I call myself a Mystic Christian these days, and use words like Divine and Divinity. I read the mystics and read the Bible as mystical. I am not attending a church and have no church membership. I miss the community but not the dogma. I am no longer pulled into dogma or religion. Some would say I am New Age. But I say only that I am still searching for Truth. Not the truth, for I also believe there is more than one Truth. There are many truths, many beliefs, but one God. This God is female and male. We were all made in this image. We all possess feminine aspects and male aspects so must God. I pray to Mother and Father God.

BUT

The purpose of birth is learning.
The purpose of learning is
to grasp the Divine.
The purpose of apprehending
The Divine
Is to maintain the endurance
of one who apprehends
with joy of apprehending. Abraham Abulafia

When I stepped out of traditional Christianity to discover God, I first determined that God is Love = Love is God. My second determination is that God is not male; God is male and female. I now search for the divine feminine that is missing in the Christian churches, Muslim mosques, Jewish temples and from many religions. Most of all, it is missing in our world and needed desperately to bring balance to the masculine structures that rule our world.

I shall continue to search for deeper meaning and understanding. I shall ask more questions. I shall continue to search for answers. I shall listen, listen to the inner voice. I have much more to learn.

Printed in the United States
By Bookmasters